# CSI: MIAMI™

Smoking Gun
Thou Shalt Not...
Blood/Money

D1217107

Mariotte
Oprisko
Avilés
Guedes
Wood
Perkins

IDW Publishing
San Diego

# CSI: Miami™

Created by Anthony E. Zuiker;
Ann Donahue; and Carol Mendelsohn

Licensed to IDW by CBS Consumer Products

Cover Photo by Robert Voets/CBS Photo

ISBN: 1-932382-54-2
08 07 06 05    1 2 3 4 5

IDW Publishing is:
**Ted Adams,** Publisher
**Chris Ryall,** Editor-in-Chief
**Robbie Robbins,** Design Director
**Kris Oprisko,** Vice President
**Alex Garner,** Art Director
**Cindy Chapman,** Operations Manager
**Tom B. Long,** Designer
**Chance Boren,** Editorial Assistant
**Yumiko Miyano,** Business Development
**Rick Privman,** Business Development

www.idwpublishing.com

CSI: Miami. February 2005. FIRST PRINTING. IDW Publishing, a division of Idea + Design Works, LLC. Editorial offices: 4411 Morena Blvd., Suite 106, San Diego, CA 92117. CSI:MIAMIand all elements and characters thereof © 2002-2004 CBS Broadcasting Inc. and Alliance Atlantis Productions, Inc. All Rights Reserved. CSI:MIAMIand related marks TM CBS Broadcasting Inc. CBS and the CBS Eye design TM CBS Broadcasting Inc. ALLIANCEATLANTIS with the Stylized "A" design TM Alliance Atlantis Communications Inc. © 2005 Idea + Design Works, LLC. All Rights Reserved. Originally published as CSI: Miami–Smoking Gun, CSI: Miami–Thou Shalt Not…, and CSI: Miami–Blood/Money. The IDW logo is registered in the U.S. Patent and Trade Office. Any similarities to persons living or dead are purely coincidental. With the exception of artwork used for review purposes, none of the contents of this publication may be reprinted without the permission of Idea + Design Works, LLC. Printed in Korea.

## CSI: Miami™
## Smoking Gun

Written by
**Jeff Mariotte**

Pencils by
**José Avilés,**
**Sulaco Studios**

Inks by
**Fran Gamboa,**
**Sulaco Studios**

Color Separations by
**JC Ruiz,**
**Sulaco Studios**

Painted Artwork by
**Ashley Wood**

Lettered by
**Cindy Chapman**

Edited by
**Kris Oprisko**

Cover Photo by
**Tony Esparza/**
**CBS Photo**

Design by
**Cindy Chapman and**
**Robbie Robbins**

## CSI: Miami™
## Thou Shalt Not...

Written by
**Kris Oprisko**

Art by
**Renato Guedes**

Painted Artwork by
**Ashley Wood**

Lettered by
**Robbie Robbins**

Edited by
**Jeff Mariotte**

Cover Photo by
**Blake Edwards**

Variant Cover Photo by
**Blake Edwards**

Design by
**Cindy Chapman**

## CSI: Miami™
## Blood/Money

Written by
**Kris Oprisko**

Art by
**Renato Guedes**

Painted Artwork by
**Steve Perkins**

Lettered by
**Robbie Robbins and**
**Cindy Chapman**

Edited by
**Chris Ryall**

Cover Photo by
**Robert Voets/**
**CBS Photo**

Design by
**Robbie Robbins and**
**Cindy Chapman**

# CSI: MIAMI™

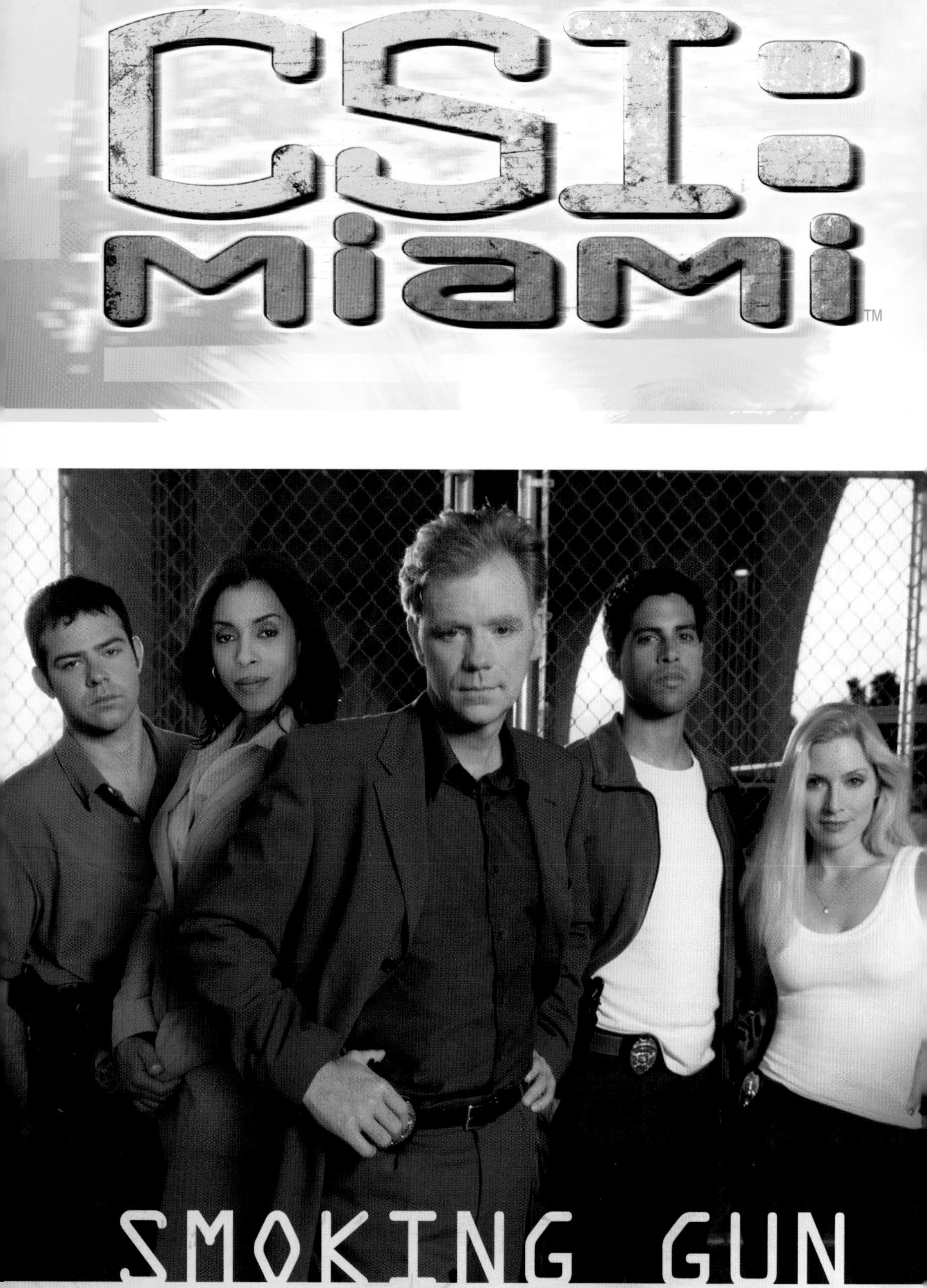

# SMOKING GUN

MARIOTTE • AVILÉS • WOOD

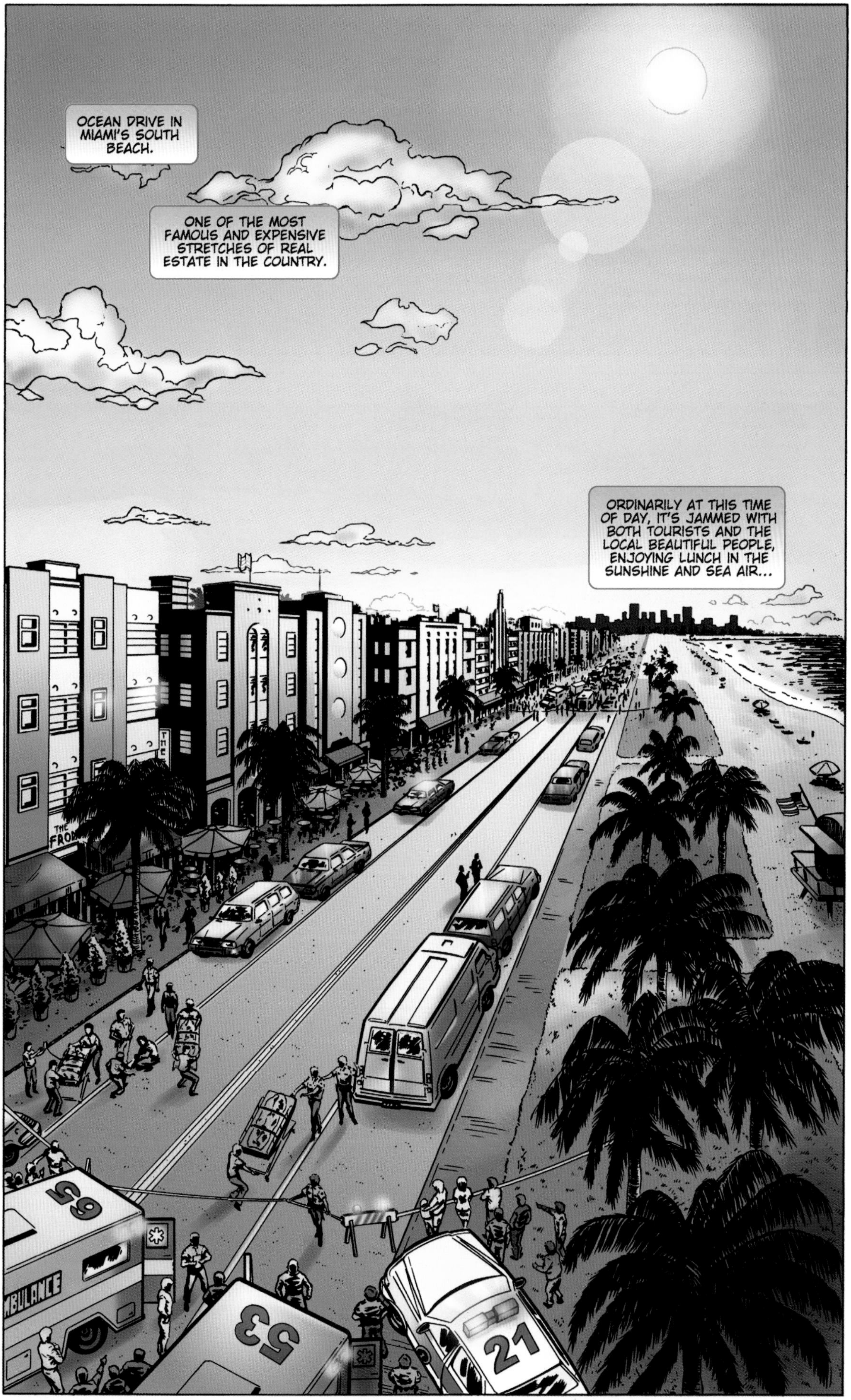
OCEAN DRIVE IN MIAMI'S SOUTH BEACH.
ONE OF THE MOST FAMOUS AND EXPENSIVE STRETCHES OF REAL ESTATE IN THE COUNTRY.
ORDINARILY AT THIS TIME OF DAY, IT'S JAMMED WITH BOTH TOURISTS AND THE LOCAL BEAUTIFUL PEOPLE, ENJOYING LUNCH IN THE SUNSHINE AND SEA AIR...
AMBULANCE

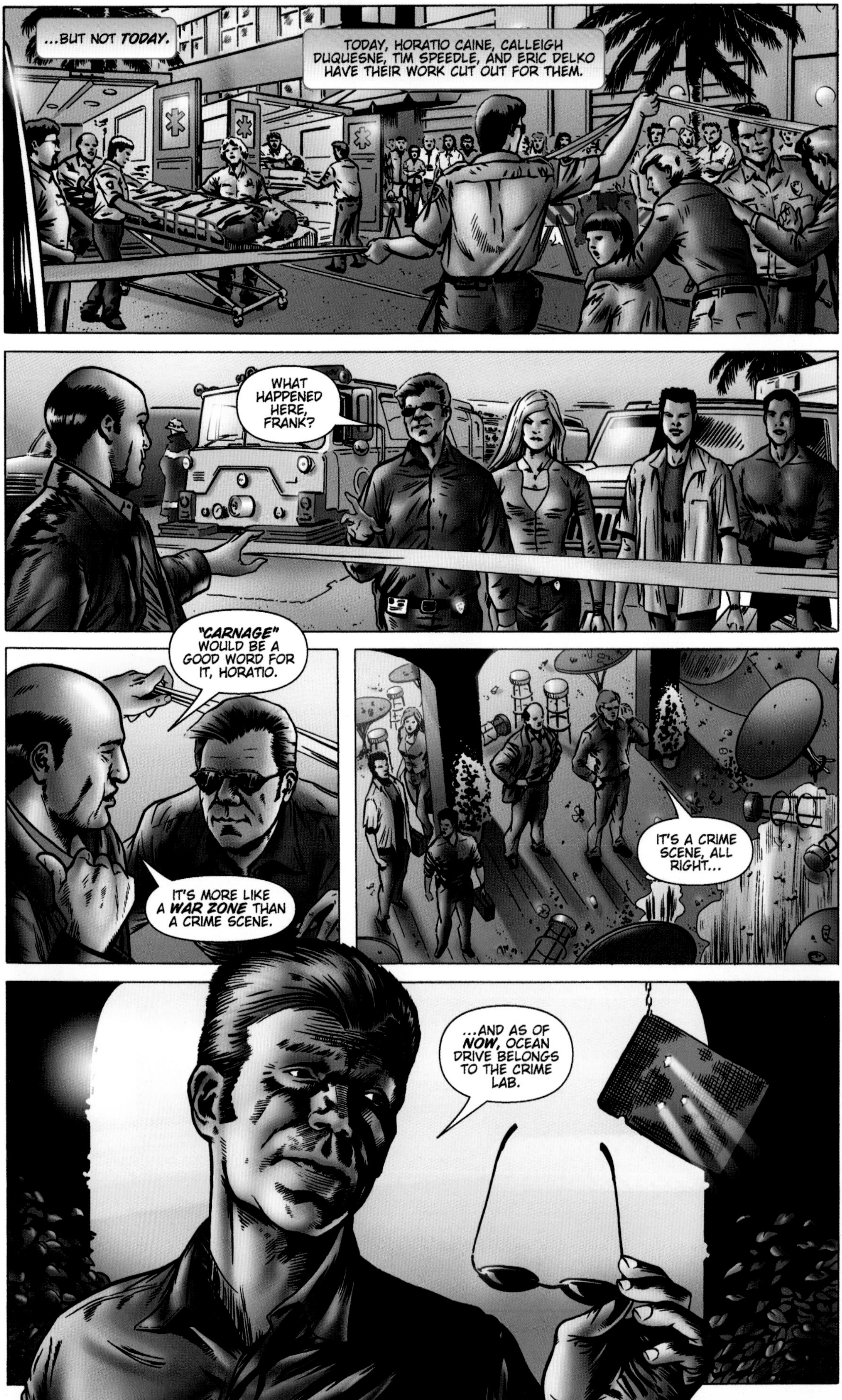
...BUT NOT TODAY.
TODAY, HORATIO CAINE, CALLEIGH DUQUESNE, TIM SPEEDLE, AND ERIC DELKO HAVE THEIR WORK CUT OUT FOR THEM.
WHAT HAPPENED HERE, FRANK?
"CARNAGE" WOULD BE A GOOD WORD FOR IT, HORATIO.
IT'S MORE LIKE A WAR ZONE THAN A CRIME SCENE.
IT'S A CRIME SCENE, ALL RIGHT...
...AND AS OF NOW, OCEAN DRIVE BELONGS TO THE CRIME LAB.

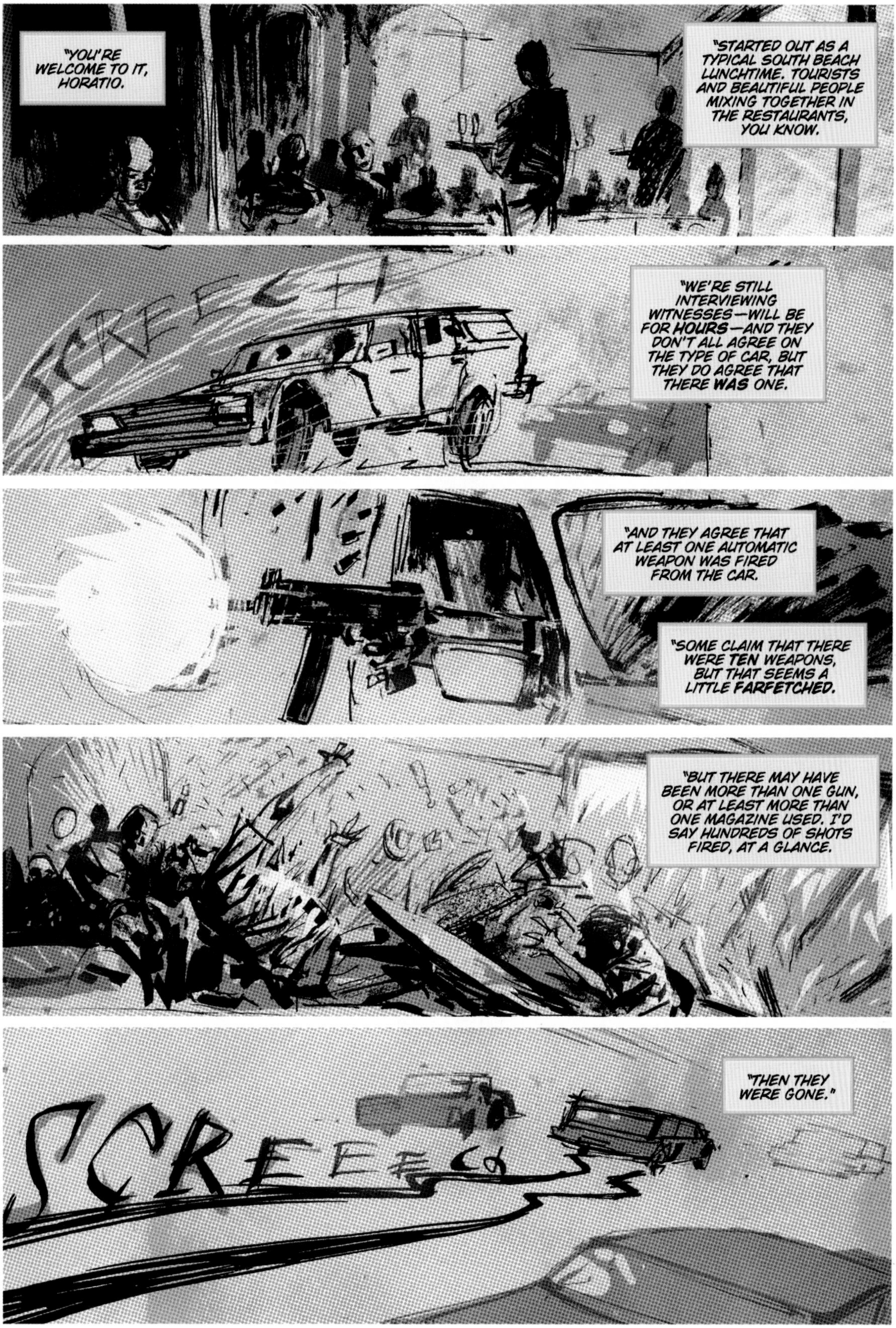
"YOU'RE WELCOME TO IT, HORATIO.
"STARTED OUT AS A TYPICAL SOUTH BEACH LUNCHTIME. TOURISTS AND BEAUTIFUL PEOPLE MIXING TOGETHER IN THE RESTAURANTS, YOU KNOW.
SCREECH
"WE'RE STILL INTERVIEWING WITNESSES—WILL BE FOR **HOURS**—AND THEY DON'T ALL AGREE ON THE TYPE OF CAR, BUT THEY DO AGREE THAT THERE **WAS** ONE.
"AND THEY AGREE THAT AT LEAST ONE AUTOMATIC WEAPON WAS FIRED FROM THE CAR.
"SOME CLAIM THAT THERE WERE **TEN** WEAPONS, BUT THAT SEEMS A LITTLE **FARFETCHED**.
"BUT THERE MAY HAVE BEEN MORE THAN ONE GUN, OR AT LEAST MORE THAN ONE MAGAZINE USED. I'D SAY HUNDREDS OF SHOTS FIRED, AT A GLANCE.
"THEN THEY WERE GONE."

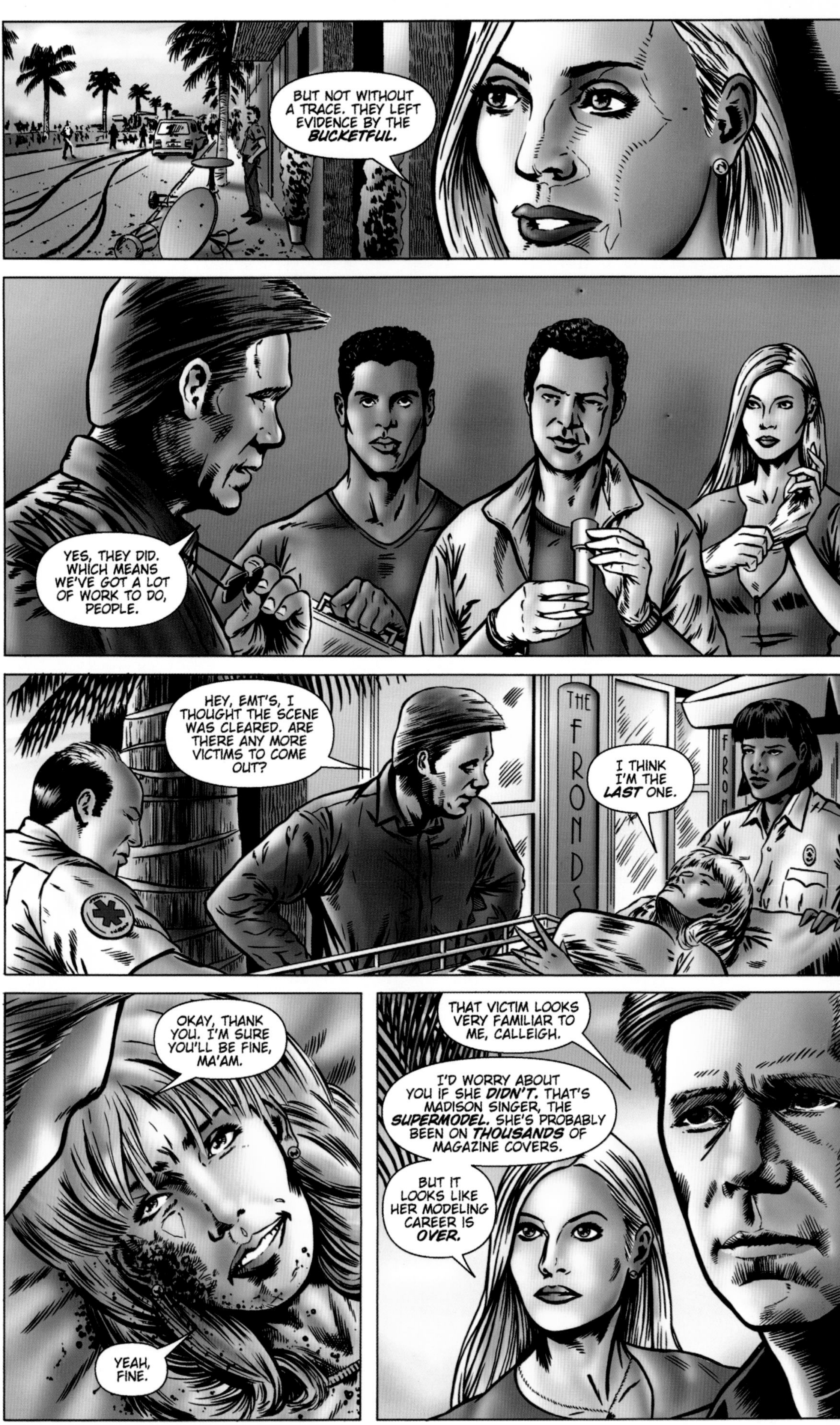
BUT NOT WITHOUT A TRACE. THEY LEFT EVIDENCE BY THE BUCKETFUL.
YES, THEY DID. WHICH MEANS WE'VE GOT A LOT OF WORK TO DO, PEOPLE.
HEY, EMT'S, I THOUGHT THE SCENE WAS CLEARED. ARE THERE ANY MORE VICTIMS TO COME OUT?
THE FRONDS
I THINK I'M THE LAST ONE.
OKAY, THANK YOU. I'M SURE YOU'LL BE FINE, MA'AM.
YEAH, FINE.
THAT VICTIM LOOKS VERY FAMILIAR TO ME, CALLEIGH.
I'D WORRY ABOUT YOU IF SHE DIDN'T. THAT'S MADISON SINGER, THE SUPERMODEL. SHE'S PROBABLY BEEN ON THOUSANDS OF MAGAZINE COVERS.
BUT IT LOOKS LIKE HER MODELING CAREER IS OVER.

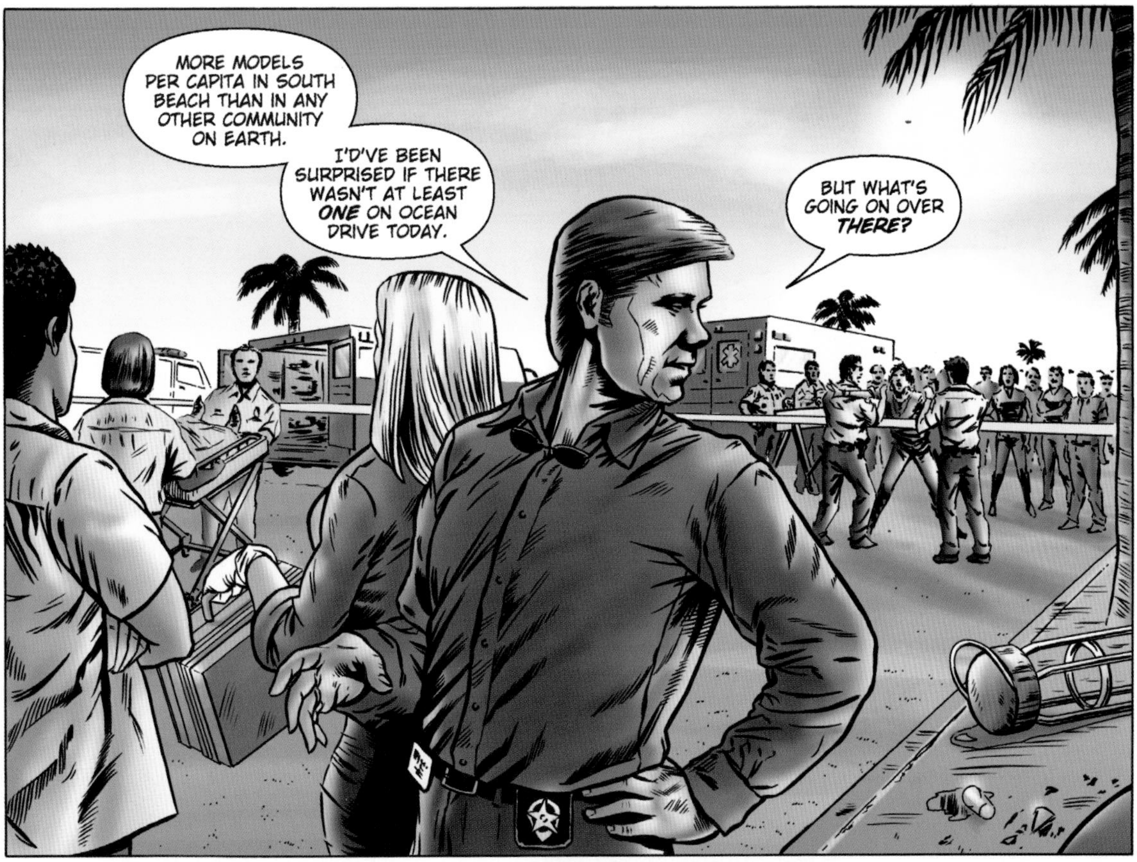
MORE MODELS PER CAPITA IN SOUTH BEACH THAN IN ANY OTHER COMMUNITY ON EARTH.
I'D'VE BEEN SURPRISED IF THERE WASN'T AT LEAST *ONE* ON OCEAN DRIVE TODAY.
BUT WHAT'S GOING ON OVER *THERE?*

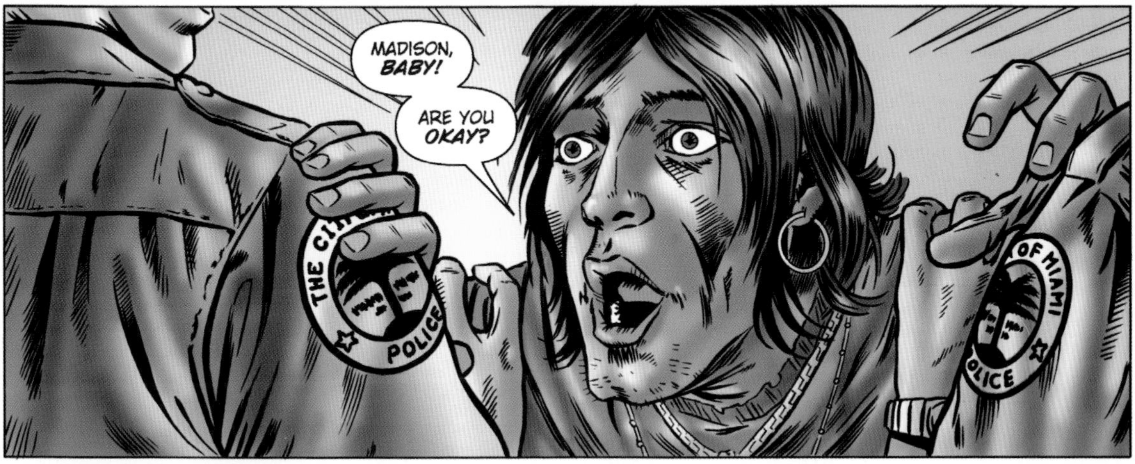
MADISON, *BABY!*
ARE YOU *OKAY?*
THE CITY OF MIAMI POLICE

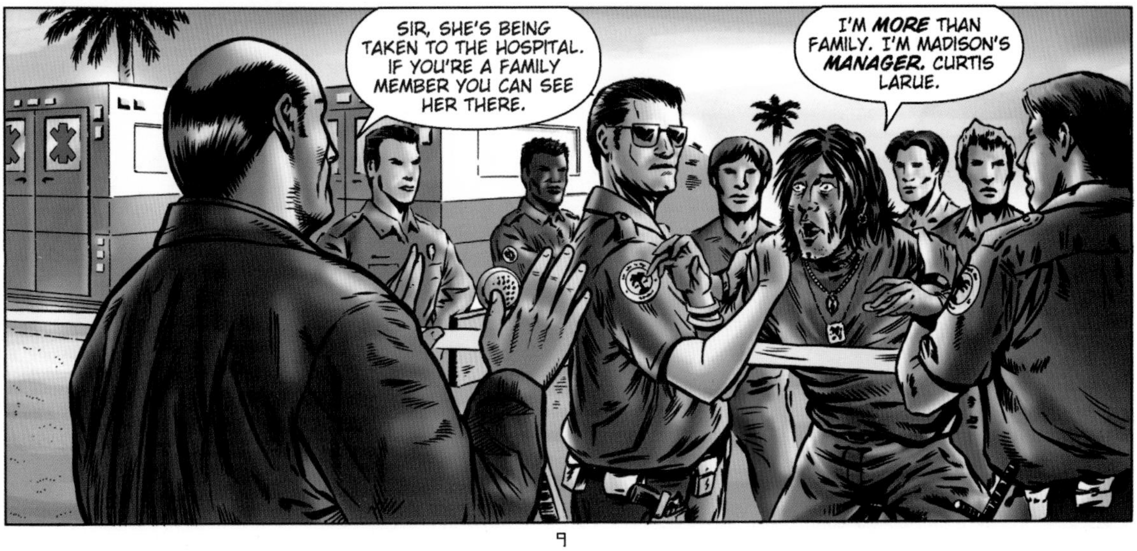
SIR, SHE'S BEING TAKEN TO THE HOSPITAL. IF YOU'RE A FAMILY MEMBER YOU CAN SEE HER THERE.
I'M *MORE* THAN FAMILY. I'M MADISON'S *MANAGER.* CURTIS LARUE.

I WAS SUPPOSED TO MEET MADISON FOR LUNCH. TRAFFIC ON THE DAMN MACARTHUR CAUSEWAY HELD ME UP. NOW LOOK!

WILL SHE BE *OKAY*?

I'M A *DETECTIVE*, MR. LARUE, NOT A DOCTOR.

OH, MAN, THIS SUCKS. THIS *REALLY* SUCKS.

SIR, YOU'LL WANT TO STAY ON *THAT* SIDE OF THE POLICE LINE. ONLY EMERGENCY WORKERS AND WITNESSES ARE ALLOWED ON THIS SIDE. IF YOU GET MIXED UP IN THIS CROWD, YOU'LL BE HERE ALL DAY.

I HEAR YOU, PAL. GUESS I'LL SEE MADISON AT THE HOSPITAL, THEN.

THAT'D BE BEST.

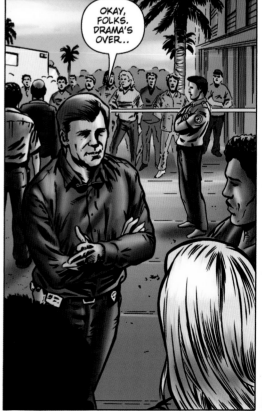

OKAY, FOLKS. DRAMA'S OVER...

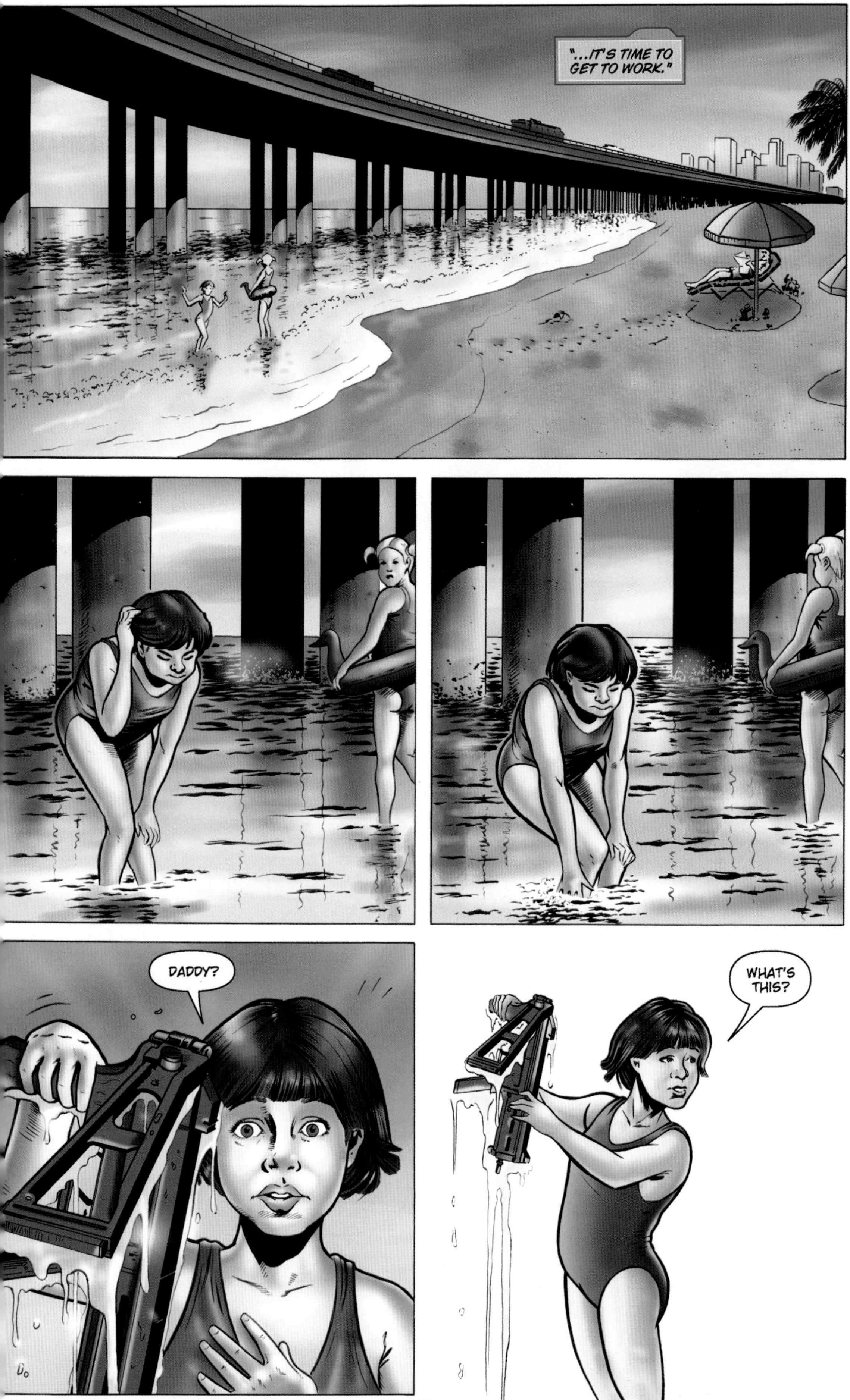
"...IT'S TIME TO GET TO WORK."
DADDY?
WHAT'S THIS?

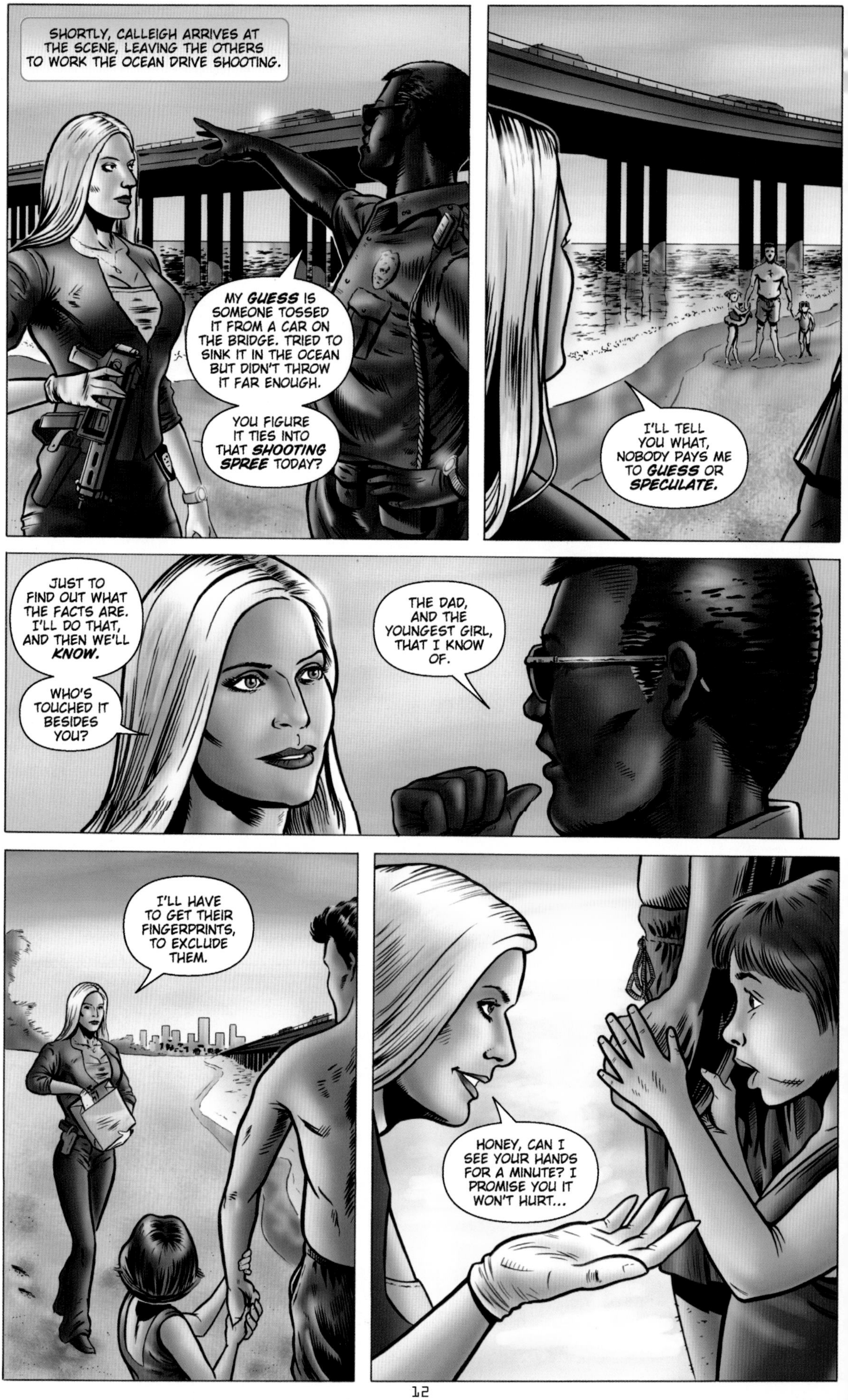
SHORTLY, CALLEIGH ARRIVES AT THE SCENE, LEAVING THE OTHERS TO WORK THE OCEAN DRIVE SHOOTING.
MY GUESS IS SOMEONE TOSSED IT FROM A CAR ON THE BRIDGE. TRIED TO SINK IT IN THE OCEAN BUT DIDN'T THROW IT FAR ENOUGH.
YOU FIGURE IT TIES INTO THAT SHOOTING SPREE TODAY?
I'LL TELL YOU WHAT, NOBODY PAYS ME TO GUESS OR SPECULATE.
JUST TO FIND OUT WHAT THE FACTS ARE. I'LL DO THAT, AND THEN WE'LL KNOW.
WHO'S TOUCHED IT BESIDES YOU?
THE DAD, AND THE YOUNGEST GIRL, THAT I KNOW OF.
I'LL HAVE TO GET THEIR FINGERPRINTS, TO EXCLUDE THEM.
HONEY, CAN I SEE YOUR HANDS FOR A MINUTE? I PROMISE YOU IT WON'T HURT...

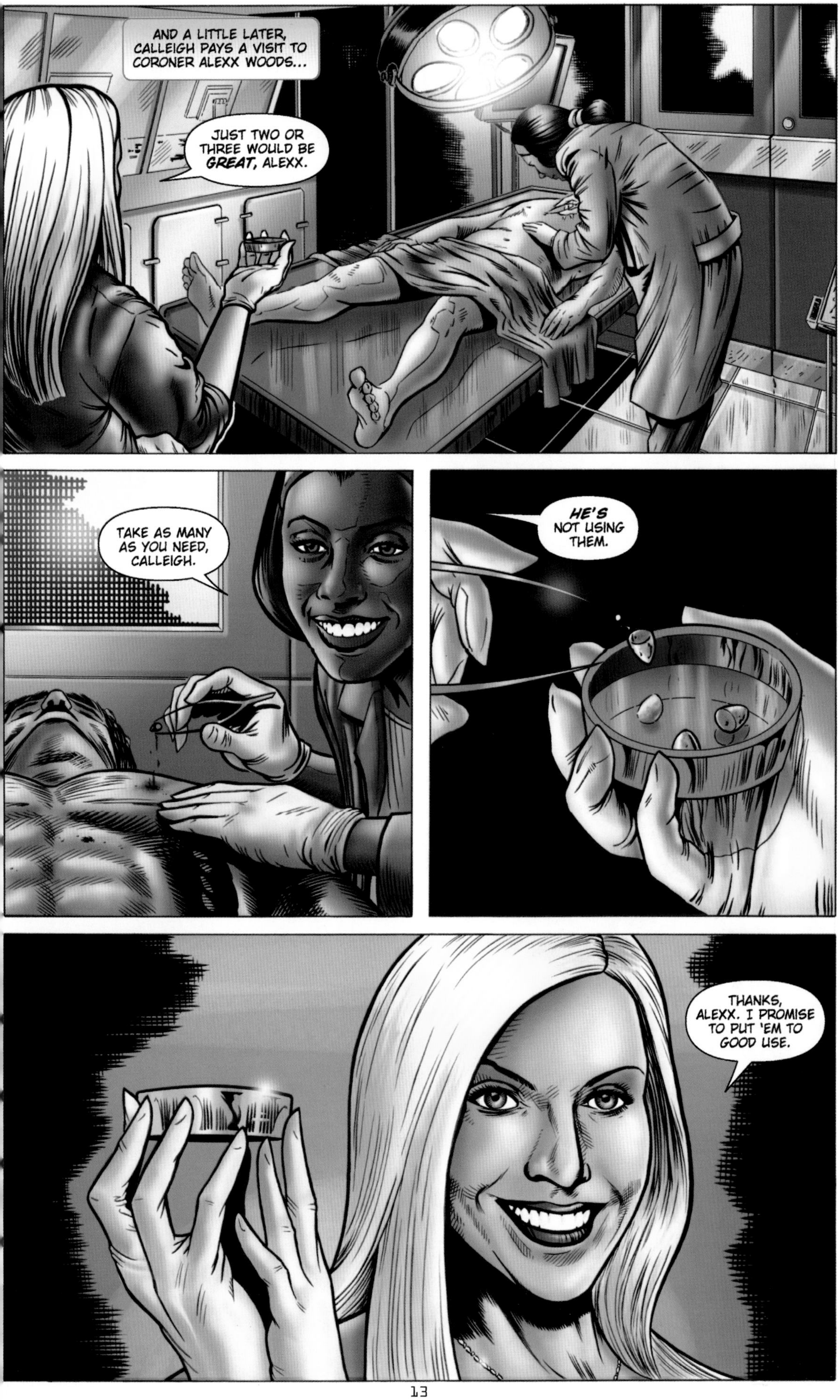
AND A LITTLE LATER, CALLEIGH PAYS A VISIT TO CORONER ALEXX WOODS...
JUST TWO OR THREE WOULD BE GREAT, ALEXX.
TAKE AS MANY AS YOU NEED, CALLEIGH.
HE'S NOT USING THEM.
THANKS, ALEXX. I PROMISE TO PUT 'EM TO GOOD USE.

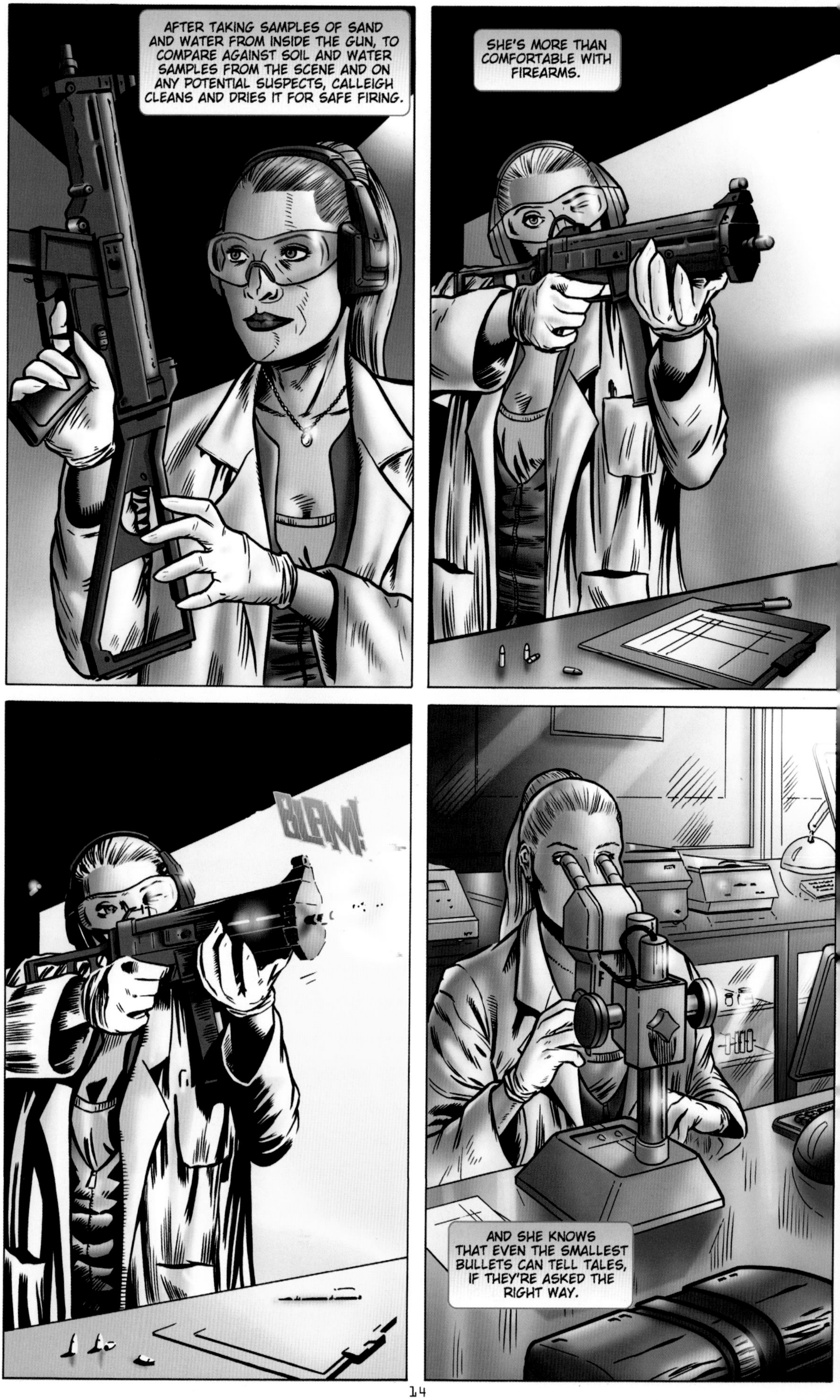
AFTER TAKING SAMPLES OF SAND AND WATER FROM INSIDE THE GUN, TO COMPARE AGAINST SOIL AND WATER SAMPLES FROM THE SCENE AND ON ANY POTENTIAL SUSPECTS, CALLEIGH CLEANS AND DRIES IT FOR SAFE FIRING.
SHE'S MORE THAN COMFORTABLE WITH FIREARMS.
BLAM!
AND SHE KNOWS THAT EVEN THE SMALLEST BULLETS CAN TELL TALES, IF THEY'RE ASKED THE RIGHT WAY.

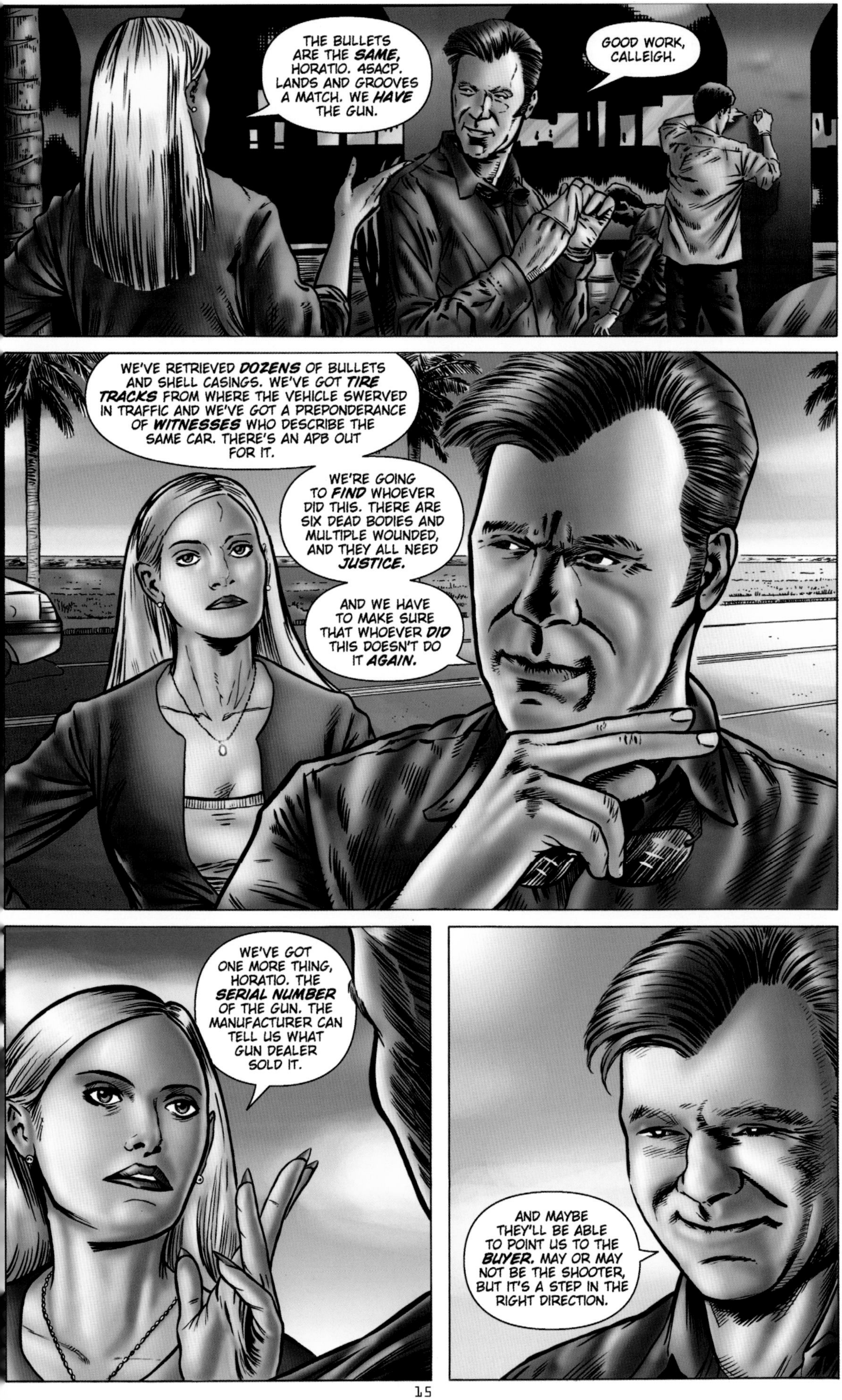
THE BULLETS ARE THE SAME, HORATIO. 45ACP. LANDS AND GROOVES A MATCH. WE HAVE THE GUN.
GOOD WORK, CALLEIGH.
WE'VE RETRIEVED DOZENS OF BULLETS AND SHELL CASINGS. WE'VE GOT TIRE TRACKS FROM WHERE THE VEHICLE SWERVED IN TRAFFIC AND WE'VE GOT A PREPONDERANCE OF WITNESSES WHO DESCRIBE THE SAME CAR. THERE'S AN APB OUT FOR IT.
WE'RE GOING TO FIND WHOEVER DID THIS. THERE ARE SIX DEAD BODIES AND MULTIPLE WOUNDED, AND THEY ALL NEED JUSTICE.
AND WE HAVE TO MAKE SURE THAT WHOEVER DID THIS DOESN'T DO IT AGAIN.
WE'VE GOT ONE MORE THING, HORATIO. THE SERIAL NUMBER OF THE GUN. THE MANUFACTURER CAN TELL US WHAT GUN DEALER SOLD IT.
AND MAYBE THEY'LL BE ABLE TO POINT US TO THE BUYER. MAY OR MAY NOT BE THE SHOOTER, BUT IT'S A STEP IN THE RIGHT DIRECTION.

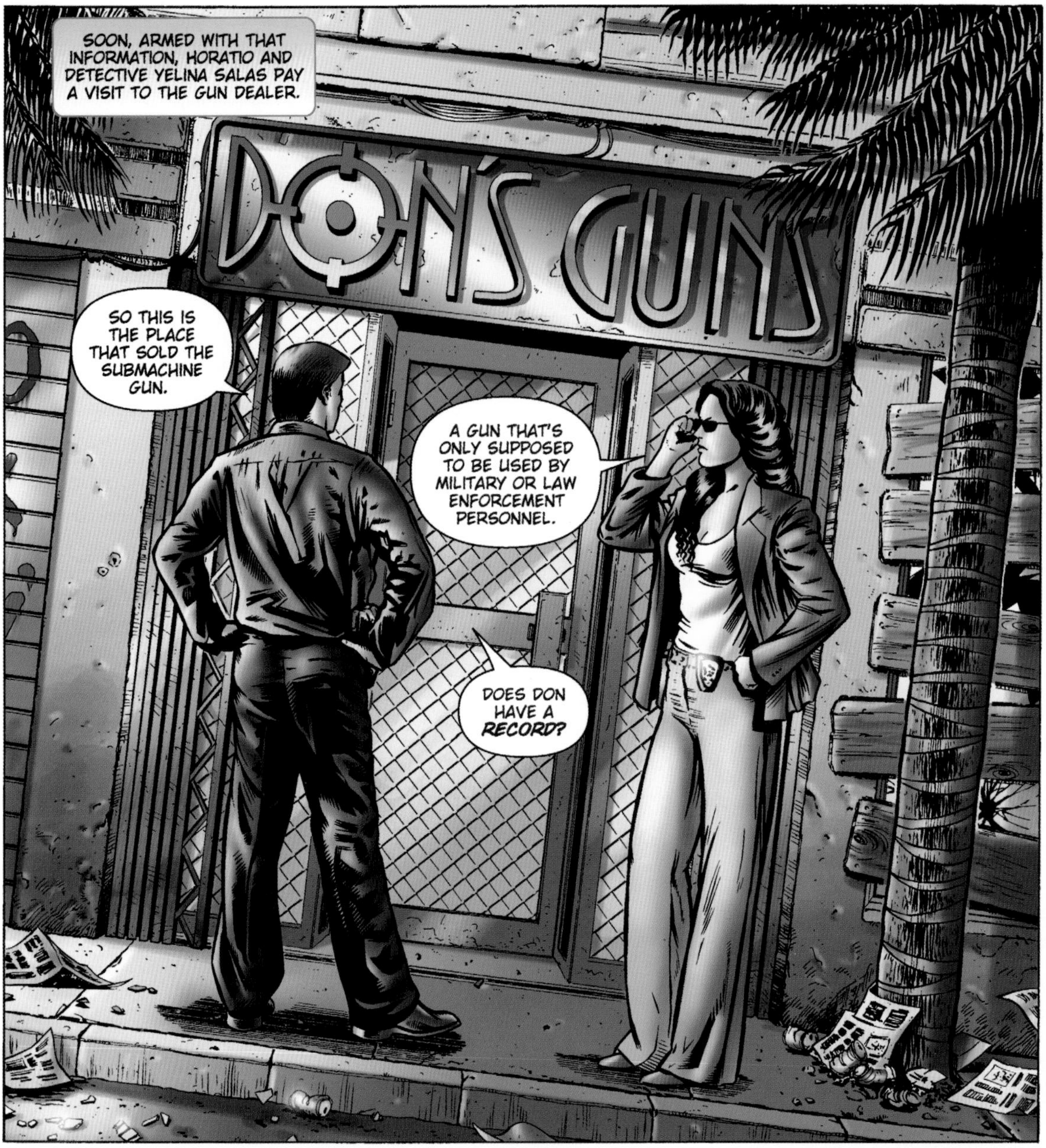
SOON, ARMED WITH THAT INFORMATION, HORATIO AND DETECTIVE YELINA SALAS PAY A VISIT TO THE GUN DEALER.
DON'S GUNS
SO THIS IS THE PLACE THAT SOLD THE SUBMACHINE GUN.
A GUN THAT'S ONLY SUPPOSED TO BE USED BY MILITARY OR LAW ENFORCEMENT PERSONNEL.
DOES DON HAVE A *RECORD?*

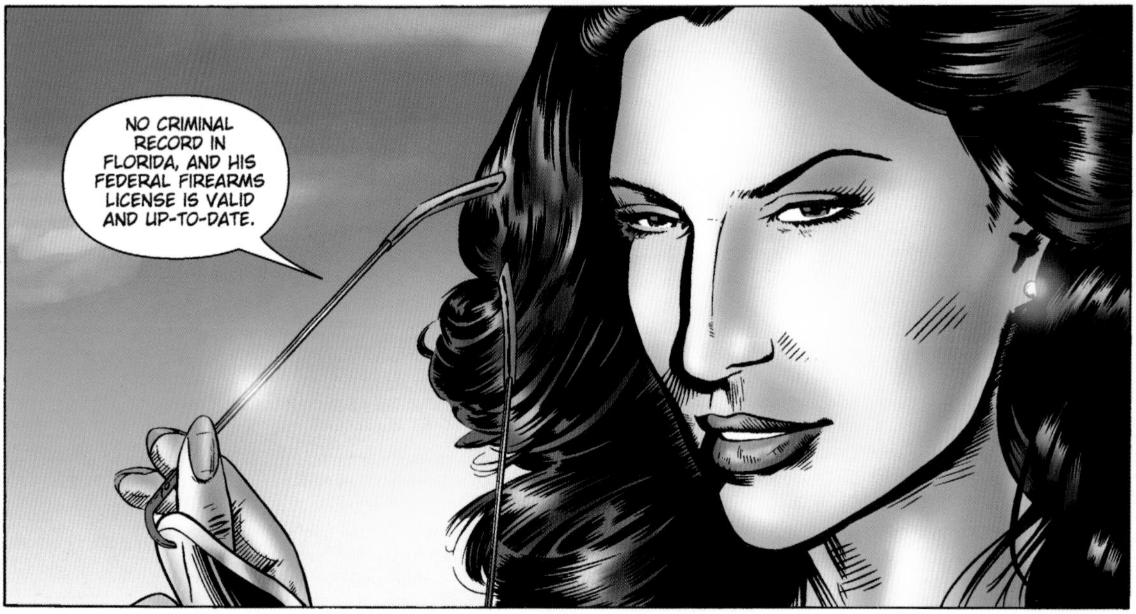
NO CRIMINAL RECORD IN FLORIDA, AND HIS FEDERAL FIREARMS LICENSE IS VALID AND UP-TO-DATE.

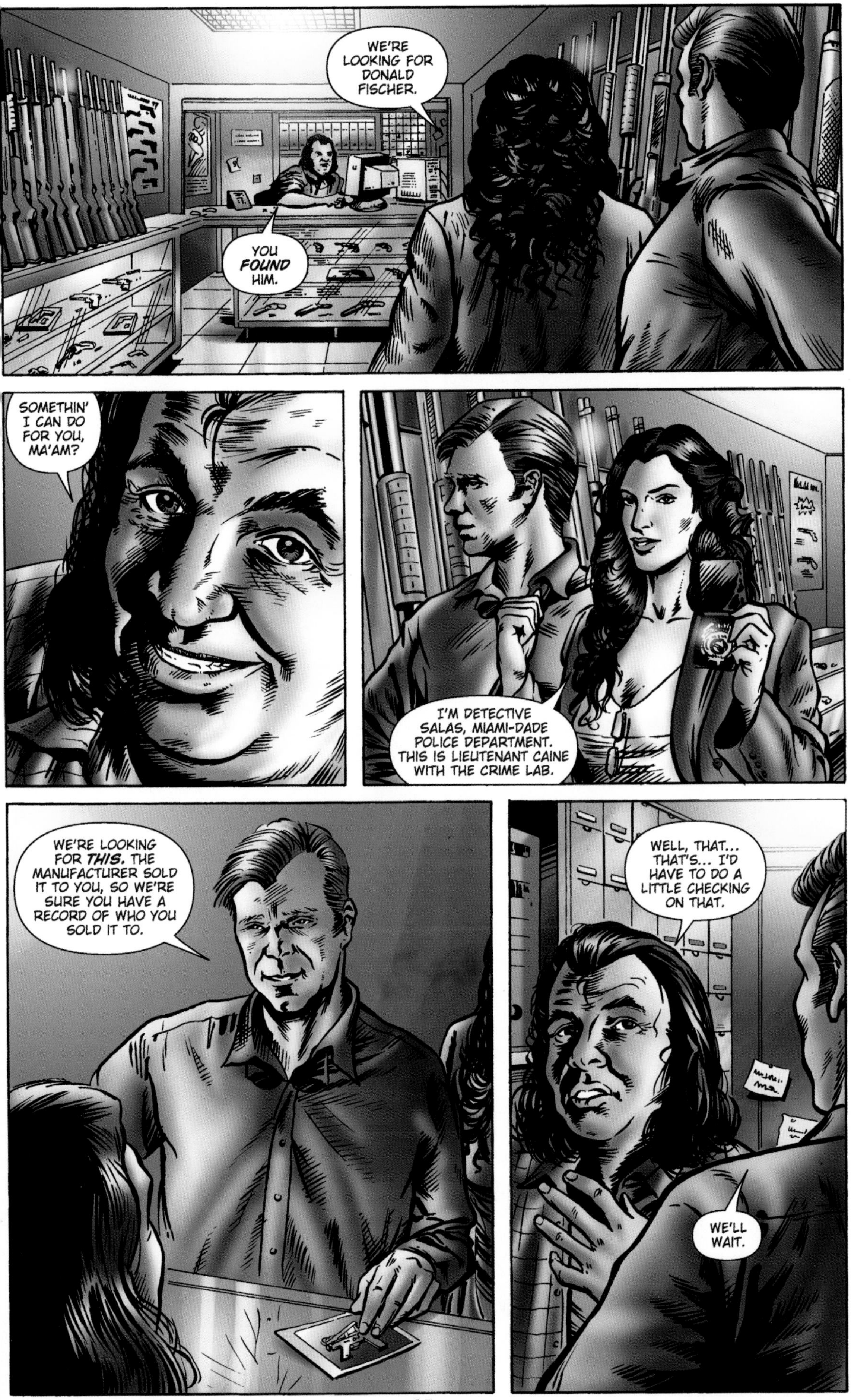
WE'RE LOOKING FOR DONALD FISCHER.
YOU FOUND HIM.
SOMETHIN' I CAN DO FOR YOU, MA'AM?
I'M DETECTIVE SALAS, MIAMI-DADE POLICE DEPARTMENT. THIS IS LIEUTENANT CAINE WITH THE CRIME LAB.
WE'RE LOOKING FOR THIS. THE MANUFACTURER SOLD IT TO YOU, SO WE'RE SURE YOU HAVE A RECORD OF WHO YOU SOLD IT TO.
WELL, THAT... THAT'S... I'D HAVE TO DO A LITTLE CHECKING ON THAT.
WE'LL WAIT.

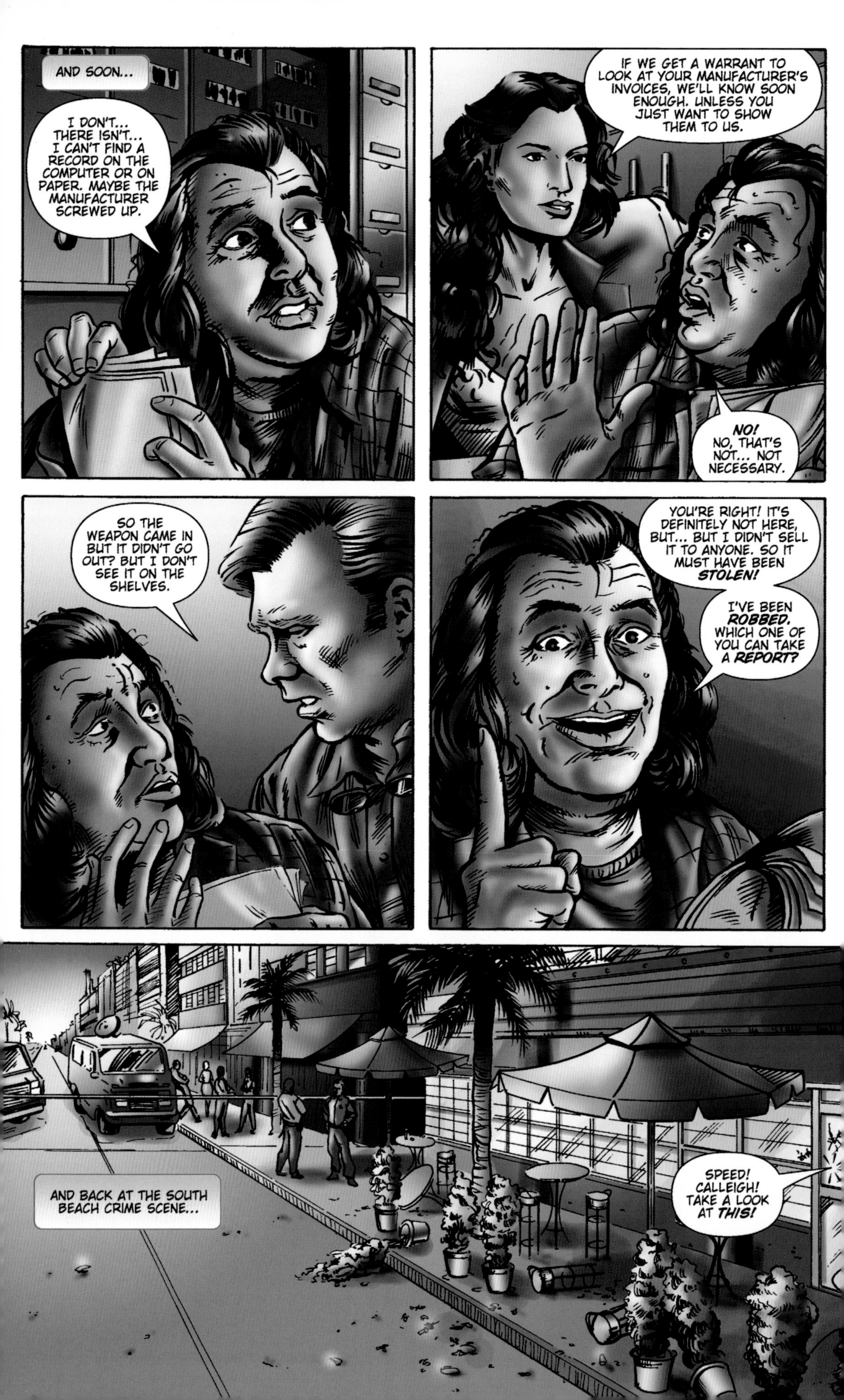
AND SOON...
I DON'T... THERE ISN'T... I CAN'T FIND A RECORD ON THE COMPUTER OR ON PAPER. MAYBE THE MANUFACTURER SCREWED UP.
IF WE GET A WARRANT TO LOOK AT YOUR MANUFACTURER'S INVOICES, WE'LL KNOW SOON ENOUGH. UNLESS YOU JUST WANT TO SHOW THEM TO US.
NO! NO, THAT'S NOT... NOT NECESSARY.
SO THE WEAPON CAME IN BUT IT DIDN'T GO OUT? BUT I DON'T SEE IT ON THE SHELVES.
YOU'RE RIGHT! IT'S DEFINITELY NOT HERE, BUT... BUT I DIDN'T SELL IT TO ANYONE. SO IT MUST HAVE BEEN STOLEN!
I'VE BEEN ROBBED. WHICH ONE OF YOU CAN TAKE A REPORT?
AND BACK AT THE SOUTH BEACH CRIME SCENE...
SPEED! CALLEIGH! TAKE A LOOK AT THIS!

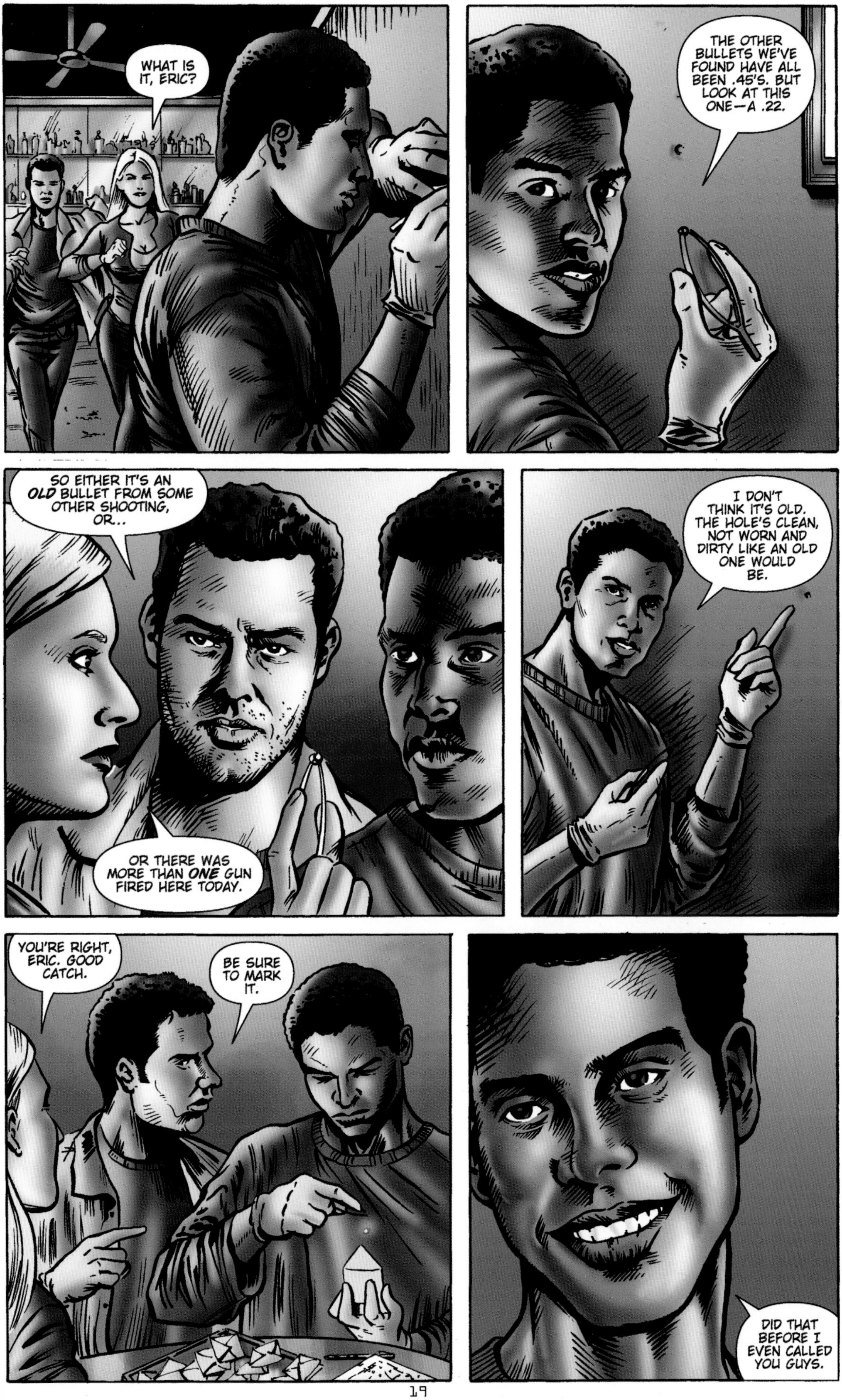
WHAT IS IT, ERIC?
THE OTHER BULLETS WE'VE FOUND HAVE ALL BEEN .45'S. BUT LOOK AT THIS ONE—A .22.
SO EITHER IT'S AN OLD BULLET FROM SOME OTHER SHOOTING, OR...
OR THERE WAS MORE THAN ONE GUN FIRED HERE TODAY.
I DON'T THINK IT'S OLD. THE HOLE'S CLEAN, NOT WORN AND DIRTY LIKE AN OLD ONE WOULD BE.
YOU'RE RIGHT, ERIC. GOOD CATCH.
BE SURE TO MARK IT.
DID THAT BEFORE I EVEN CALLED YOU GUYS.

"SHE'S STILL HEAVILY SEDATED, LT. CAINE."

WHAT'S HER PROGNOSIS, DOCTOR?

YOU HATE TO SEE SOMETHING LIKE THIS HAPPEN TO ANYONE, MUCH LESS A BEAUTIFUL YOUNG WOMAN.

EVEN MORE SO, ONE WHO MAKES HER LIVING WITH HER FACE.

HER LIFE ISN'T IN DANGER. BUT SHE'LL NEED A *LOT* OF RECONSTRUCTIVE SURGERY BEFORE HER FACE WILL EVEN BEGIN TO LOOK THE SAME.

I DOUBT THAT SHE'LL EVER GET HER LOOKS BACK COMPLETELY.

SHE'S NOT... A *SUSPECT* IN ANYTHING, IS SHE?

THE UNIFORM? NO, SHE'S NOT A SUSPECT.

BUT UNTIL SHE'S AWAKE AND COHERENT WE DON'T KNOW IF SHE'S A WITNESS AS WELL AS A VICTIM.

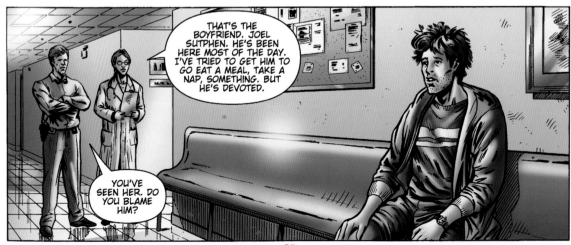

THAT'S THE BOYFRIEND. JOEL SUTPHEN. HE'S BEEN HERE MOST OF THE DAY. I'VE TRIED TO GET HIM TO GO EAT A MEAL, TAKE A NAP, SOMETHING. BUT HE'S DEVOTED.

YOU'VE SEEN HER. DO YOU BLAME HIM?

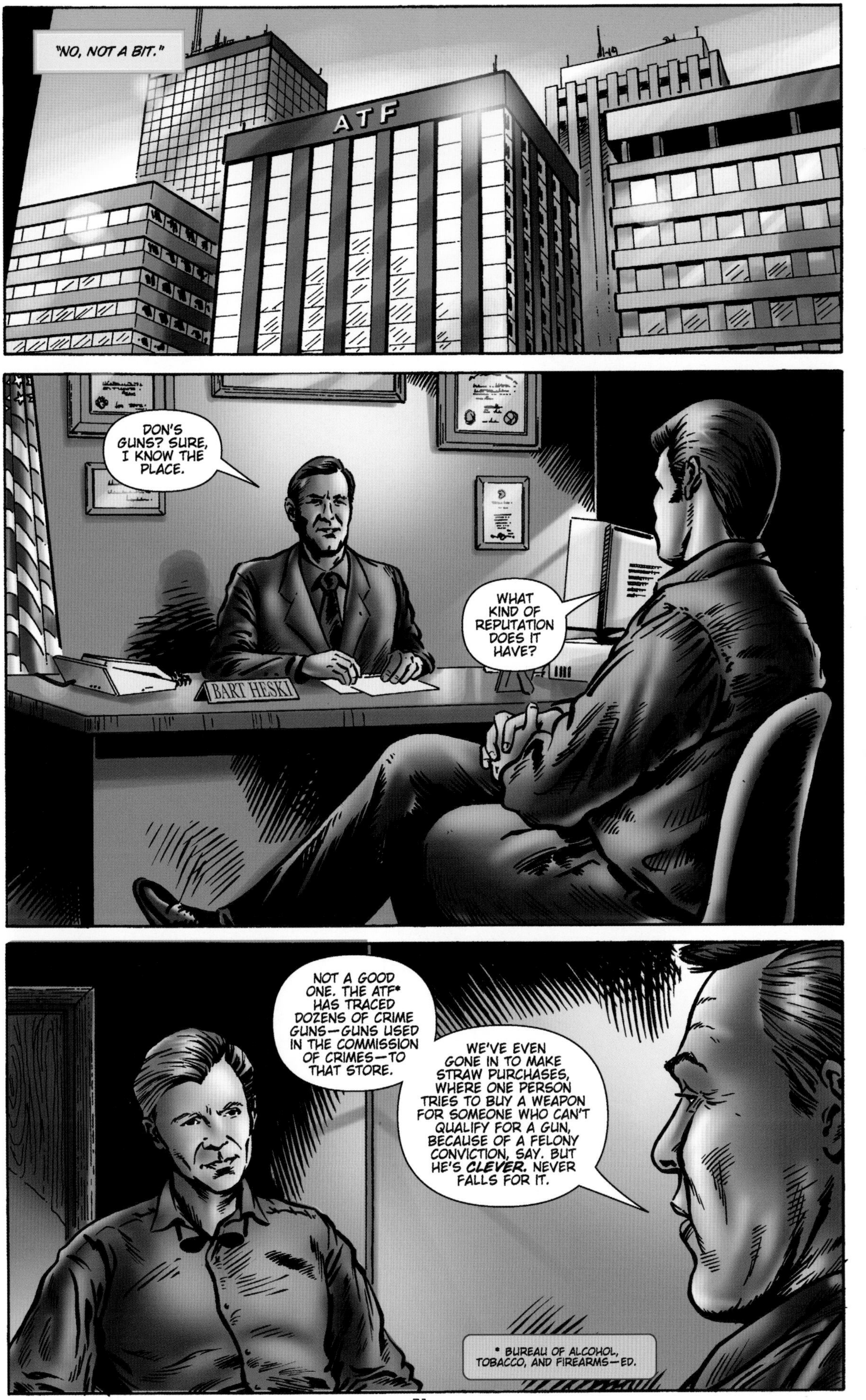
"NO, NOT A BIT."
ATF
DON'S GUNS? SURE, I KNOW THE PLACE.
BART HESKI
WHAT KIND OF REPUTATION DOES IT HAVE?
NOT A GOOD ONE. THE ATF* HAS TRACED DOZENS OF CRIME GUNS—GUNS USED IN THE COMMISSION OF CRIMES—TO THAT STORE.
WE'VE EVEN GONE IN TO MAKE STRAW PURCHASES, WHERE ONE PERSON TRIES TO BUY A WEAPON FOR SOMEONE WHO CAN'T QUALIFY FOR A GUN, BECAUSE OF A FELONY CONVICTION, SAY. BUT HE'S CLEVER. NEVER FALLS FOR IT.
* BUREAU OF ALCOHOL, TOBACCO, AND FIREARMS—ED.

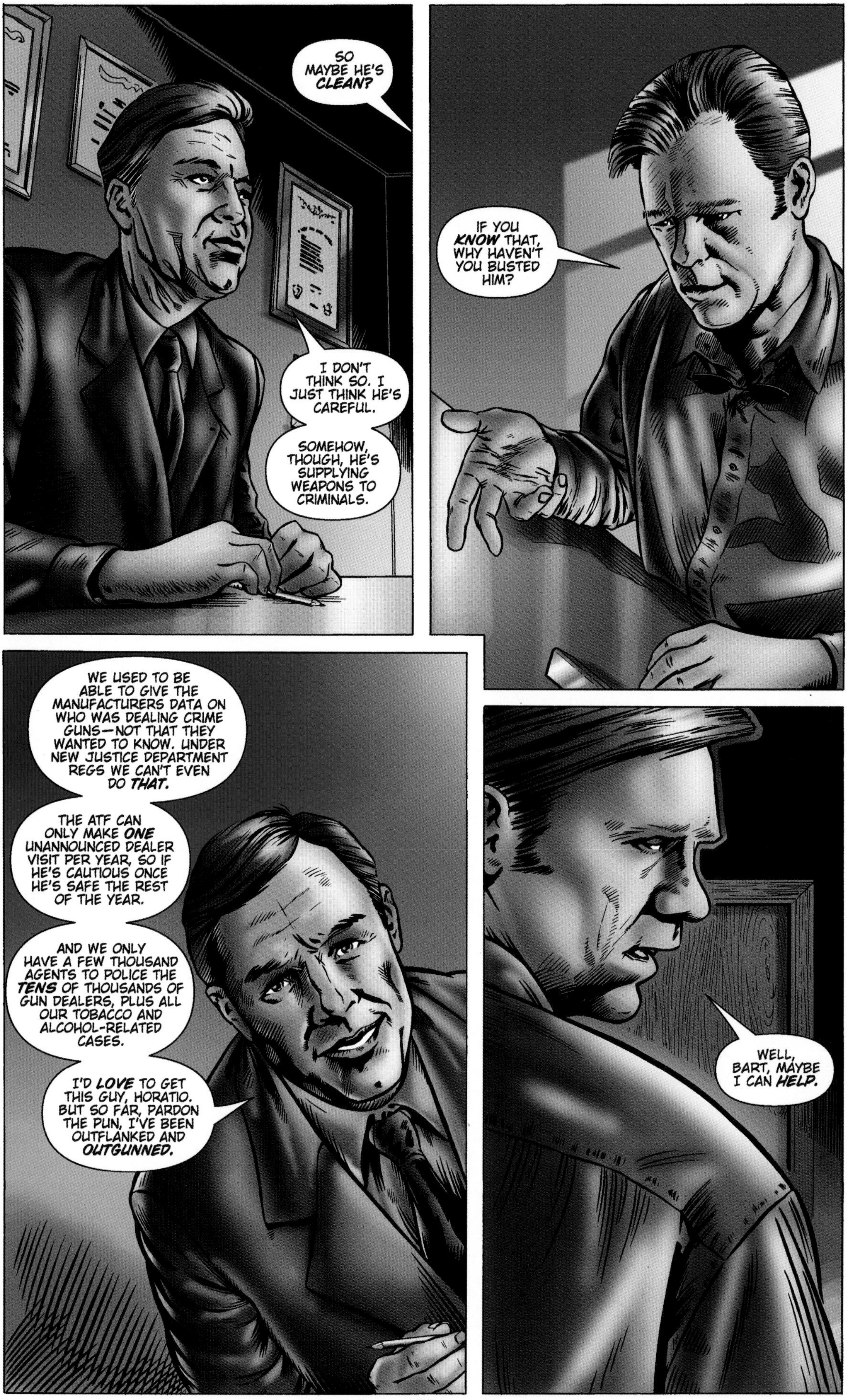
SO MAYBE HE'S CLEAN?
I DON'T THINK SO. I JUST THINK HE'S CAREFUL.
SOMEHOW, THOUGH, HE'S SUPPLYING WEAPONS TO CRIMINALS.
IF YOU KNOW THAT, WHY HAVEN'T YOU BUSTED HIM?
WE USED TO BE ABLE TO GIVE THE MANUFACTURERS DATA ON WHO WAS DEALING CRIME GUNS—NOT THAT THEY WANTED TO KNOW. UNDER NEW JUSTICE DEPARTMENT REGS WE CAN'T EVEN DO THAT.
THE ATF CAN ONLY MAKE ONE UNANNOUNCED DEALER VISIT PER YEAR, SO IF HE'S CAUTIOUS ONCE HE'S SAFE THE REST OF THE YEAR.
AND WE ONLY HAVE A FEW THOUSAND AGENTS TO POLICE THE TENS OF THOUSANDS OF GUN DEALERS, PLUS ALL OUR TOBACCO AND ALCOHOL-RELATED CASES.
I'D LOVE TO GET THIS GUY, HORATIO. BUT SO FAR, PARDON THE PUN, I'VE BEEN OUTFLANKED AND OUTGUNNED.
WELL, BART, MAYBE I CAN HELP.

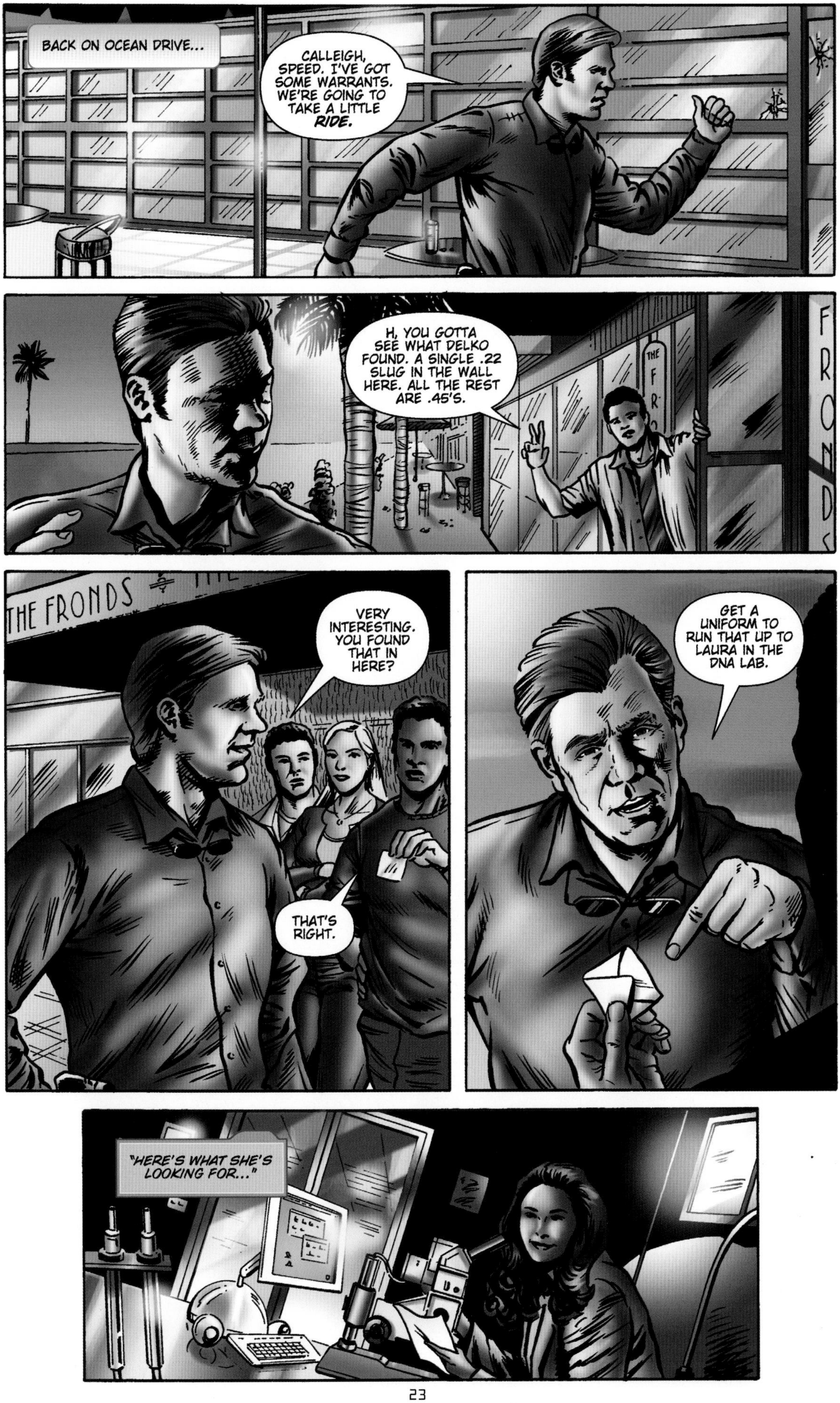
BACK ON OCEAN DRIVE...
CALLEIGH, SPEED. I'VE GOT SOME WARRANTS. WE'RE GOING TO TAKE A LITTLE RIDE.
H, YOU GOTTA SEE WHAT DELKO FOUND. A SINGLE .22 SLUG IN THE WALL HERE. ALL THE REST ARE .45'S.
THE FRONDS
VERY INTERESTING. YOU FOUND THAT IN HERE?
THAT'S RIGHT.
GET A UNIFORM TO RUN THAT UP TO LAURA IN THE DNA LAB.
"HERE'S WHAT SHE'S LOOKING FOR..."

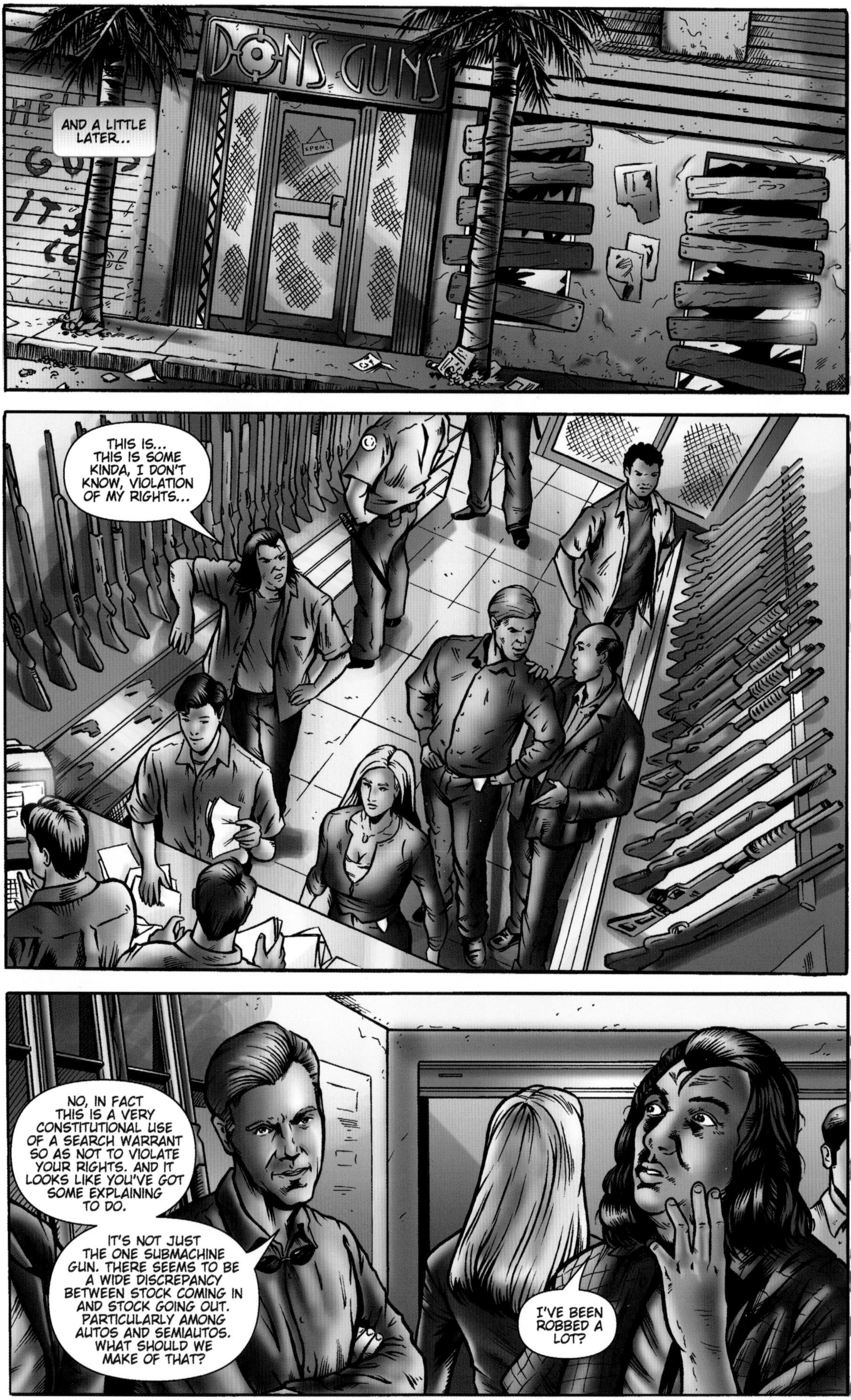
DON'S GUNS
AND A LITTLE LATER...
THIS IS... THIS IS SOME KINDA, I DON'T KNOW, VIOLATION OF MY RIGHTS...
NO, IN FACT THIS IS A VERY CONSTITUTIONAL USE OF A SEARCH WARRANT SO AS NOT TO VIOLATE YOUR RIGHTS. AND IT LOOKS LIKE YOU'VE GOT SOME EXPLAINING TO DO.
IT'S NOT JUST THE ONE SUBMACHINE GUN. THERE SEEMS TO BE A WIDE DISCREPANCY BETWEEN STOCK COMING IN AND STOCK GOING OUT. PARTICULARLY AMONG AUTOS AND SEMIAUTOS. WHAT SHOULD WE MAKE OF THAT?
I'VE BEEN ROBBED A LOT?

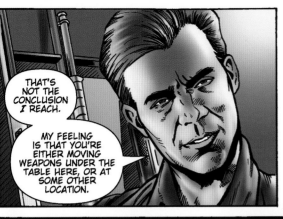

THAT'S NOT THE CONCLUSION *I* REACH.

MY FEELING IS THAT YOU'RE EITHER MOVING WEAPONS UNDER THE TABLE HERE, OR AT SOME OTHER LOCATION.

WHICH IS WHY WE GOT ANOTHER WARRANT, FOR YOUR HOUSE.

"DO YOU WANT TO GIVE ME THE KEY, OR COME WITH US?"

YOU MAY BE RIGHT ABOUT DONNY HERE, HORATIO. LORD KNOWS HE'S NO PILLAR OF SOCIETY.

BUT I DO WORRY ABOUT OVERLY AGGRESSIVE TACTICS BEING USED AGAINST LAW-ABIDING FIREARMS DEALERS AND OWNERS, WHICH ARE THE VAST *MAJORITY*.

YOU MAKE A GOOD POINT, CALLEIGH.

BUT I KEEP SEEING MADISON SINGER'S RUINED *FACE*, AND SUDDENLY THE RIGHTS OF SOMEONE LIKE DON TAKE A BACK SEAT.

WHAT DO YOU THINK, DON?

I'M NOT SAYING A WORD UNTIL I SEE MY LAWYER.

HE'S MEETING YOU AT YOUR HOUSE. NOT MUCH FARTHER TO GO.

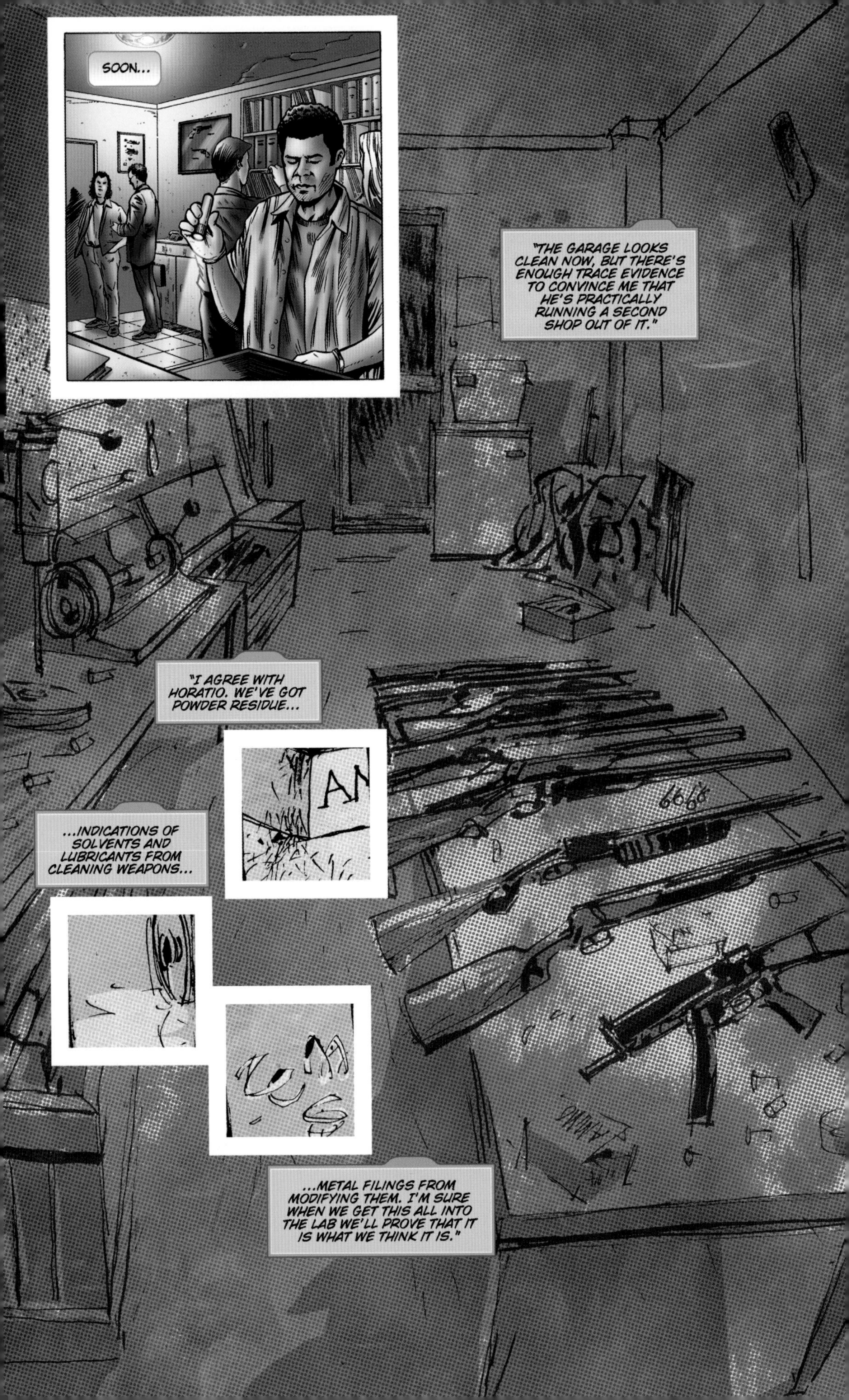
SOON...
"THE GARAGE LOOKS CLEAN NOW, BUT THERE'S ENOUGH TRACE EVIDENCE TO CONVINCE ME THAT HE'S PRACTICALLY RUNNING A SECOND SHOP OUT OF IT."
"I AGREE WITH HORATIO. WE'VE GOT POWDER RESIDUE...
...INDICATIONS OF SOLVENTS AND LUBRICANTS FROM CLEANING WEAPONS...
...METAL FILINGS FROM MODIFYING THEM. I'M SURE WHEN WE GET THIS ALL INTO THE LAB WE'LL PROVE THAT IT IS WHAT WE THINK IT IS."

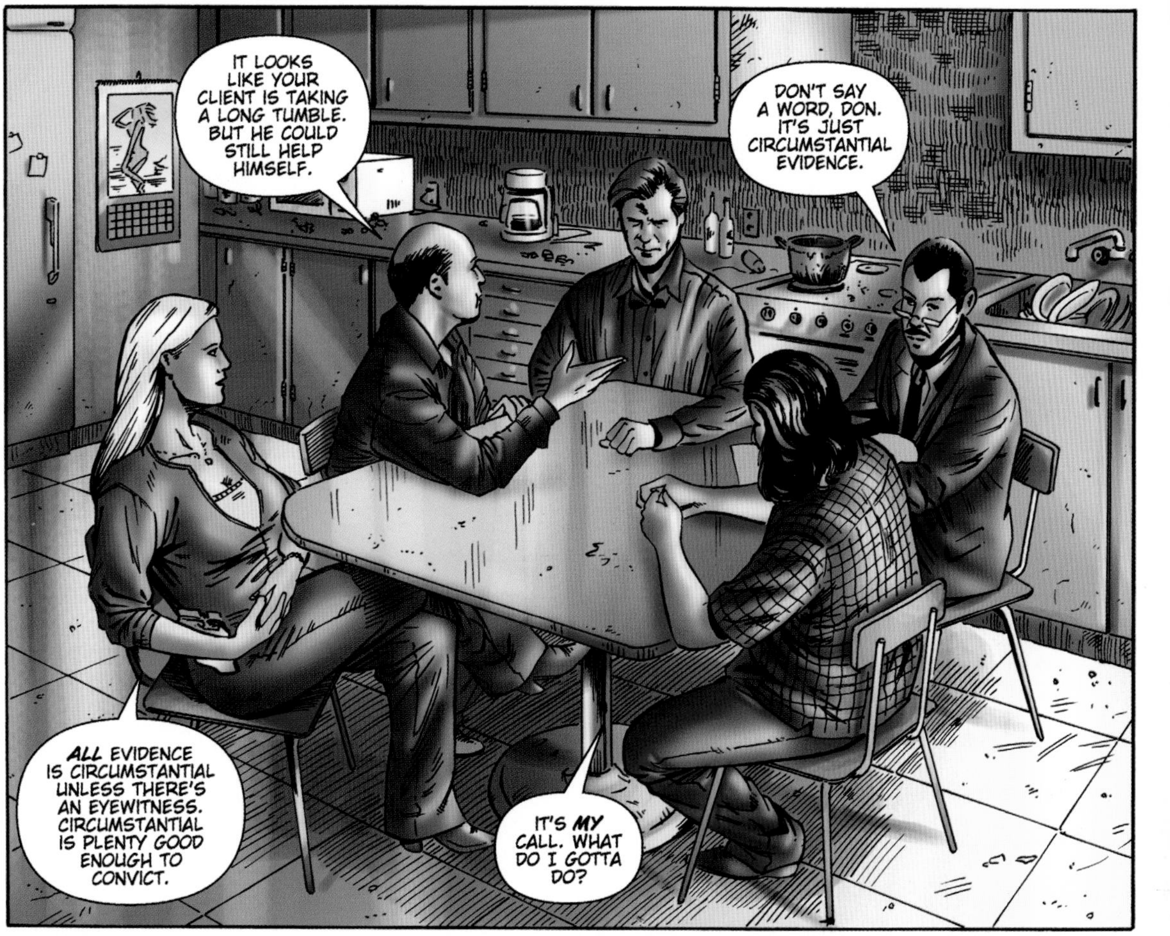
IT LOOKS LIKE YOUR CLIENT IS TAKING A LONG TUMBLE. BUT HE COULD STILL HELP HIMSELF.
DON'T SAY A WORD, DON. IT'S JUST CIRCUMSTANTIAL EVIDENCE.
ALL EVIDENCE IS CIRCUMSTANTIAL UNLESS THERE'S AN EYEWITNESS. CIRCUMSTANTIAL IS PLENTY GOOD ENOUGH TO CONVICT.
IT'S MY CALL. WHAT DO I GOTTA DO?

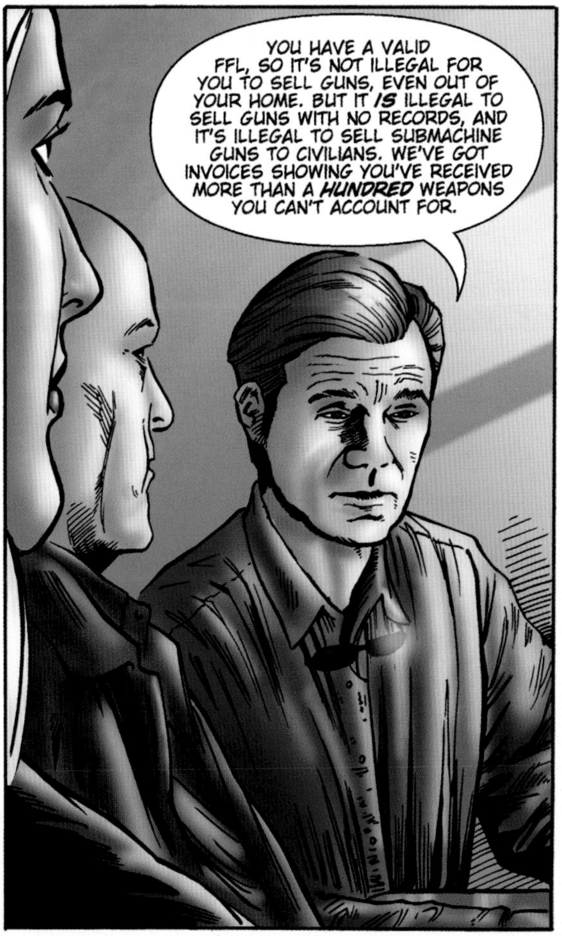
YOU HAVE A VALID FFL, SO IT'S NOT ILLEGAL FOR YOU TO SELL GUNS, EVEN OUT OF YOUR HOME. BUT IT IS ILLEGAL TO SELL GUNS WITH NO RECORDS, AND IT'S ILLEGAL TO SELL SUBMACHINE GUNS TO CIVILIANS. WE'VE GOT INVOICES SHOWING YOU'VE RECEIVED MORE THAN A HUNDRED WEAPONS YOU CAN'T ACCOUNT FOR.

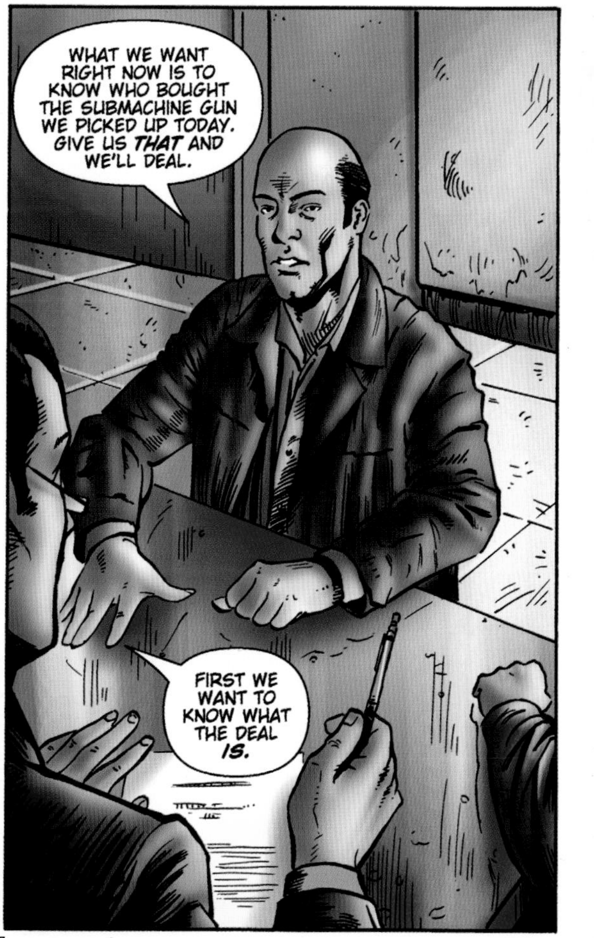
WHAT WE WANT RIGHT NOW IS TO KNOW WHO BOUGHT THE SUBMACHINE GUN WE PICKED UP TODAY. GIVE US THAT AND WE'LL DEAL.
FIRST WE WANT TO KNOW WHAT THE DEAL IS.

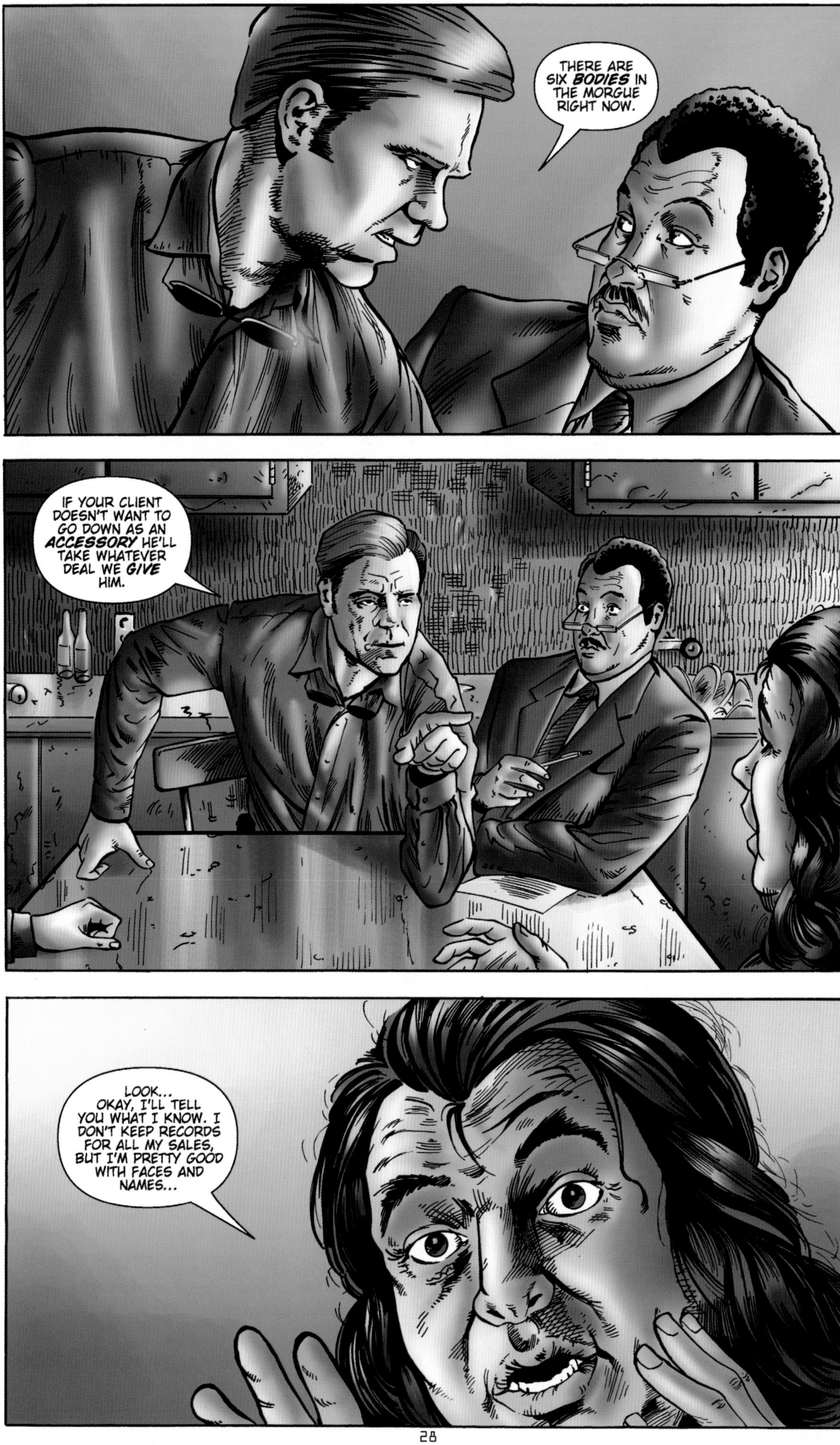
THERE ARE SIX BODIES IN THE MORGUE RIGHT NOW.
IF YOUR CLIENT DOESN'T WANT TO GO DOWN AS AN ACCESSORY HE'LL TAKE WHATEVER DEAL WE GIVE HIM.
LOOK... OKAY, I'LL TELL YOU WHAT I KNOW. I DON'T KEEP RECORDS FOR ALL MY SALES, BUT I'M PRETTY GOOD WITH FACES AND NAMES...

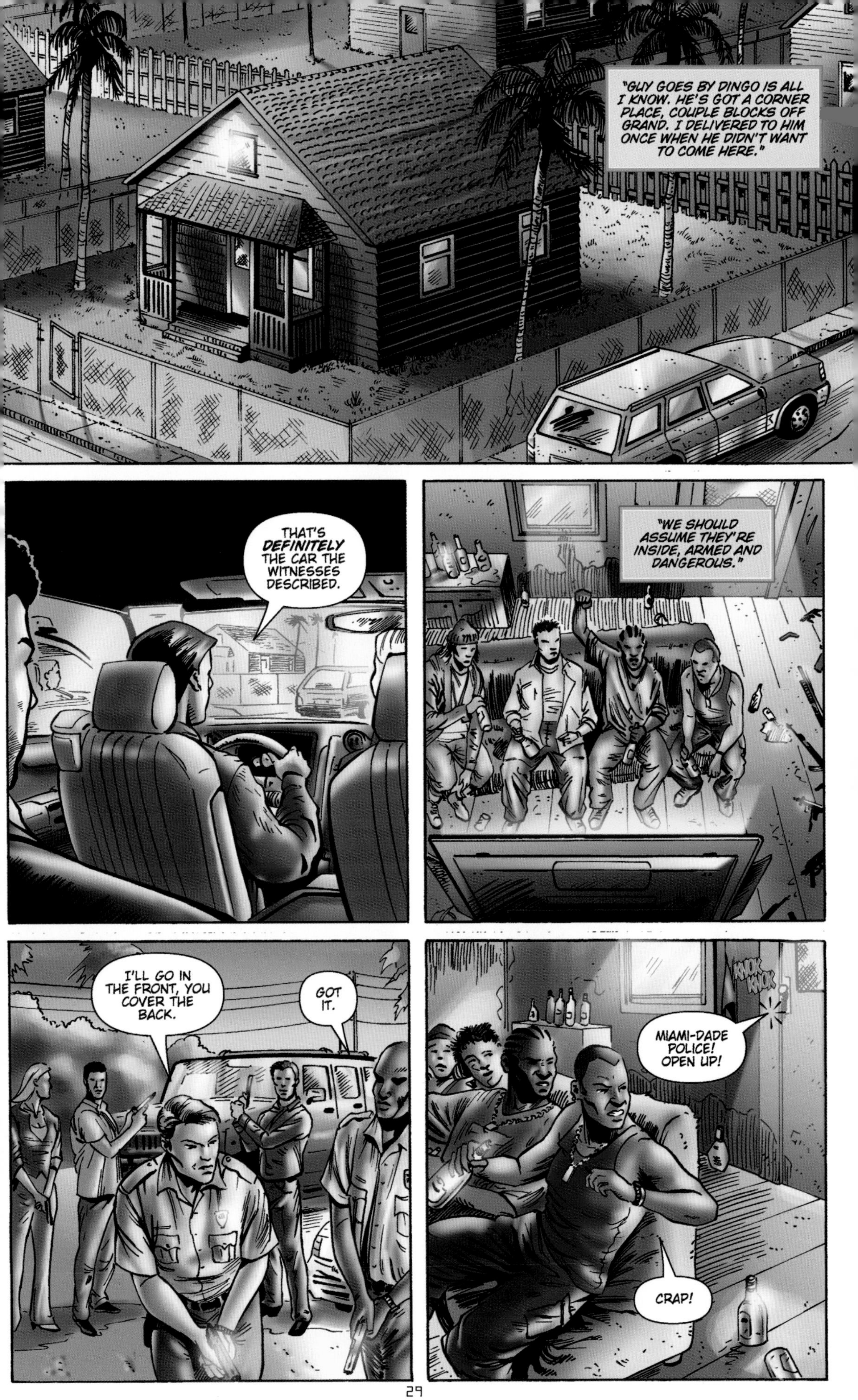
"GUY GOES BY DINGO IS ALL I KNOW. HE'S GOT A CORNER PLACE, COUPLE BLOCKS OFF GRAND. I DELIVERED TO HIM ONCE WHEN HE DIDN'T WANT TO COME HERE."
THAT'S DEFINITELY THE CAR THE WITNESSES DESCRIBED.
"WE SHOULD ASSUME THEY'RE INSIDE, ARMED AND DANGEROUS."
I'LL GO IN THE FRONT, YOU COVER THE BACK.
GOT IT.
KNOK KNOK
MIAMI-DADE POLICE! OPEN UP!
CRAP!

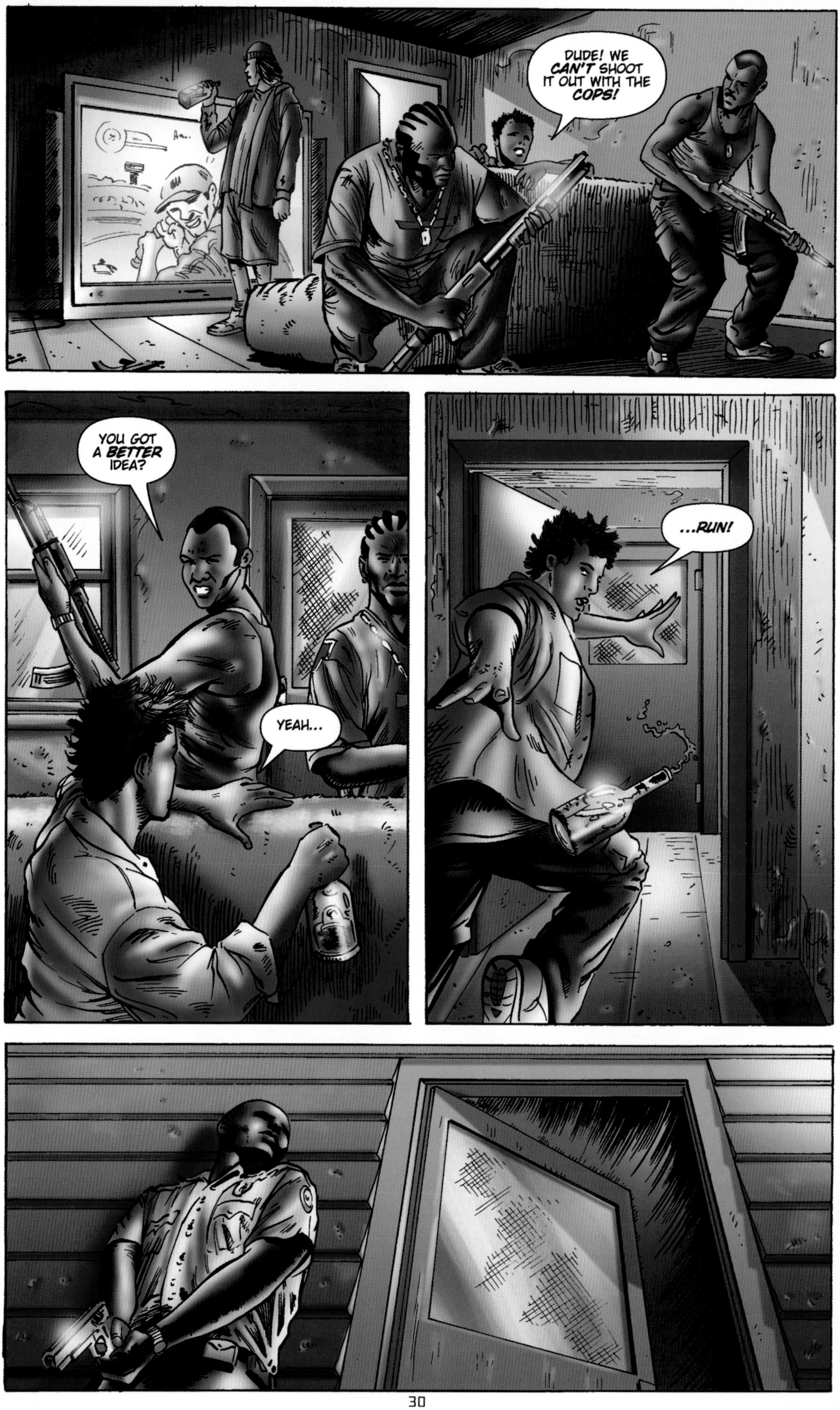
DUDE! WE CAN'T SHOOT IT OUT WITH THE COPS!
YOU GOT A BETTER IDEA?
YEAH...
...RUN!

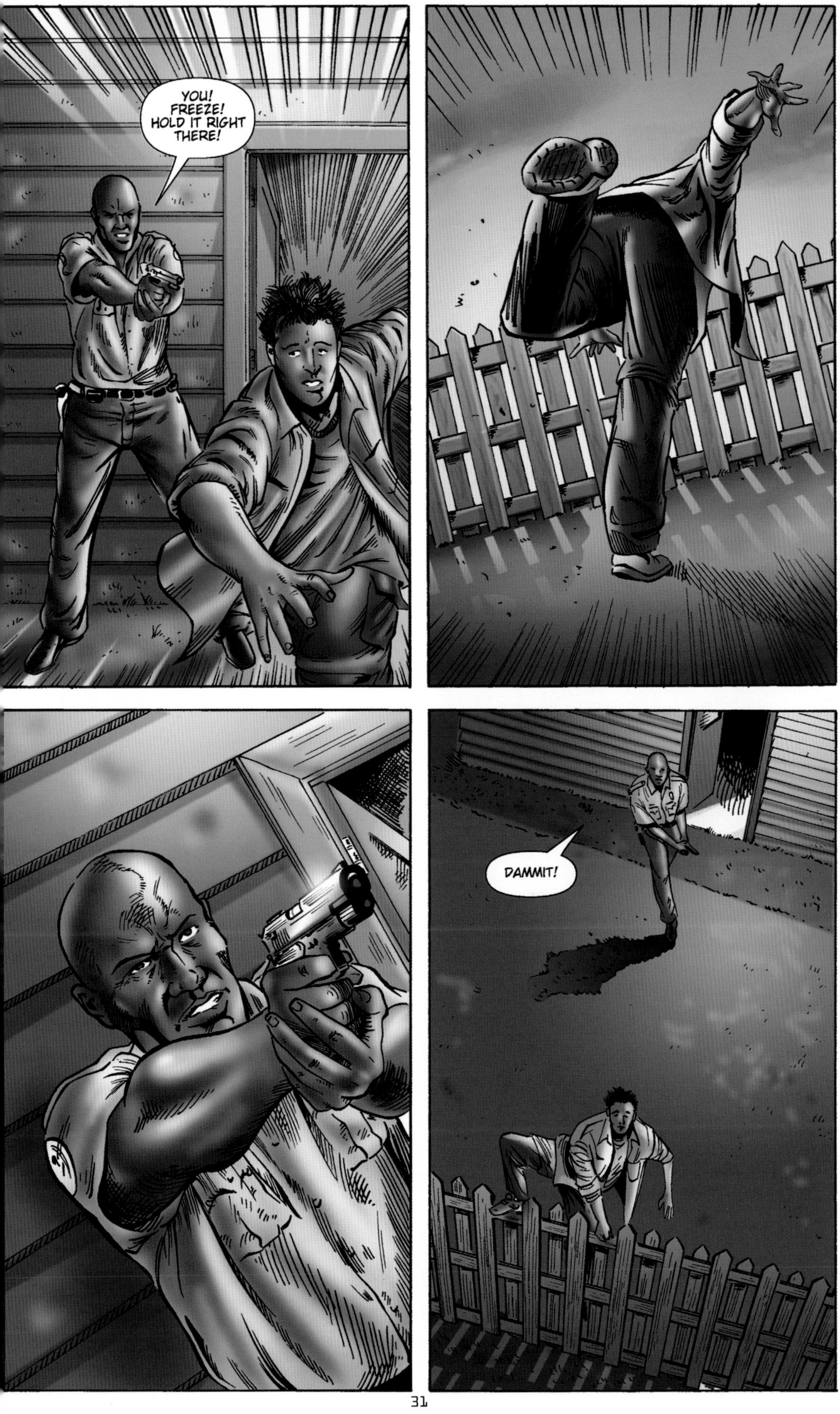
YOU! FREEZE! HOLD IT RIGHT THERE!
DAMMIT!

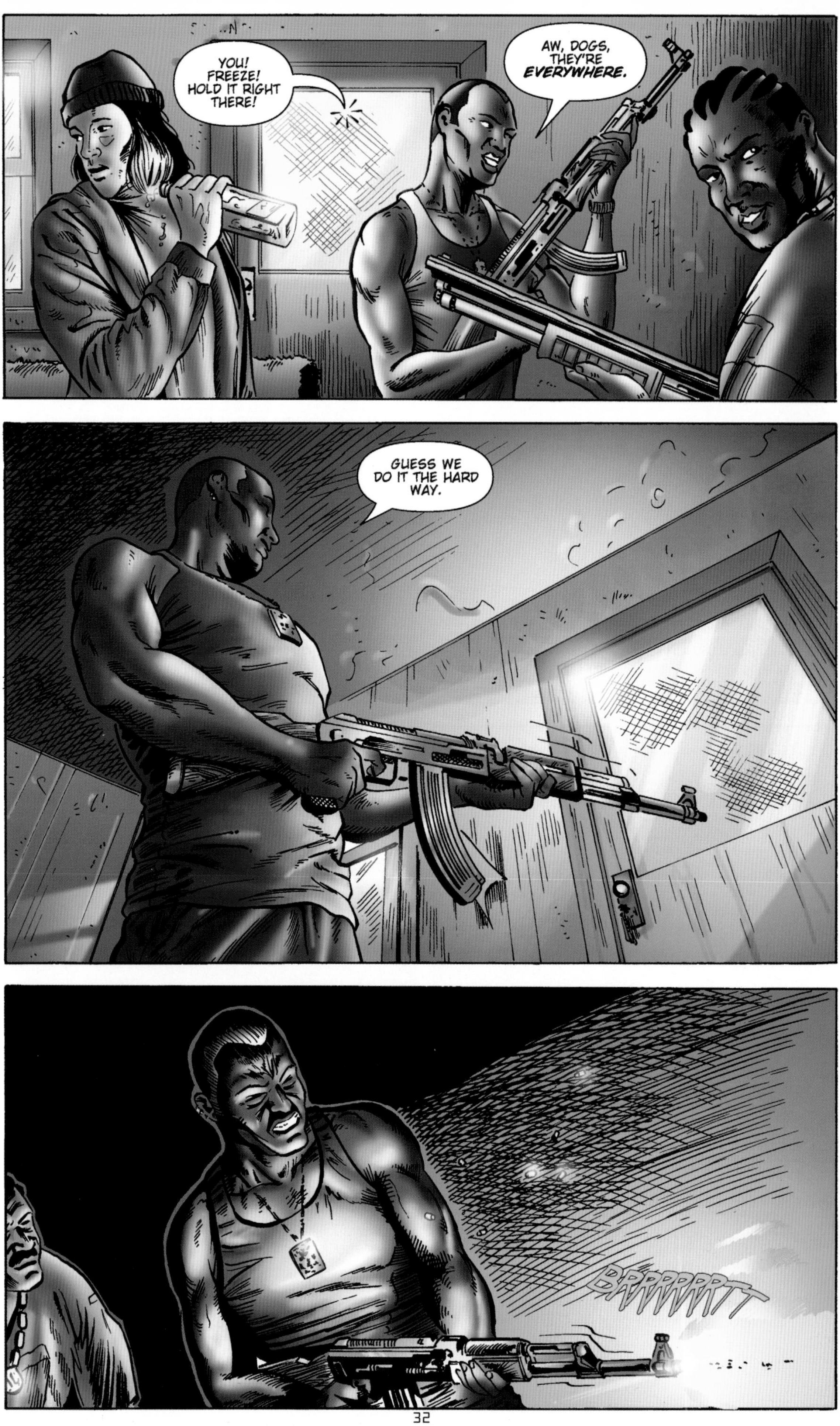
YOU! FREEZE! HOLD IT RIGHT THERE!
AW, DOGS, THEY'RE *EVERYWHERE.*
GUESS WE DO IT THE HARD WAY.
BRRRRRRTT

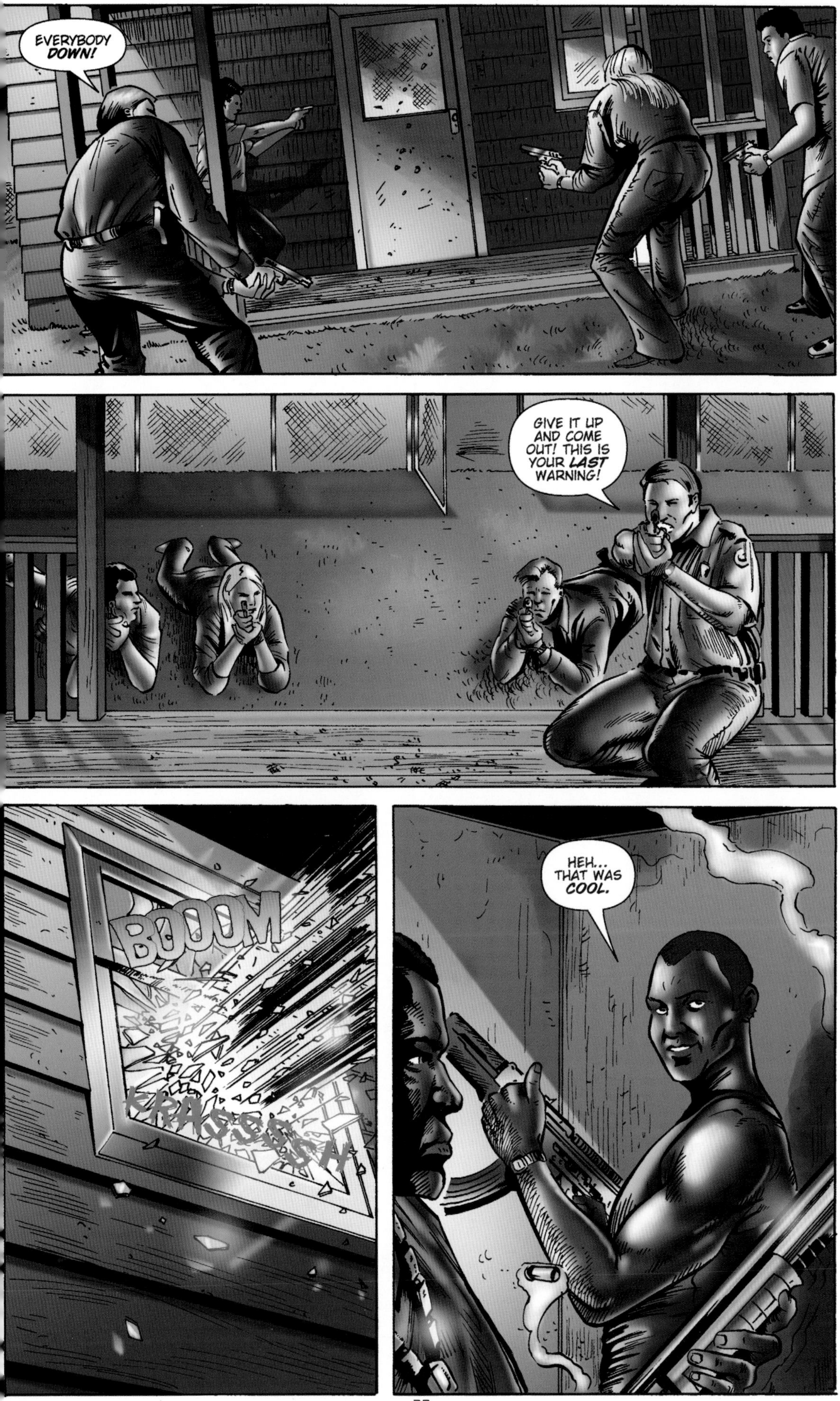
EVERYBODY DOWN!
GIVE IT UP AND COME OUT! THIS IS YOUR LAST WARNING!
BOOOM
KRASSSSH
HEH... THAT WAS COOL.

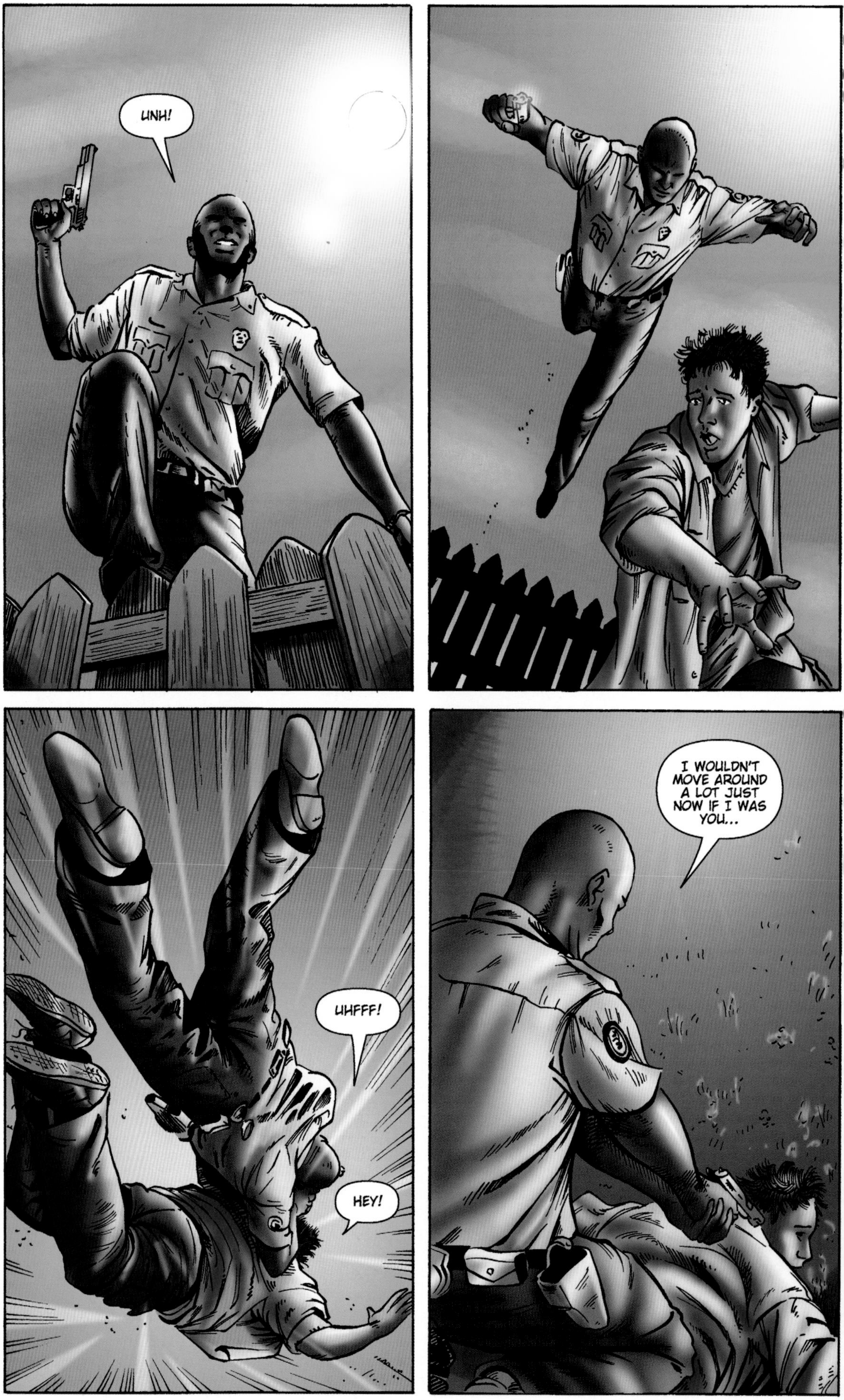
UNH!
UHFFF!
HEY!
I WOULDN'T MOVE AROUND A LOT JUST NOW IF I WAS YOU...

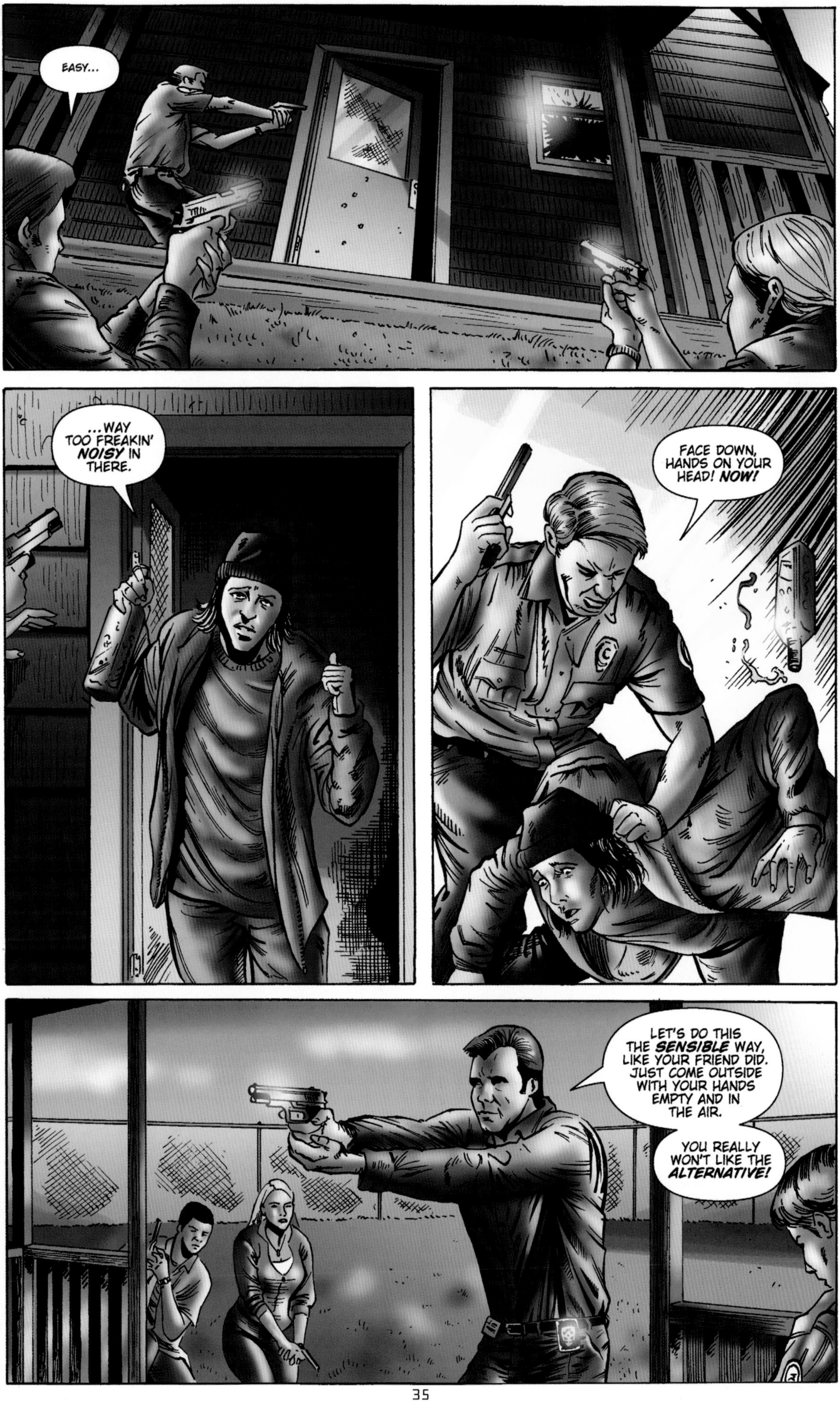
EASY...
...WAY TOO FREAKIN' NOISY IN THERE.
FACE DOWN, HANDS ON YOUR HEAD! NOW!
LET'S DO THIS THE SENSIBLE WAY, LIKE YOUR FRIEND DID. JUST COME OUTSIDE WITH YOUR HANDS EMPTY AND IN THE AIR.
YOU REALLY WON'T LIKE THE ALTERNATIVE!

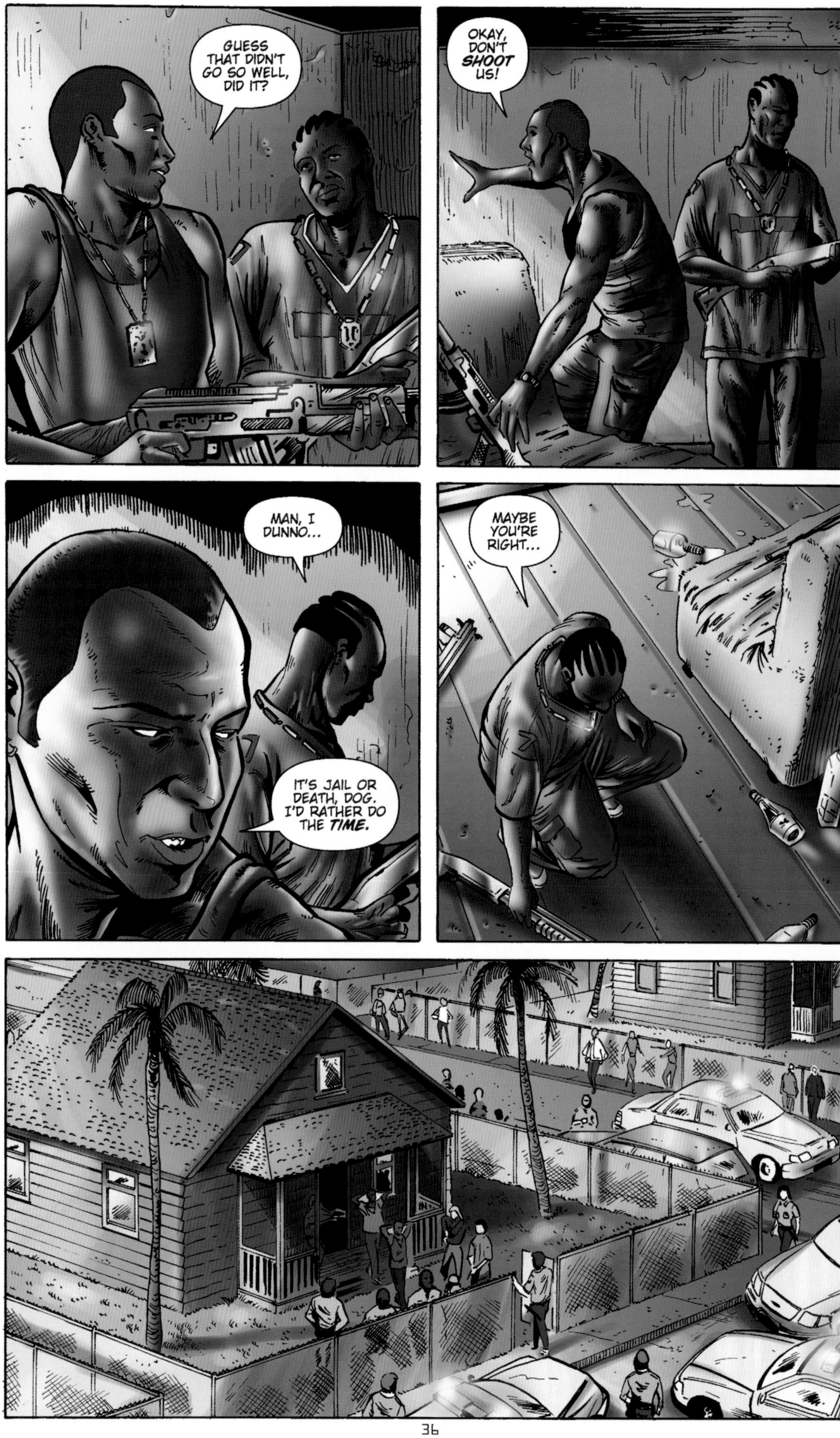
GUESS THAT DIDN'T GO SO WELL, DID IT?
OKAY, DON'T SHOOT US!
MAN, I DUNNO...
IT'S JAIL OR DEATH, DOG. I'D RATHER DO THE TIME.
MAYBE YOU'RE RIGHT...

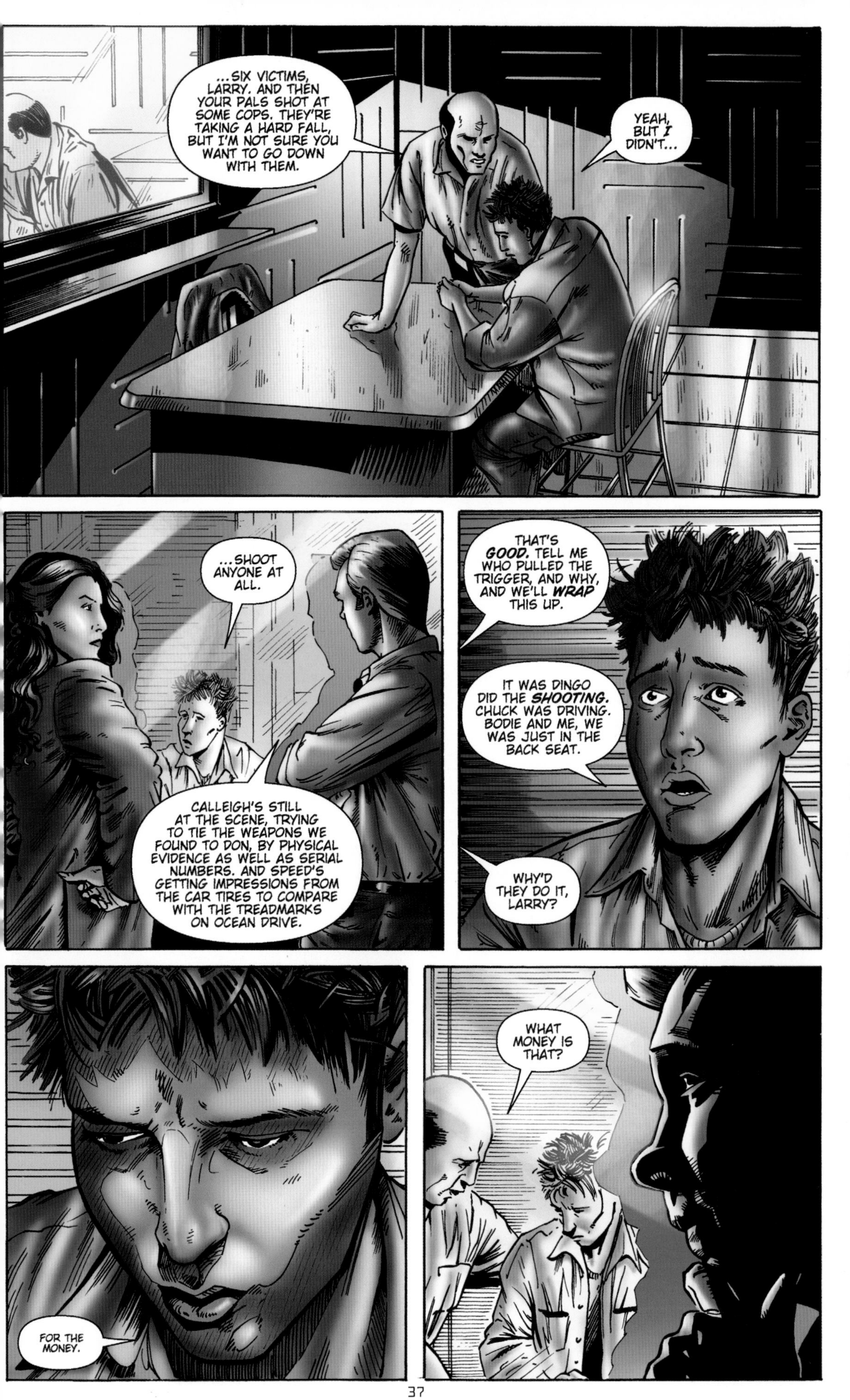
...SIX VICTIMS, LARRY. AND THEN YOUR PALS SHOT AT SOME COPS. THEY'RE TAKING A HARD FALL, BUT I'M NOT SURE YOU WANT TO GO DOWN WITH THEM.
YEAH, BUT *I* DIDN'T...
...SHOOT ANYONE AT ALL.
CALLEIGH'S STILL AT THE SCENE, TRYING TO TIE THE WEAPONS WE FOUND TO DON, BY PHYSICAL EVIDENCE AS WELL AS SERIAL NUMBERS. AND SPEED'S GETTING IMPRESSIONS FROM THE CAR TIRES TO COMPARE WITH THE TREADMARKS ON OCEAN DRIVE.
THAT'S ***GOOD.*** TELL ME WHO PULLED THE TRIGGER, AND WHY, AND WE'LL ***WRAP*** THIS UP.
IT WAS DINGO DID THE ***SHOOTING.*** CHUCK WAS DRIVING. BODIE AND ME, WE WAS JUST IN THE BACK SEAT.
WHY'D THEY DO IT, LARRY?
FOR THE MONEY.
WHAT MONEY IS THAT?

THIS SHOULD BE GOOD.

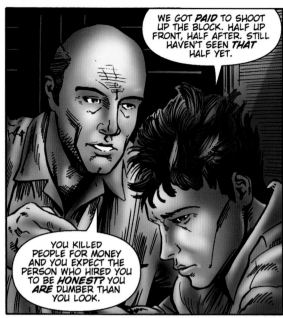

WE GOT *PAID* TO SHOOT UP THE BLOCK. HALF UP FRONT, HALF AFTER. STILL HAVEN'T SEEN *THAT* HALF YET.

YOU KILLED PEOPLE FOR MONEY AND YOU EXPECT THE PERSON WHO HIRED YOU TO BE *HONEST?* YOU *ARE* DUMBER THAN YOU LOOK.

WE DIDN'T *MEAN* TO KILL ANYONE. WE WAS JUST STIRRING UP SOME TROUBLE, Y'KNOW? *SCARING* PEOPLE.

WHO WAS IT?

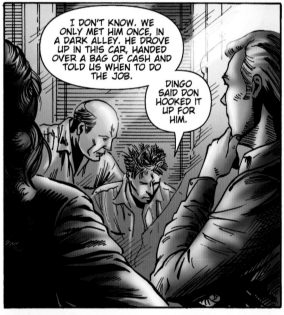

I DON'T KNOW. WE ONLY MET HIM ONCE, IN A DARK ALLEY. HE DROVE UP IN THIS CAR, HANDED OVER A BAG OF CASH AND TOLD US WHEN TO DO THE JOB.

DINGO SAID DON HOOKED IT UP FOR HIM.

DON FISCHER, THE *GUN SHOP* OWNER?

THAT'S RIGHT. DINGO'S BEEN A CUSTOMER OF HIS FOR YEARS.

IT LOOKS LIKE WHATEVER DEAL DON CUT JUST WENT OUT THE *WINDOW.*

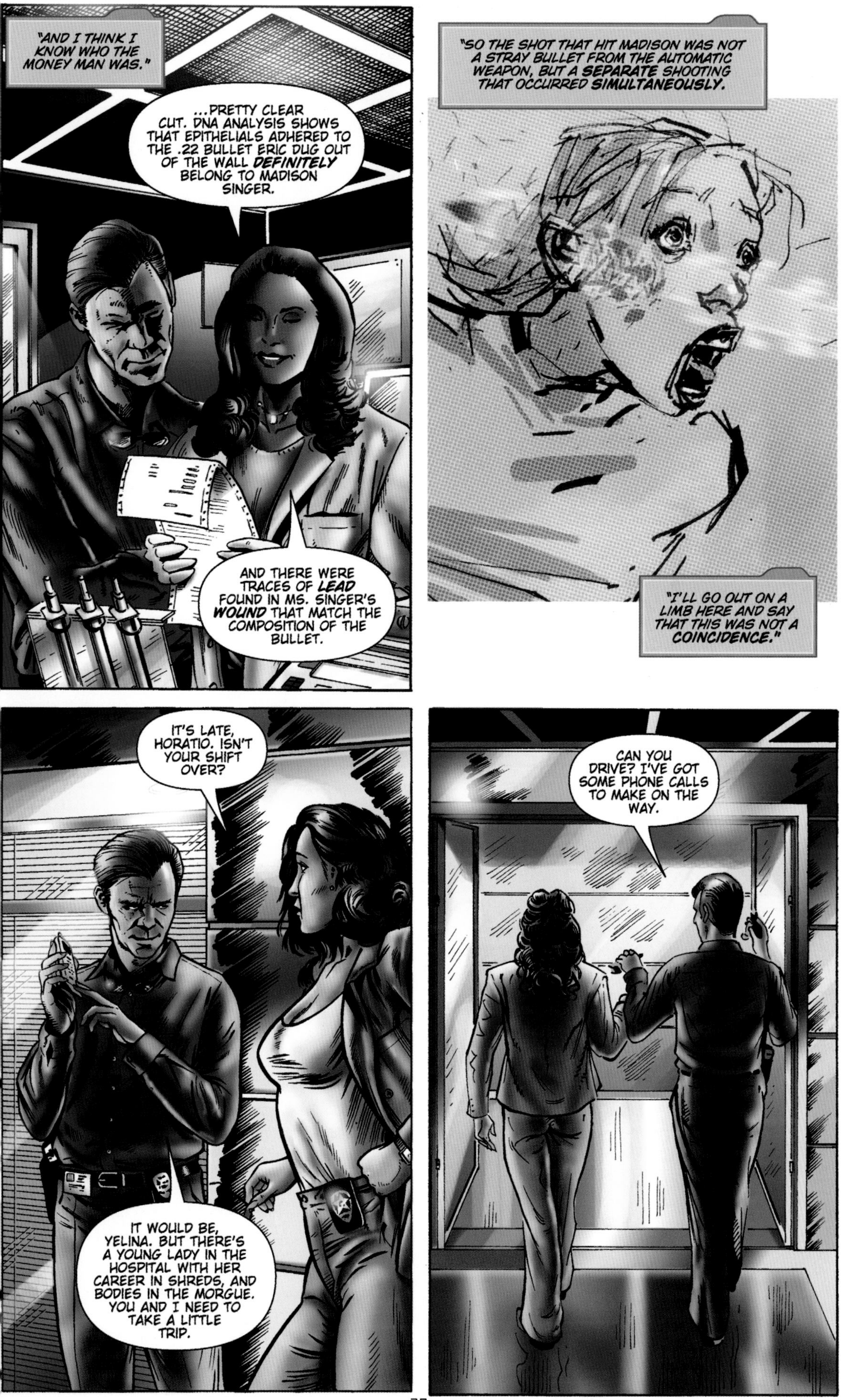
"AND I THINK I KNOW WHO THE MONEY MAN WAS."
...PRETTY CLEAR CUT. DNA ANALYSIS SHOWS THAT EPITHELIALS ADHERED TO THE .22 BULLET ERIC DUG OUT OF THE WALL *DEFINITELY* BELONG TO MADISON SINGER.
AND THERE WERE TRACES OF *LEAD* FOUND IN MS. SINGER'S *WOUND* THAT MATCH THE COMPOSITION OF THE BULLET.
"SO THE SHOT THAT HIT MADISON WAS NOT A STRAY BULLET FROM THE AUTOMATIC WEAPON, BUT A *SEPARATE* SHOOTING THAT OCCURRED *SIMULTANEOUSLY.*
"I'LL GO OUT ON A LIMB HERE AND SAY THAT THIS WAS NOT A *COINCIDENCE.*"
IT'S LATE, HORATIO. ISN'T YOUR SHIFT OVER?
IT WOULD BE, YELINA. BUT THERE'S A YOUNG LADY IN THE HOSPITAL WITH HER CAREER IN SHREDS, AND BODIES IN THE MORGUE. YOU AND I NEED TO TAKE A LITTLE TRIP.
CAN YOU DRIVE? I'VE GOT SOME PHONE CALLS TO MAKE ON THE WAY.

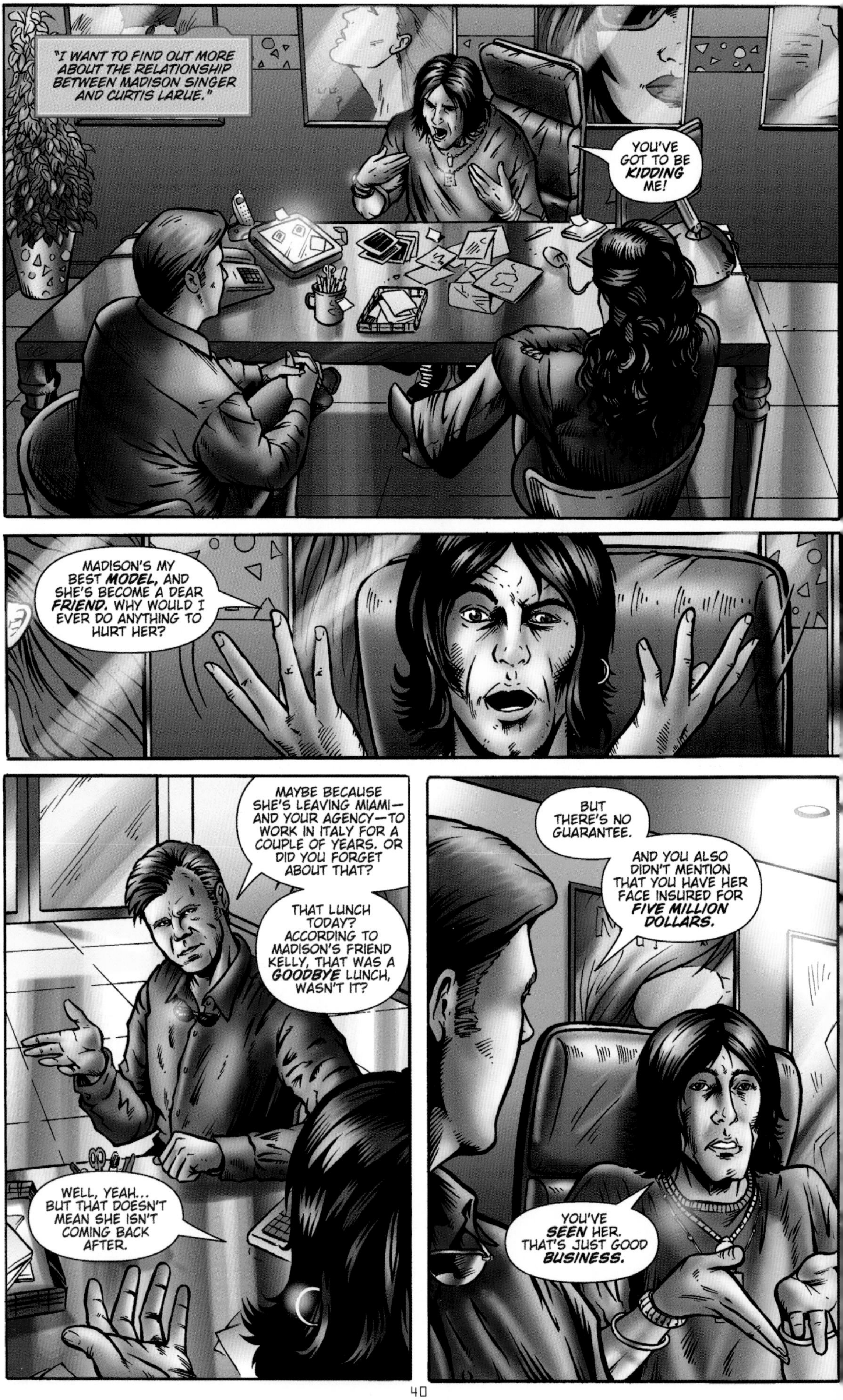
"I WANT TO FIND OUT MORE ABOUT THE RELATIONSHIP BETWEEN MADISON SINGER AND CURTIS LARUE."
YOU'VE GOT TO BE KIDDING ME!
MADISON'S MY BEST MODEL, AND SHE'S BECOME A DEAR FRIEND. WHY WOULD I EVER DO ANYTHING TO HURT HER?
MAYBE BECAUSE SHE'S LEAVING MIAMI— AND YOUR AGENCY—TO WORK IN ITALY FOR A COUPLE OF YEARS. OR DID YOU FORGET ABOUT THAT?
THAT LUNCH TODAY? ACCORDING TO MADISON'S FRIEND KELLY, THAT WAS A GOODBYE LUNCH, WASN'T IT?
WELL, YEAH... BUT THAT DOESN'T MEAN SHE ISN'T COMING BACK AFTER.
BUT THERE'S NO GUARANTEE.
AND YOU ALSO DIDN'T MENTION THAT YOU HAVE HER FACE INSURED FOR FIVE MILLION DOLLARS.
YOU'VE SEEN HER. THAT'S JUST GOOD BUSINESS.

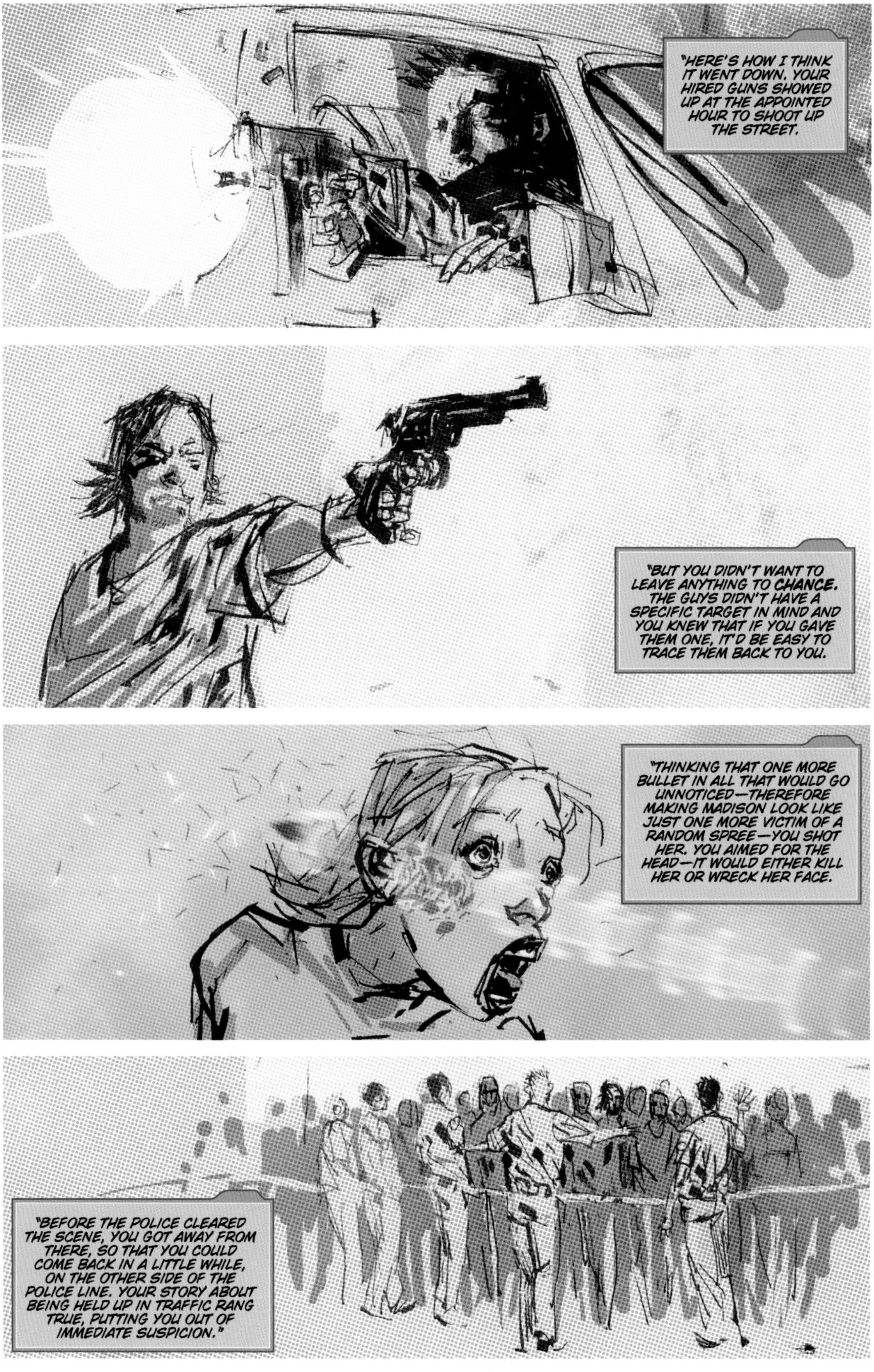
"HERE'S HOW I THINK IT WENT DOWN. YOUR HIRED GUNS SHOWED UP AT THE APPOINTED HOUR TO SHOOT UP THE STREET.
"BUT YOU DIDN'T WANT TO LEAVE ANYTHING TO CHANCE. THE GUYS DIDN'T HAVE A SPECIFIC TARGET IN MIND AND YOU KNEW THAT IF YOU GAVE THEM ONE, IT'D BE EASY TO TRACE THEM BACK TO YOU.
"THINKING THAT ONE MORE BULLET IN ALL THAT WOULD GO UNNOTICED—THEREFORE MAKING MADISON LOOK LIKE JUST ONE MORE VICTIM OF A RANDOM SPREE—YOU SHOT HER. YOU AIMED FOR THE HEAD—IT WOULD EITHER KILL HER OR WRECK HER FACE.
"BEFORE THE POLICE CLEARED THE SCENE, YOU GOT AWAY FROM THERE, SO THAT YOU COULD COME BACK IN A LITTLE WHILE, ON THE OTHER SIDE OF THE POLICE LINE. YOUR STORY ABOUT BEING HELD UP IN TRAFFIC RANG TRUE, PUTTING YOU OUT OF IMMEDIATE SUSPICION."

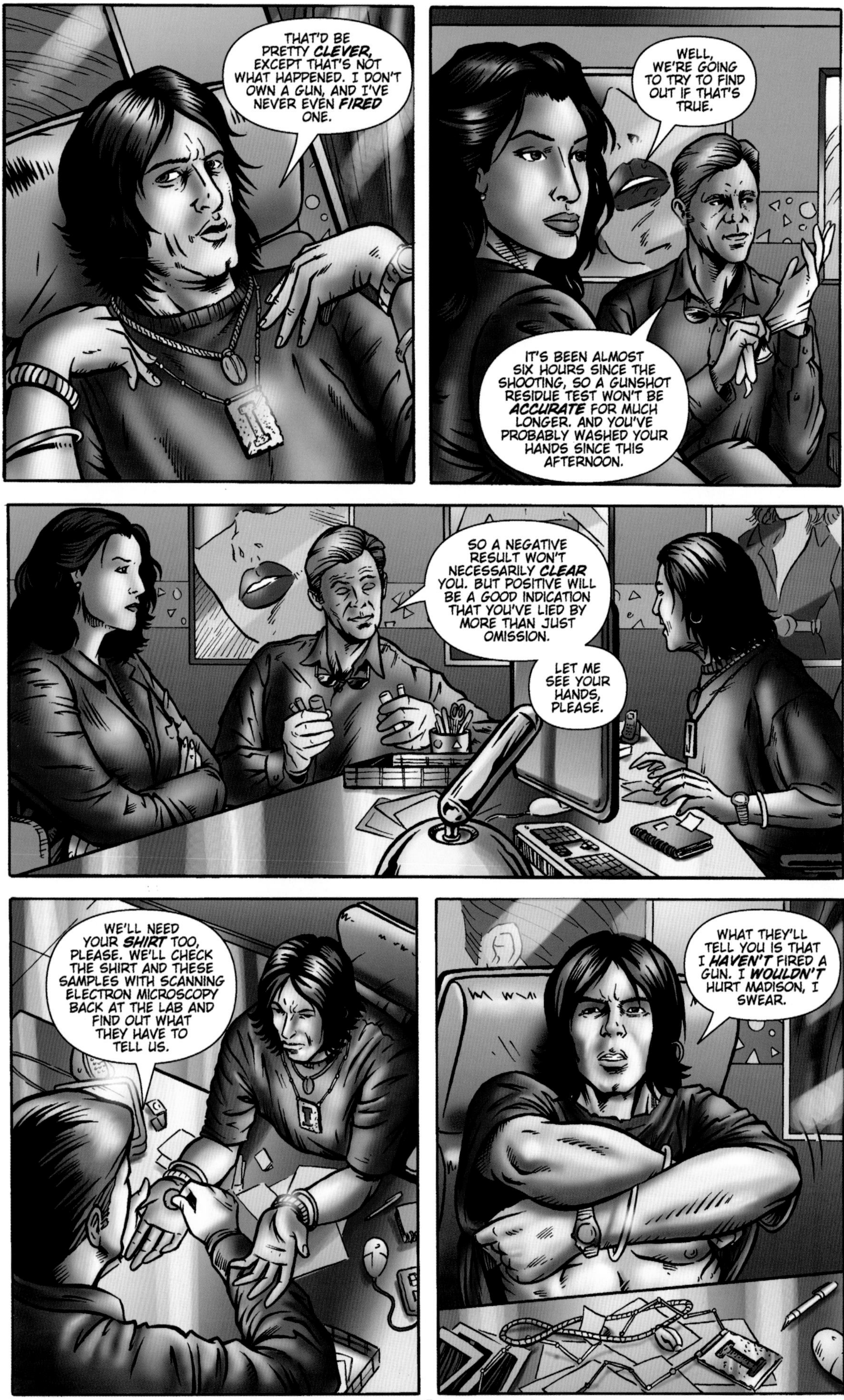
THAT'D BE PRETTY CLEVER, EXCEPT THAT'S NOT WHAT HAPPENED. I DON'T OWN A GUN, AND I'VE NEVER EVEN FIRED ONE.
WELL, WE'RE GOING TO TRY TO FIND OUT IF THAT'S TRUE.
IT'S BEEN ALMOST SIX HOURS SINCE THE SHOOTING, SO A GUNSHOT RESIDUE TEST WON'T BE ACCURATE FOR MUCH LONGER. AND YOU'VE PROBABLY WASHED YOUR HANDS SINCE THIS AFTERNOON.
SO A NEGATIVE RESULT WON'T NECESSARILY CLEAR YOU. BUT POSITIVE WILL BE A GOOD INDICATION THAT YOU'VE LIED BY MORE THAN JUST OMISSION.
LET ME SEE YOUR HANDS, PLEASE.
WE'LL NEED YOUR SHIRT TOO, PLEASE. WE'LL CHECK THE SHIRT AND THESE SAMPLES WITH SCANNING ELECTRON MICROSCOPY BACK AT THE LAB AND FIND OUT WHAT THEY HAVE TO TELL US.
WHAT THEY'LL TELL YOU IS THAT I HAVEN'T FIRED A GUN. I WOULDN'T HURT MADISON, I SWEAR.

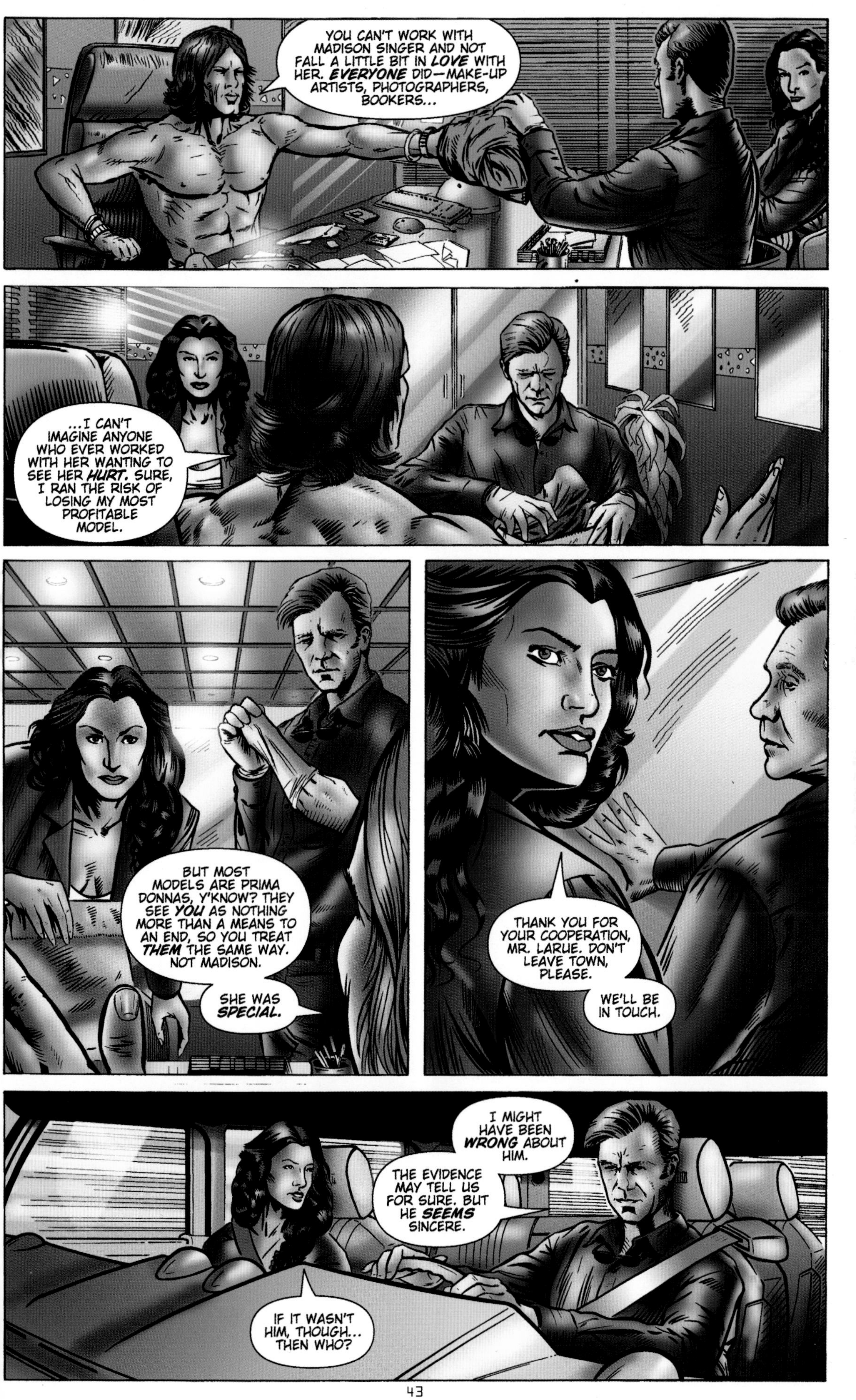

YOU CAN'T WORK WITH MADISON SINGER AND NOT FALL A LITTLE BIT IN LOVE WITH HER. EVERYONE DID—MAKE-UP ARTISTS, PHOTOGRAPHERS, BOOKERS...
...I CAN'T IMAGINE ANYONE WHO EVER WORKED WITH HER WANTING TO SEE HER HURT. SURE, I RAN THE RISK OF LOSING MY MOST PROFITABLE MODEL.
BUT MOST MODELS ARE PRIMA DONNAS, Y'KNOW? THEY SEE YOU AS NOTHING MORE THAN A MEANS TO AN END, SO YOU TREAT THEM THE SAME WAY. NOT MADISON.
SHE WAS SPECIAL.
THANK YOU FOR YOUR COOPERATION, MR. LARUE. DON'T LEAVE TOWN, PLEASE.
WE'LL BE IN TOUCH.
I MIGHT HAVE BEEN WRONG ABOUT HIM.
THE EVIDENCE MAY TELL US FOR SURE. BUT HE SEEMS SINCERE.
IF IT WASN'T HIM, THOUGH... THEN WHO?

"I HAVE A BAD FEELING ABOUT THAT."

TIME FOR A REFILL. I'LL BE BACK IN A MOMENT, MS. SINGER.

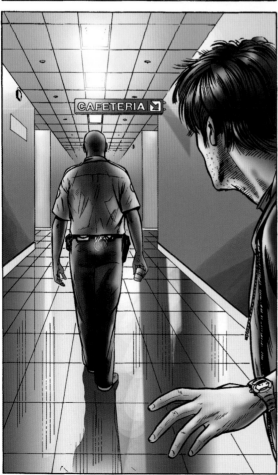

CAFETERIA

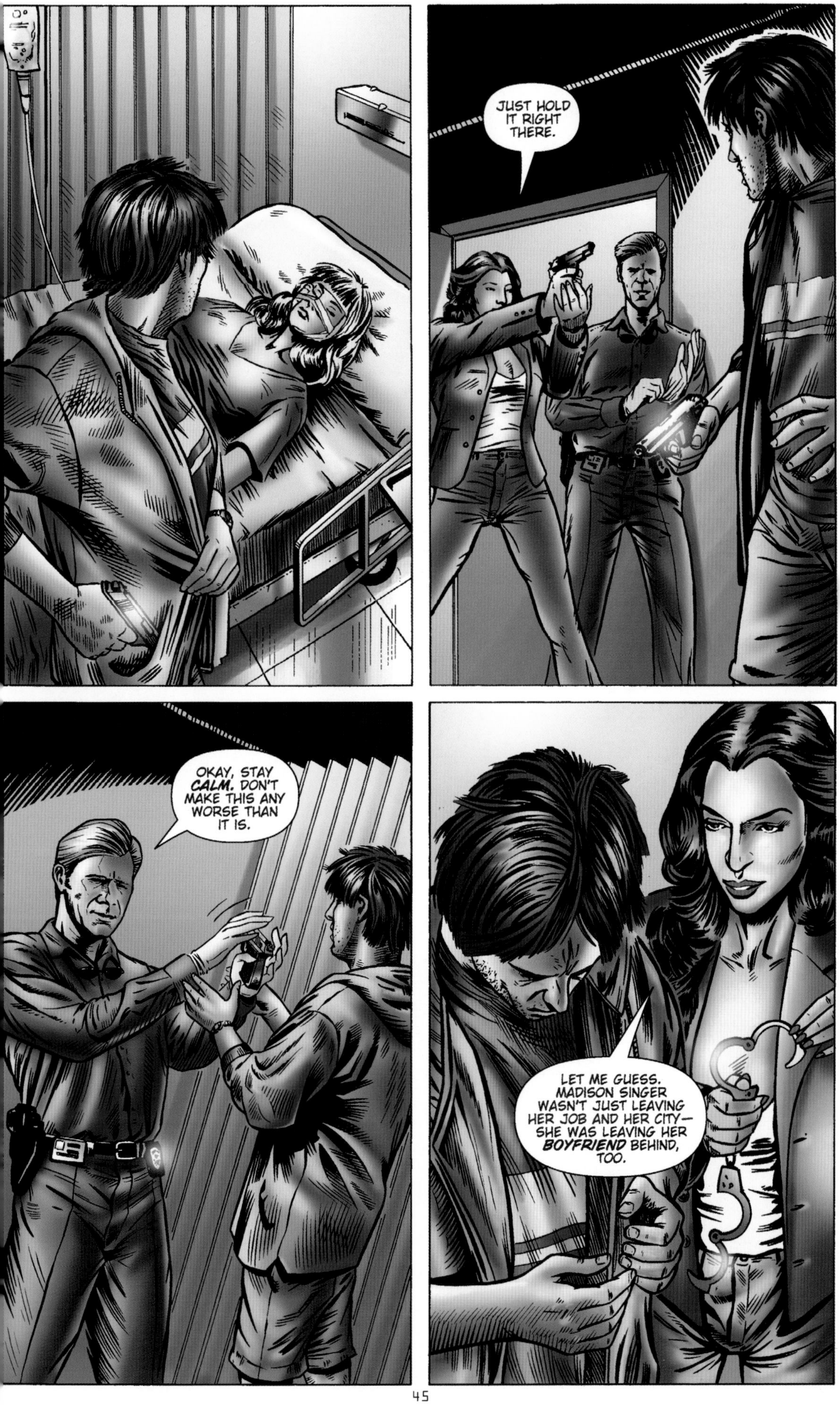
JUST HOLD IT RIGHT THERE.
OKAY, STAY CALM. DON'T MAKE THIS ANY WORSE THAN IT IS.
LET ME GUESS. MADISON SINGER WASN'T JUST LEAVING HER JOB AND HER CITY— SHE WAS LEAVING HER BOYFRIEND BEHIND, TOO.

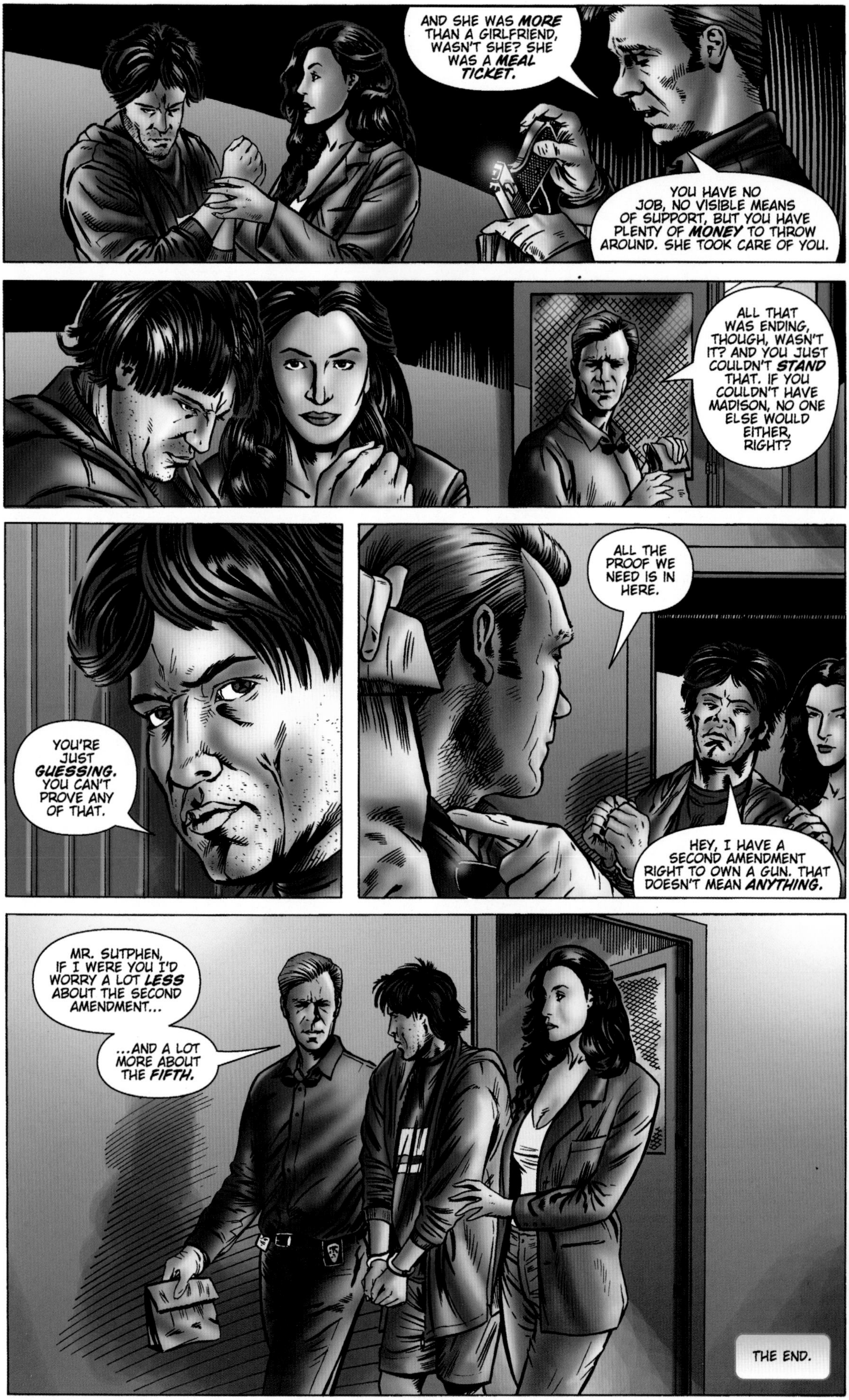
AND SHE WAS MORE THAN A GIRLFRIEND, WASN'T SHE? SHE WAS A MEAL TICKET.
YOU HAVE NO JOB, NO VISIBLE MEANS OF SUPPORT, BUT YOU HAVE PLENTY OF MONEY TO THROW AROUND. SHE TOOK CARE OF YOU.
ALL THAT WAS ENDING, THOUGH, WASN'T IT? AND YOU JUST COULDN'T STAND THAT. IF YOU COULDN'T HAVE MADISON, NO ONE ELSE WOULD EITHER, RIGHT?
YOU'RE JUST GUESSING. YOU CAN'T PROVE ANY OF THAT.
ALL THE PROOF WE NEED IS IN HERE.
HEY, I HAVE A SECOND AMENDMENT RIGHT TO OWN A GUN. THAT DOESN'T MEAN ANYTHING.
MR. SUTPHEN, IF I WERE YOU I'D WORRY A LOT LESS ABOUT THE SECOND AMENDMENT...
...AND A LOT MORE ABOUT THE FIFTH.
THE END.

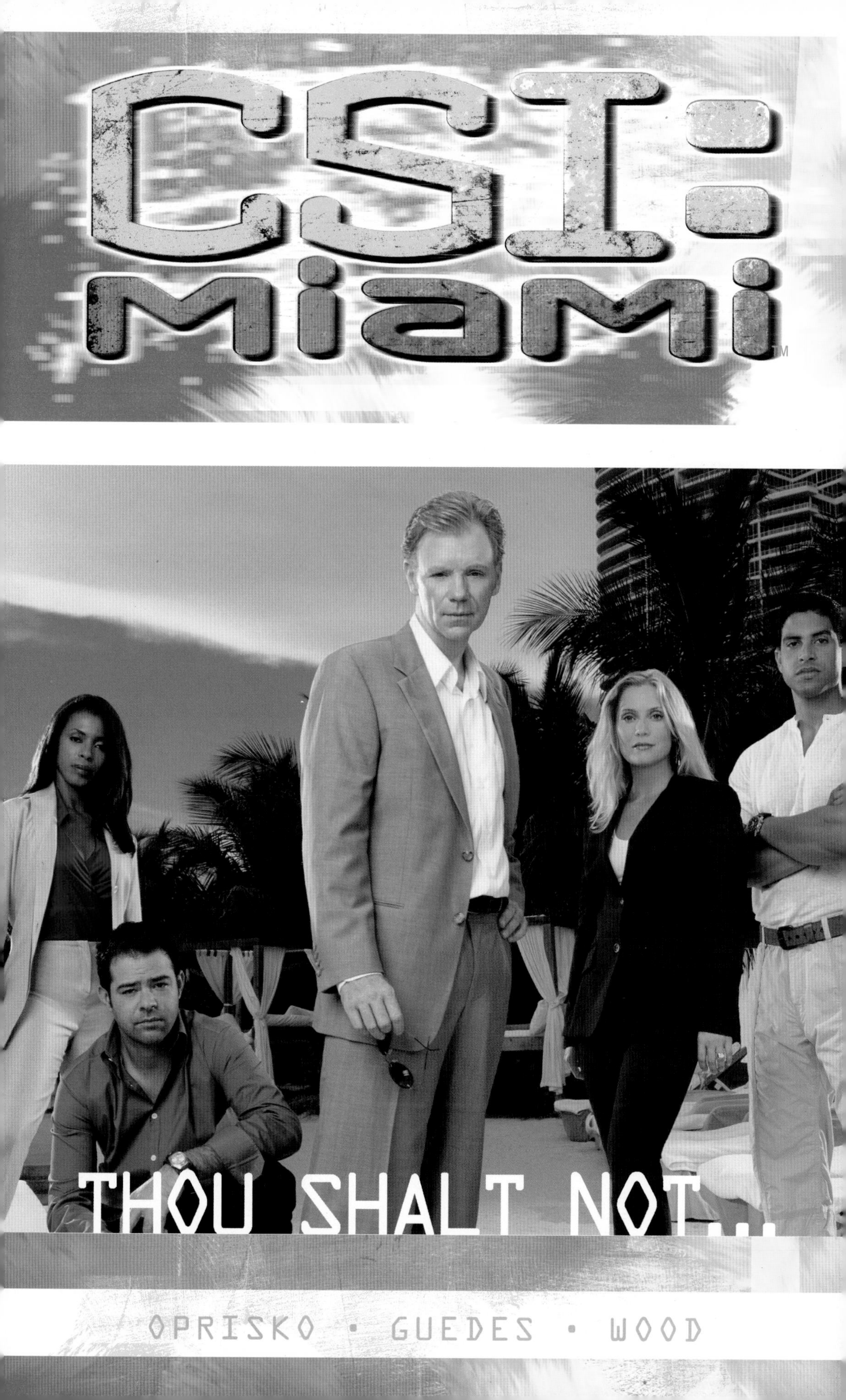
CSI:
Miami™
THOU SHALT NOT...
OPRISKO • GUEDES • WOOD

CSI: Miami™
THOU SHALT NOT...
EXCLUSIVE VARIANT COVER
COMIC-CON 2004 SAN DIEGO
OPRISKO • GUEDES • WOOD

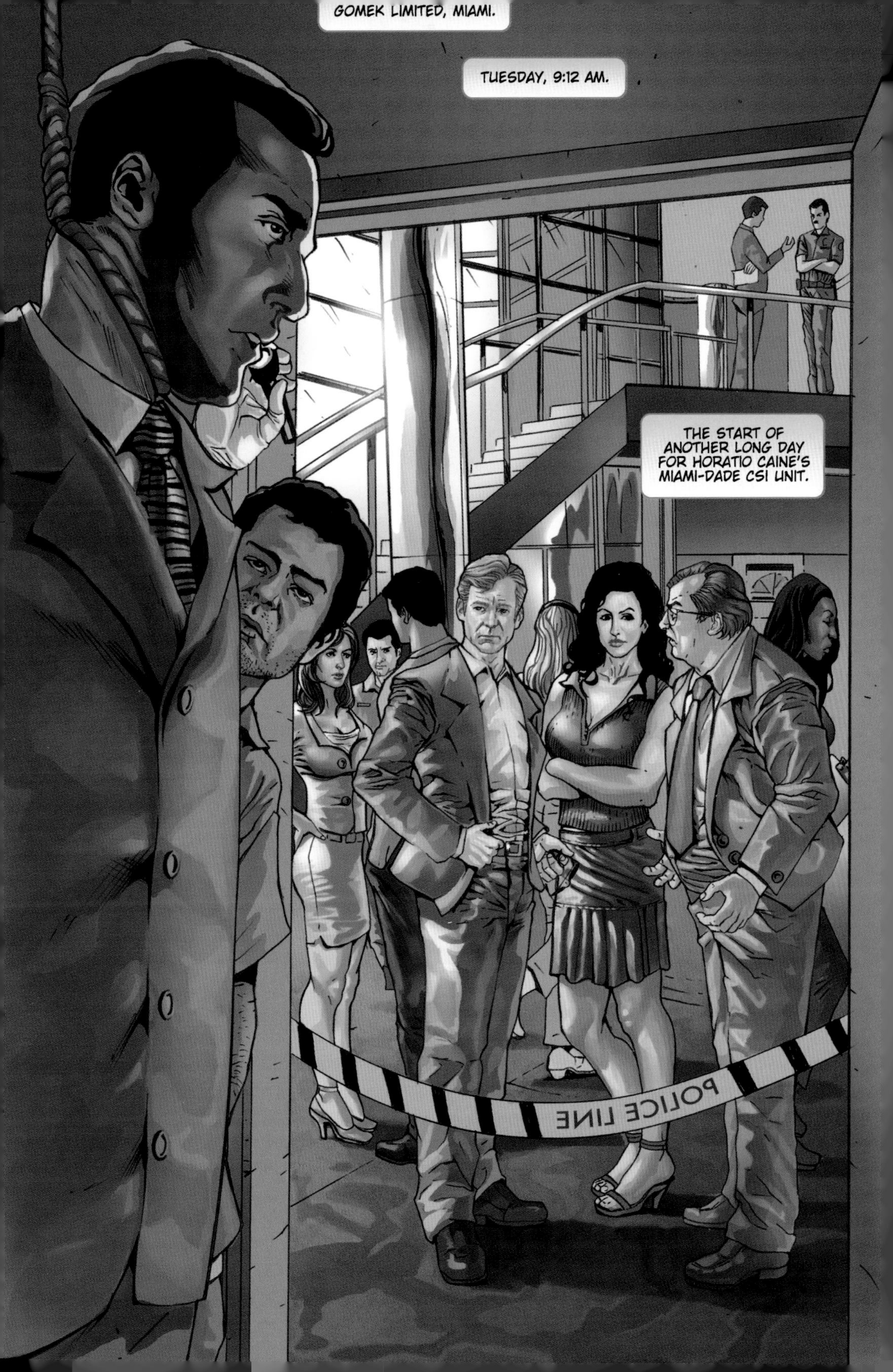
GOMEK LIMITED, MIAMI.
TUESDAY, 9:12 AM.
THE START OF ANOTHER LONG DAY FOR HORATIO CAINE'S MIAMI-DADE CSI UNIT.
POLICE LINE

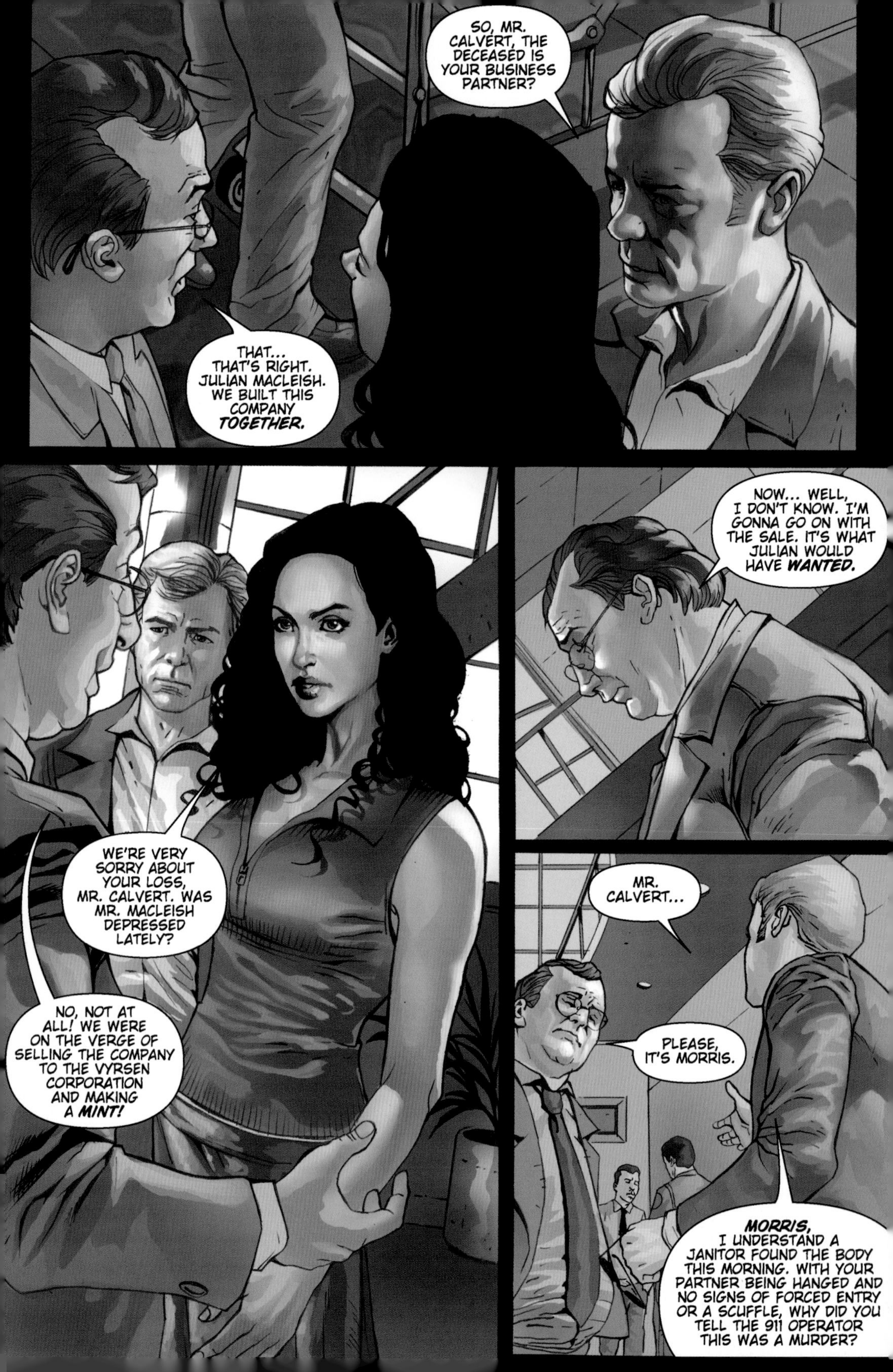
SO, MR. CALVERT, THE DECEASED IS YOUR BUSINESS PARTNER?
THAT... THAT'S RIGHT. JULIAN MACLEISH. WE BUILT THIS COMPANY *TOGETHER.*
WE'RE VERY SORRY ABOUT YOUR LOSS, MR. CALVERT. WAS MR. MACLEISH DEPRESSED LATELY?
NO, NOT AT ALL! WE WERE ON THE VERGE OF SELLING THE COMPANY TO THE VYRSEN CORPORATION AND MAKING A *MINT!*
NOW... WELL, I DON'T KNOW. I'M GONNA GO ON WITH THE SALE. IT'S WHAT JULIAN WOULD HAVE *WANTED.*
MR. CALVERT...
PLEASE, IT'S MORRIS.
*MORRIS,* I UNDERSTAND A JANITOR FOUND THE BODY THIS MORNING. WITH YOUR PARTNER BEING HANGED AND NO SIGNS OF FORCED ENTRY OR A SCUFFLE, WHY DID YOU TELL THE 911 OPERATOR THIS WAS A MURDER?

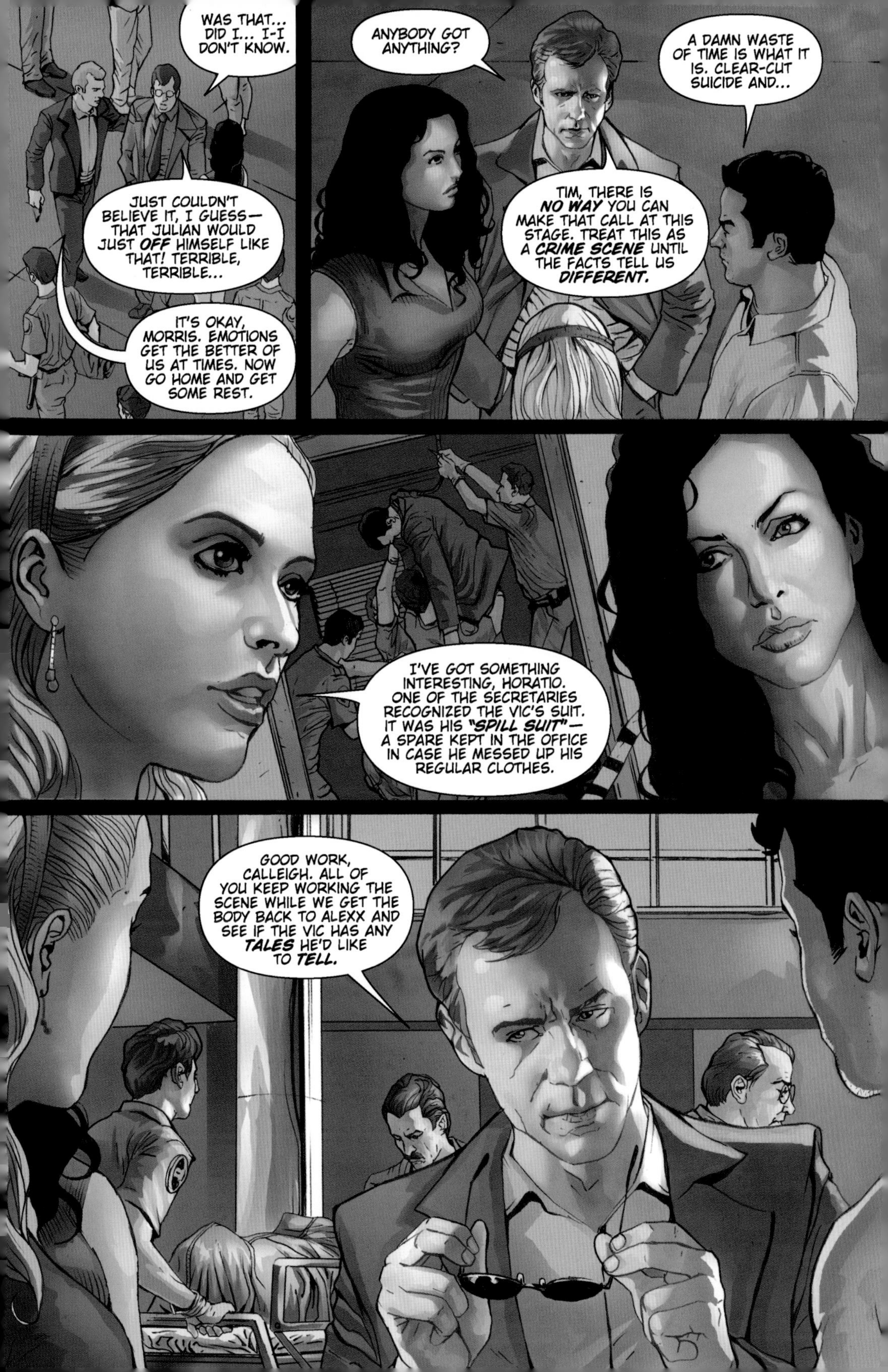
WAS THAT... DID I... I-I DON'T KNOW.
JUST COULDN'T BELIEVE IT, I GUESS— THAT JULIAN WOULD JUST OFF HIMSELF LIKE THAT! TERRIBLE, TERRIBLE...
IT'S OKAY, MORRIS. EMOTIONS GET THE BETTER OF US AT TIMES. NOW GO HOME AND GET SOME REST.
ANYBODY GOT ANYTHING?
A DAMN WASTE OF TIME IS WHAT IT IS. CLEAR-CUT SUICIDE AND...
TIM, THERE IS NO WAY YOU CAN MAKE THAT CALL AT THIS STAGE. TREAT THIS AS A CRIME SCENE UNTIL THE FACTS TELL US DIFFERENT.
I'VE GOT SOMETHING INTERESTING, HORATIO. ONE OF THE SECRETARIES RECOGNIZED THE VIC'S SUIT. IT WAS HIS "SPILL SUIT"— A SPARE KEPT IN THE OFFICE IN CASE HE MESSED UP HIS REGULAR CLOTHES.
GOOD WORK, CALLEIGH. ALL OF YOU KEEP WORKING THE SCENE WHILE WE GET THE BODY BACK TO ALEXX AND SEE IF THE VIC HAS ANY TALES HE'D LIKE TO TELL.

...SO I PLACE THE TIME OF DEATH SOMETIME ON MONDAY EVENING. BUT THAT'S NOT THE MOST *INTERESTING* THING I'VE FOUND.

THE HYOID BONE'S BROKEN. THAT *ALMOST NEVER* HAPPENS WITH A HANGING...

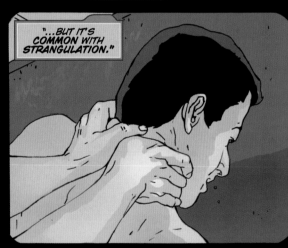

"...BUT IT'S *COMMON* WITH *STRANGULATION*."

TRUE, BUT IT'S STILL *POSSIBLE.* WE CAN'T JUMP TO CONCLUSIONS WITHOUT MORE *FACTS.* GOT ANYTHING ELSE?

OH, YES, HORATIO...

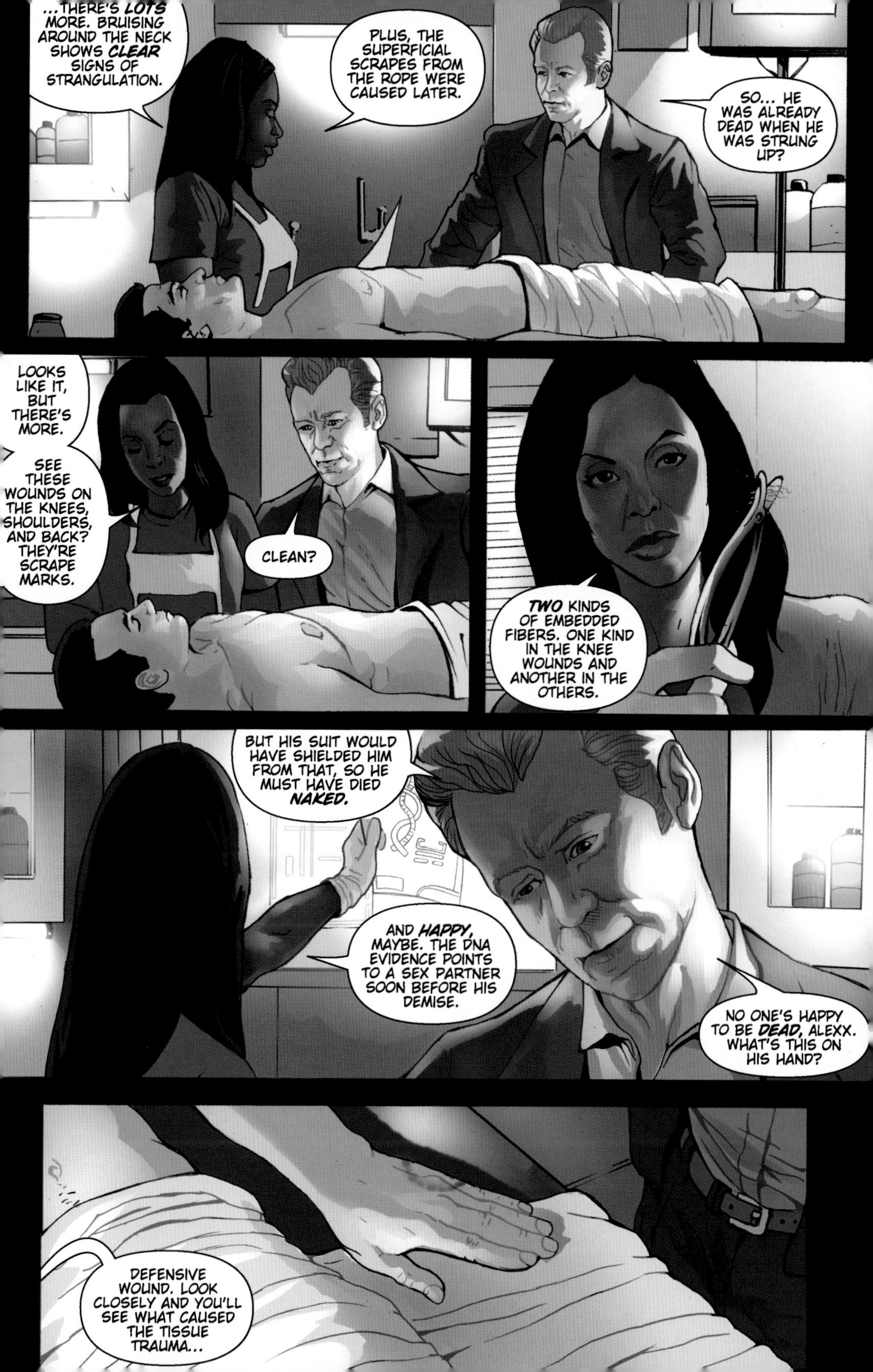
...THERE'S LOTS MORE. BRUISING AROUND THE NECK SHOWS CLEAR SIGNS OF STRANGULATION.
PLUS, THE SUPERFICIAL SCRAPES FROM THE ROPE WERE CAUSED LATER.
SO... HE WAS ALREADY DEAD WHEN HE WAS STRUNG UP?
LOOKS LIKE IT, BUT THERE'S MORE.
SEE THESE WOUNDS ON THE KNEES, SHOULDERS, AND BACK? THEY'RE SCRAPE MARKS.
CLEAN?
TWO KINDS OF EMBEDDED FIBERS. ONE KIND IN THE KNEE WOUNDS AND ANOTHER IN THE OTHERS.
BUT HIS SUIT WOULD HAVE SHIELDED HIM FROM THAT, SO HE MUST HAVE DIED NAKED.
AND HAPPY, MAYBE. THE DNA EVIDENCE POINTS TO A SEX PARTNER SOON BEFORE HIS DEMISE.
NO ONE'S HAPPY TO BE DEAD, ALEXX. WHAT'S THIS ON HIS HAND?
DEFENSIVE WOUND. LOOK CLOSELY AND YOU'LL SEE WHAT CAUSED THE TISSUE TRAUMA...

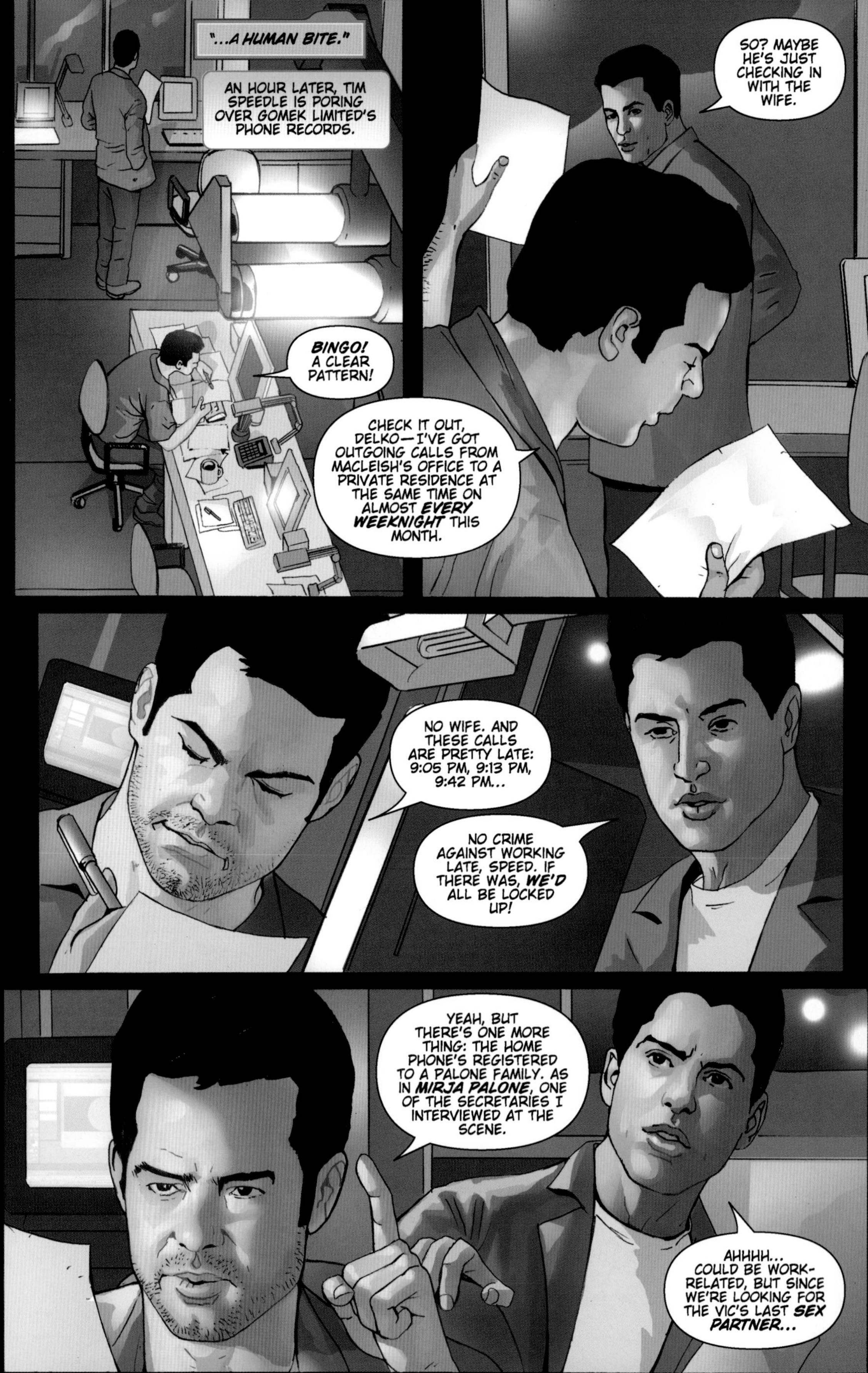
"...A HUMAN BITE."
AN HOUR LATER, TIM SPEEDLE IS PORING OVER GOMEK LIMITED'S PHONE RECORDS.
BINGO! A CLEAR PATTERN!
CHECK IT OUT, DELKO—I'VE GOT OUTGOING CALLS FROM MACLEISH'S OFFICE TO A PRIVATE RESIDENCE AT THE SAME TIME ON ALMOST EVERY WEEKNIGHT THIS MONTH.
SO? MAYBE HE'S JUST CHECKING IN WITH THE WIFE.
NO WIFE. AND THESE CALLS ARE PRETTY LATE: 9:05 PM, 9:13 PM, 9:42 PM...
NO CRIME AGAINST WORKING LATE, SPEED. IF THERE WAS, WE'D ALL BE LOCKED UP!
YEAH, BUT THERE'S ONE MORE THING: THE HOME PHONE'S REGISTERED TO A PALONE FAMILY. AS IN MIRJA PALONE, ONE OF THE SECRETARIES I INTERVIEWED AT THE SCENE.
AHHHH... COULD BE WORK-RELATED, BUT SINCE WE'RE LOOKING FOR THE VIC'S LAST SEX PARTNER...

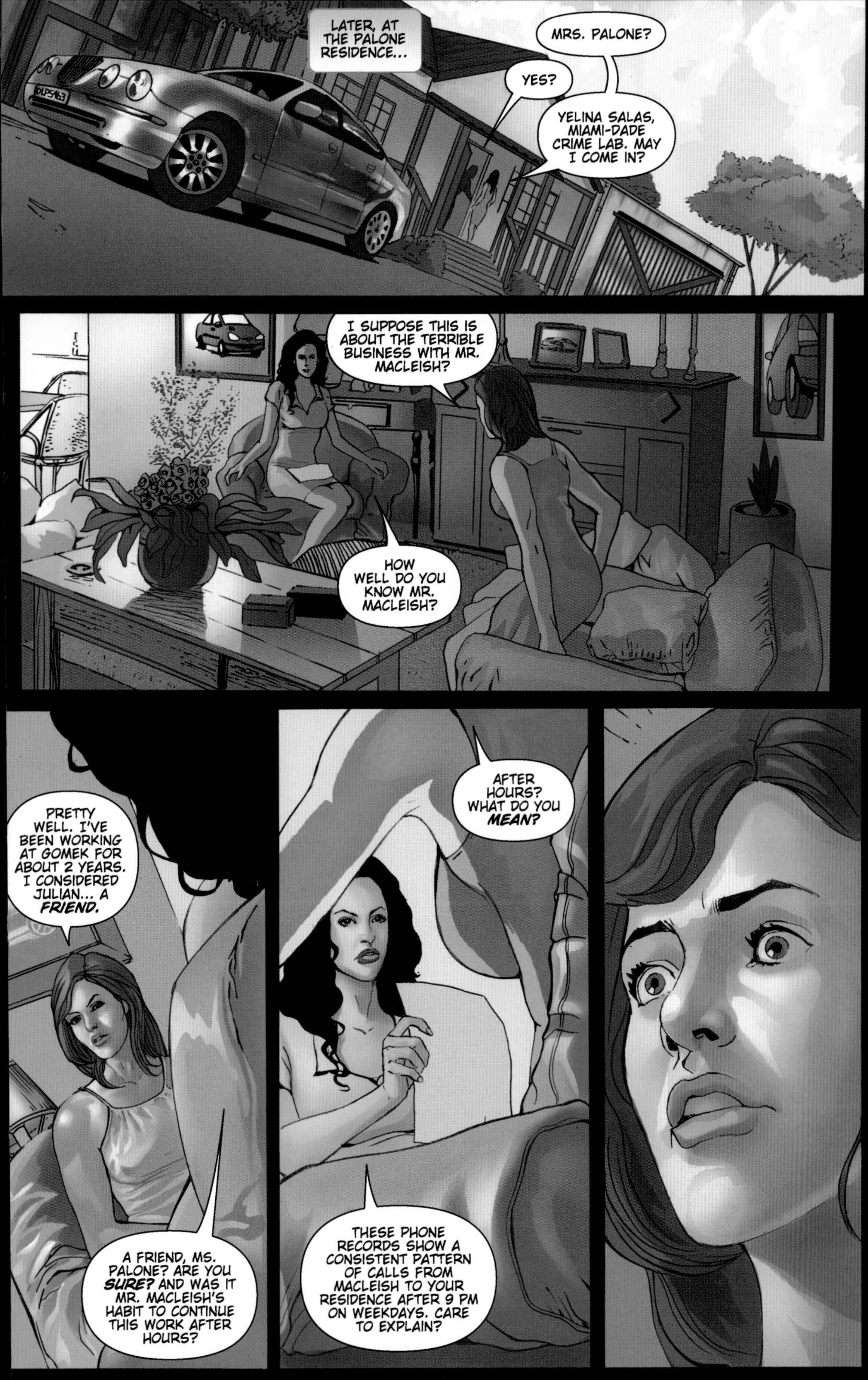
LATER, AT THE PALONE RESIDENCE...
MRS. PALONE?
YES?
YELINA SALAS, MIAMI-DADE CRIME LAB. MAY I COME IN?
I SUPPOSE THIS IS ABOUT THE TERRIBLE BUSINESS WITH MR. MACLEISH?
HOW WELL DO YOU KNOW MR. MACLEISH?
PRETTY WELL. I'VE BEEN WORKING AT GOMEK FOR ABOUT 2 YEARS. I CONSIDERED JULIAN... A ***FRIEND.***
A FRIEND, MS. PALONE? ARE YOU ***SURE?*** AND WAS IT MR. MACLEISH'S HABIT TO CONTINUE THIS WORK AFTER HOURS?
AFTER HOURS? WHAT DO YOU ***MEAN?***
THESE PHONE RECORDS SHOW A CONSISTENT PATTERN OF CALLS FROM MACLEISH TO YOUR RESIDENCE AFTER 9 PM ON WEEKDAYS. CARE TO EXPLAIN?

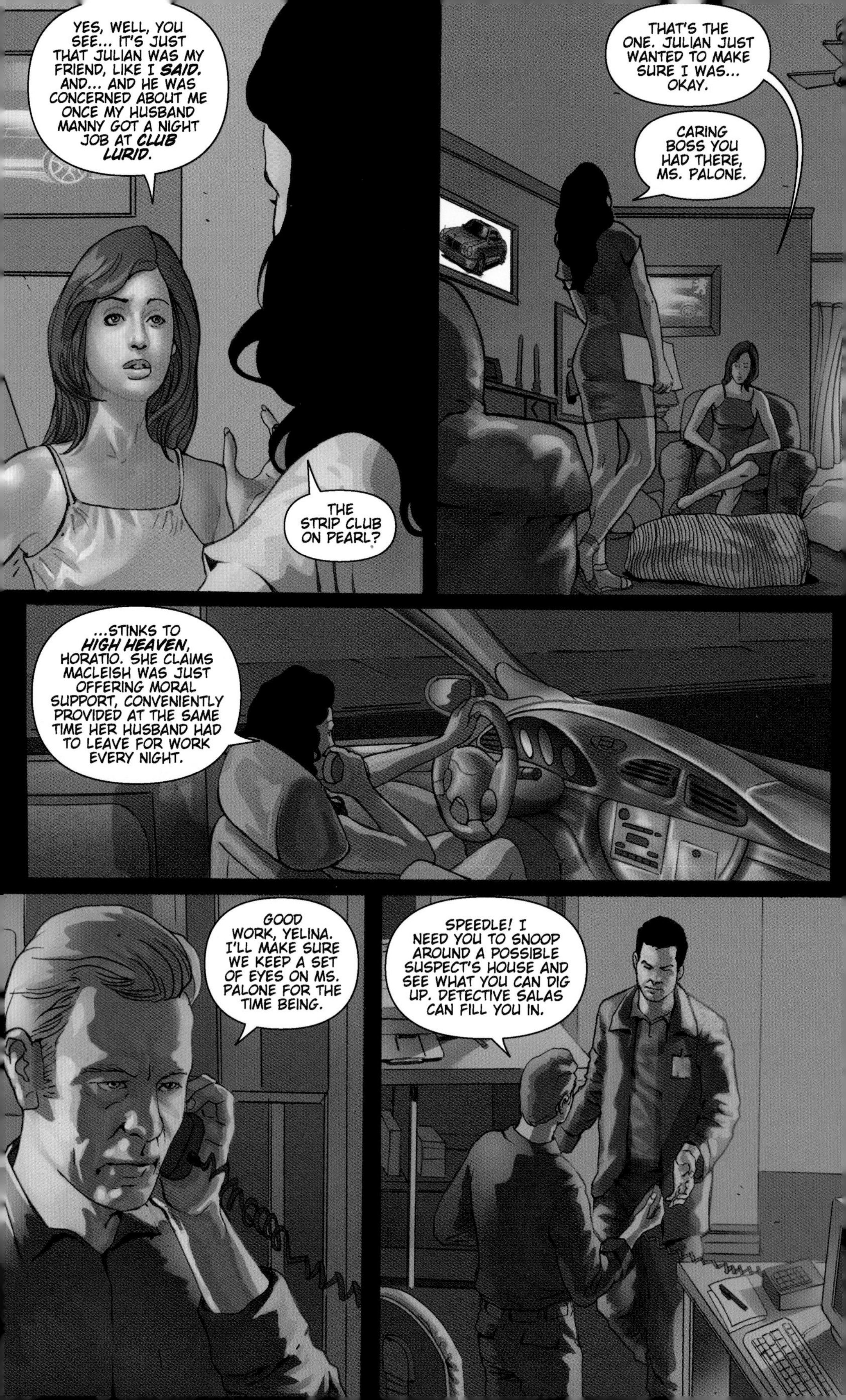
YES, WELL, YOU SEE... IT'S JUST THAT JULIAN WAS MY FRIEND, LIKE I SAID. AND... AND HE WAS CONCERNED ABOUT ME ONCE MY HUSBAND MANNY GOT A NIGHT JOB AT CLUB LURID.
THE STRIP CLUB ON PEARL?
THAT'S THE ONE. JULIAN JUST WANTED TO MAKE SURE I WAS... OKAY.
CARING BOSS YOU HAD THERE, MS. PALONE.
...STINKS TO HIGH HEAVEN, HORATIO. SHE CLAIMS MACLEISH WAS JUST OFFERING MORAL SUPPORT, CONVENIENTLY PROVIDED AT THE SAME TIME HER HUSBAND HAD TO LEAVE FOR WORK EVERY NIGHT.
GOOD WORK, YELINA. I'LL MAKE SURE WE KEEP A SET OF EYES ON MS. PALONE FOR THE TIME BEING.
SPEEDLE! I NEED YOU TO SNOOP AROUND A POSSIBLE SUSPECT'S HOUSE AND SEE WHAT YOU CAN DIG UP. DETECTIVE SALAS CAN FILL YOU IN.

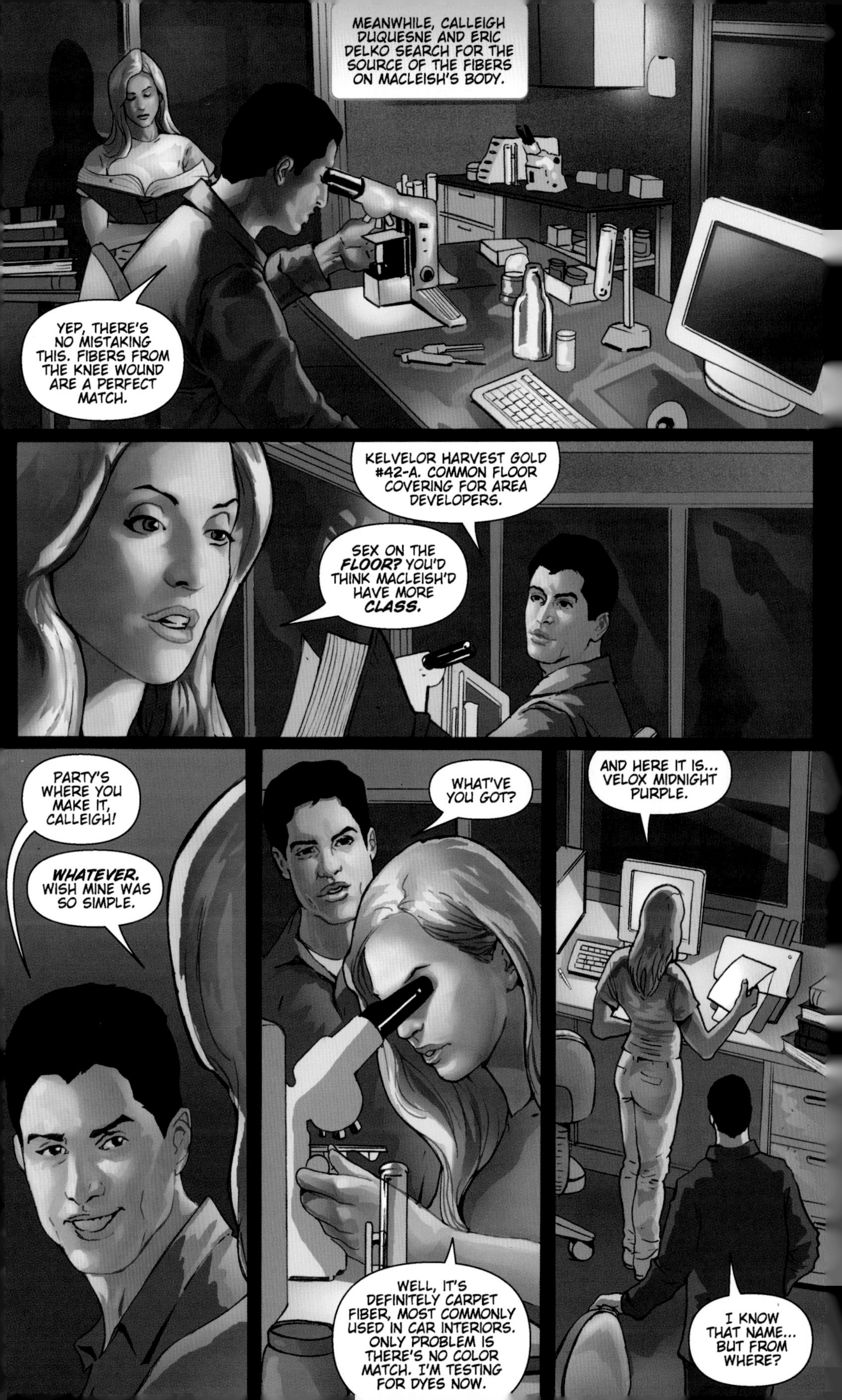
MEANWHILE, CALLEIGH DUQUESNE AND ERIC DELKO SEARCH FOR THE SOURCE OF THE FIBERS ON MACLEISH'S BODY.
YEP, THERE'S NO MISTAKING THIS. FIBERS FROM THE KNEE WOUND ARE A PERFECT MATCH.
KELVELOR HARVEST GOLD #42-A. COMMON FLOOR COVERING FOR AREA DEVELOPERS.
SEX ON THE FLOOR? YOU'D THINK MACLEISH'D HAVE MORE CLASS.
PARTY'S WHERE YOU MAKE IT, CALLEIGH!
WHATEVER. WISH MINE WAS SO SIMPLE.
WHAT'VE YOU GOT?
WELL, IT'S DEFINITELY CARPET FIBER, MOST COMMONLY USED IN CAR INTERIORS. ONLY PROBLEM IS THERE'S NO COLOR MATCH. I'M TESTING FOR DYES NOW.
AND HERE IT IS... VELOX MIDNIGHT PURPLE.
I KNOW THAT NAME... BUT FROM WHERE?

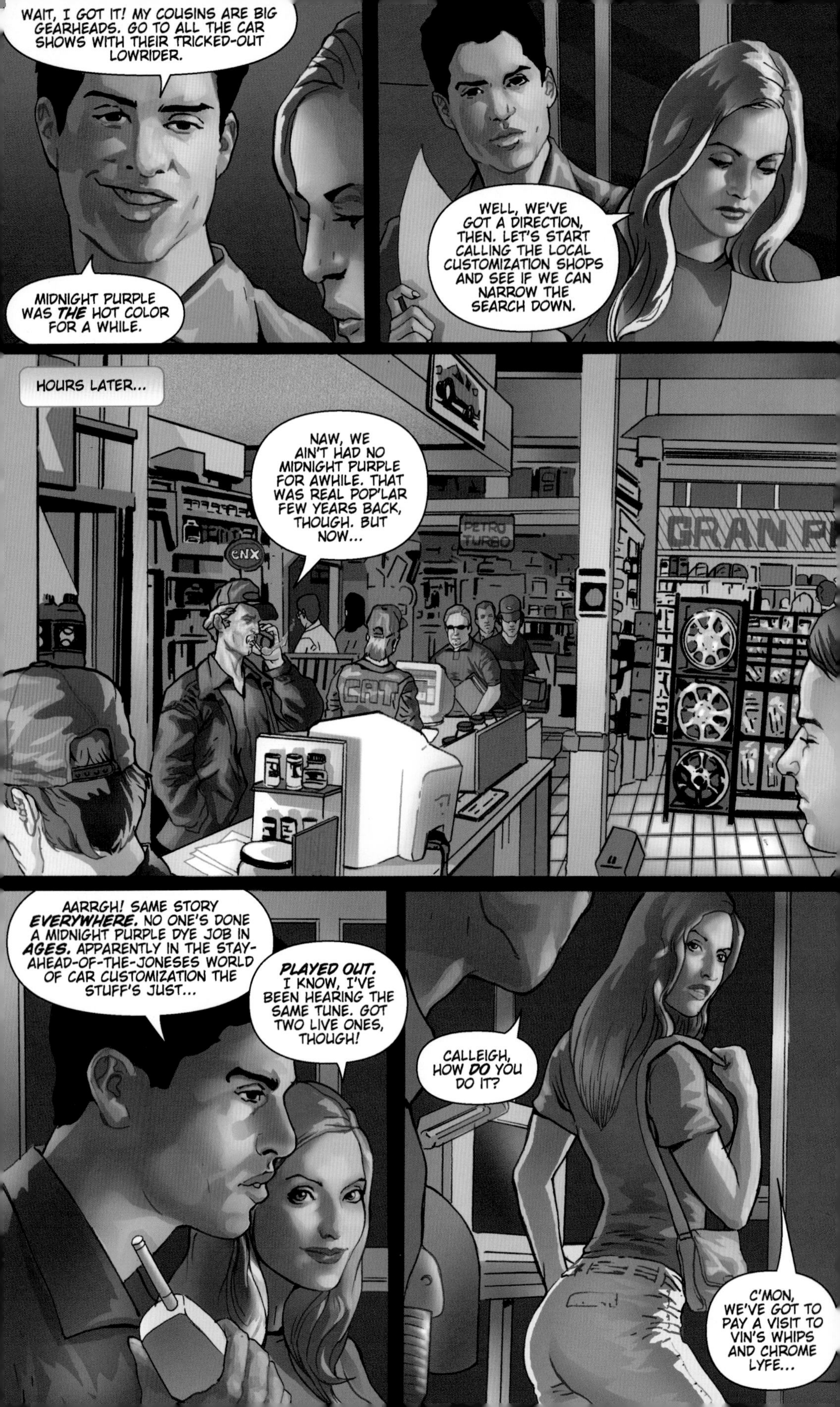
WAIT, I GOT IT! MY COUSINS ARE BIG GEARHEADS. GO TO ALL THE CAR SHOWS WITH THEIR TRICKED-OUT LOWRIDER.
MIDNIGHT PURPLE WAS ***THE*** HOT COLOR FOR A WHILE.
WELL, WE'VE GOT A DIRECTION, THEN. LET'S START CALLING THE LOCAL CUSTOMIZATION SHOPS AND SEE IF WE CAN NARROW THE SEARCH DOWN.
HOURS LATER...
NAW, WE AIN'T HAD NO MIDNIGHT PURPLE FOR AWHILE. THAT WAS REAL POP'LAR FEW YEARS BACK, THOUGH. BUT NOW...
CNX
PETRO TURBO
GRAN P
CAT
AARRGH! SAME STORY ***EVERYWHERE.*** NO ONE'S DONE A MIDNIGHT PURPLE DYE JOB IN ***AGES.*** APPARENTLY IN THE STAY-AHEAD-OF-THE-JONESES WORLD OF CAR CUSTOMIZATION THE STUFF'S JUST...
***PLAYED OUT.*** I KNOW, I'VE BEEN HEARING THE SAME TUNE. GOT TWO LIVE ONES, THOUGH!
CALLEIGH, HOW ***DO*** YOU DO IT?
C'MON, WE'VE GOT TO PAY A VISIT TO VIN'S WHIPS AND CHROME LYFE...

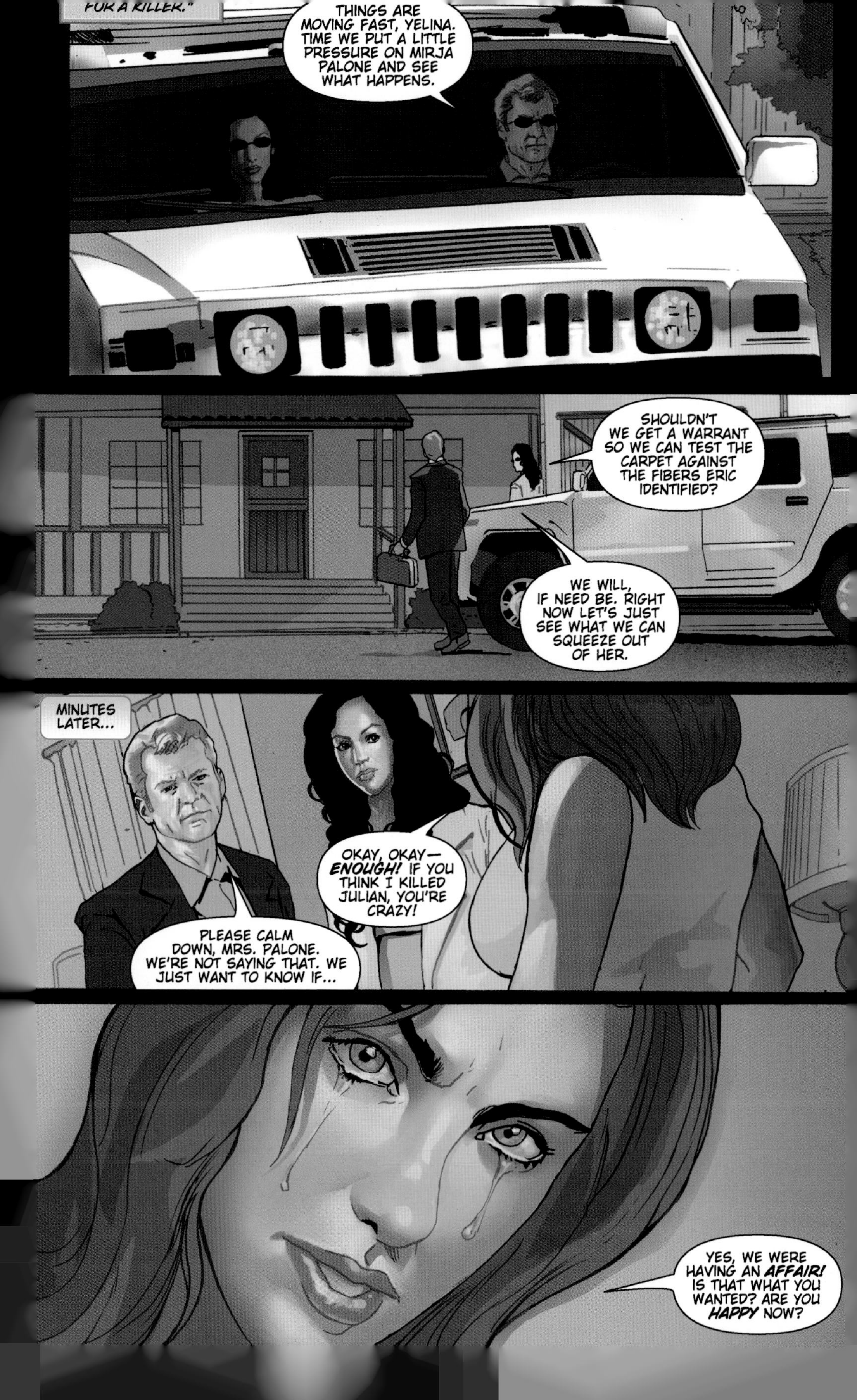
FOR A KILLER."
THINGS ARE MOVING FAST, YELINA. TIME WE PUT A LITTLE PRESSURE ON MIRJA PALONE AND SEE WHAT HAPPENS.
SHOULDN'T WE GET A WARRANT SO WE CAN TEST THE CARPET AGAINST THE FIBERS ERIC IDENTIFIED?
WE WILL, IF NEED BE. RIGHT NOW LET'S JUST SEE WHAT WE CAN SQUEEZE OUT OF HER.
MINUTES LATER...
OKAY, OKAY— ENOUGH! IF YOU THINK I KILLED JULIAN, YOU'RE CRAZY!
PLEASE CALM DOWN, MRS. PALONE. WE'RE NOT SAYING THAT. WE JUST WANT TO KNOW IF...
YES, WE WERE HAVING AN AFFAIR! IS THAT WHAT YOU WANTED? ARE YOU HAPPY NOW?

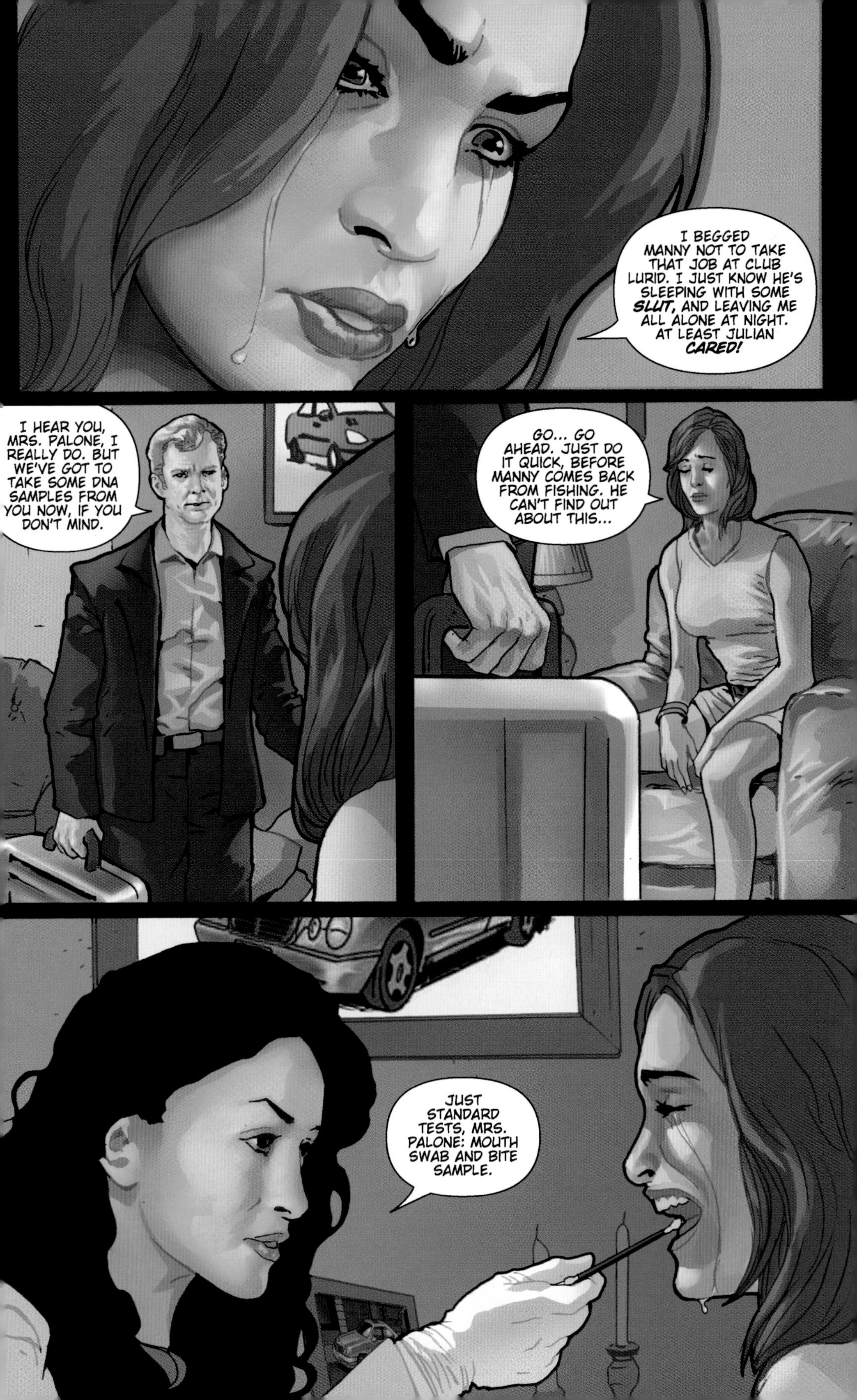
I BEGGED MANNY NOT TO TAKE THAT JOB AT CLUB LURID. I JUST KNOW HE'S SLEEPING WITH SOME *SLUT,* AND LEAVING ME ALL ALONE AT NIGHT. AT LEAST JULIAN *CARED!*
I HEAR YOU, MRS. PALONE, I REALLY DO. BUT WE'VE GOT TO TAKE SOME DNA SAMPLES FROM YOU NOW, IF YOU DON'T MIND.
GO... GO AHEAD. JUST DO IT QUICK, BEFORE MANNY COMES BACK FROM FISHING. HE CAN'T FIND OUT ABOUT THIS...
JUST STANDARD TESTS, MRS. PALONE: MOUTH SWAB AND BITE SAMPLE.

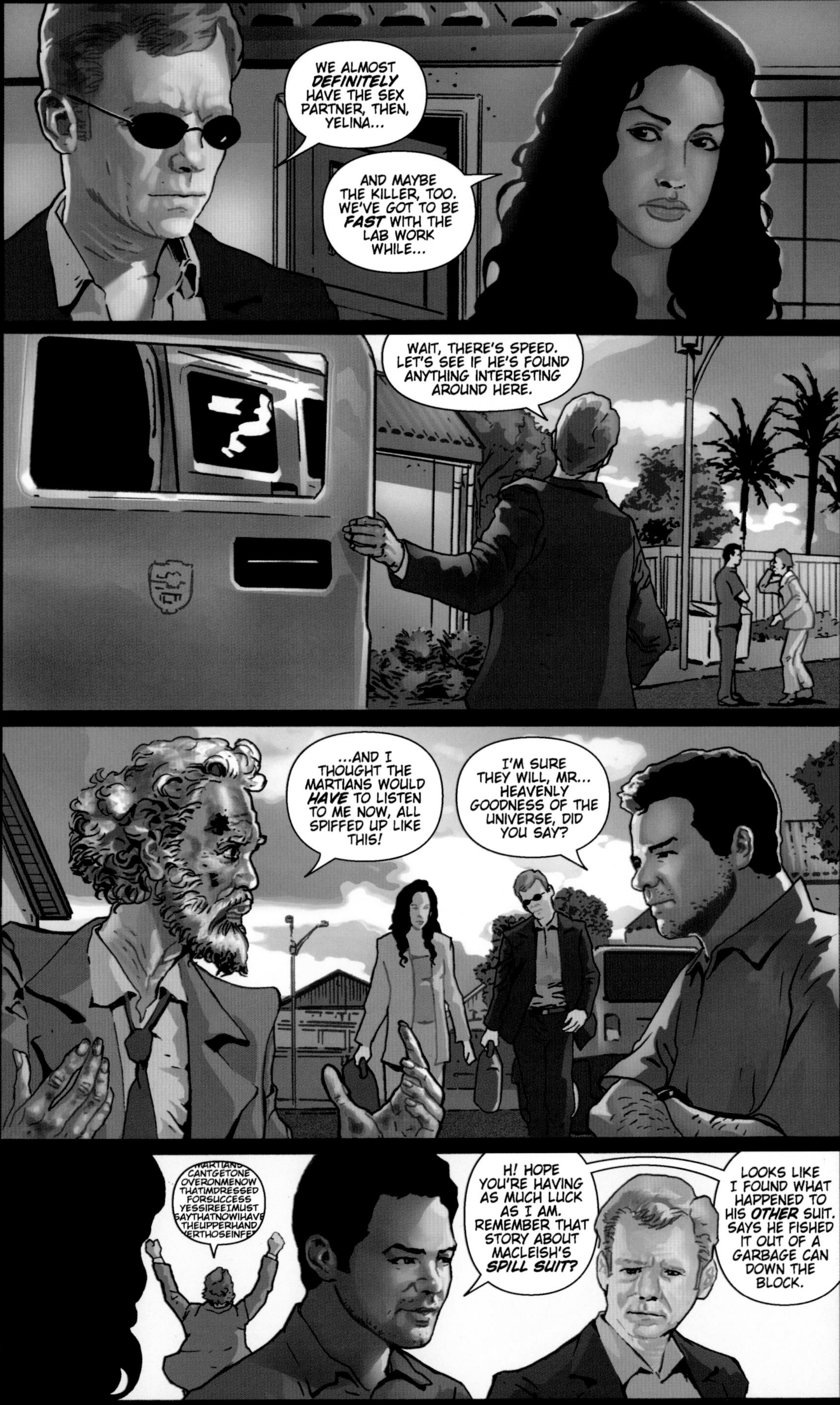
WE ALMOST DEFINITELY HAVE THE SEX PARTNER, THEN, YELINA...
AND MAYBE THE KILLER, TOO. WE'VE GOT TO BE FAST WITH THE LAB WORK WHILE...
WAIT, THERE'S SPEED. LET'S SEE IF HE'S FOUND ANYTHING INTERESTING AROUND HERE.
...AND I THOUGHT THE MARTIANS WOULD HAVE TO LISTEN TO ME NOW, ALL SPIFFED UP LIKE THIS!
I'M SURE THEY WILL, MR... HEAVENLY GOODNESS OF THE UNIVERSE, DID YOU SAY?
CANTGETONE OVERONMENOW THATIMDRESSED FORSUCCESS YESSIREEIMUST AYTHATNOWIHAV THEUPPERHAND ERTHOSEINF
H! HOPE YOU'RE HAVING AS MUCH LUCK AS I AM. REMEMBER THAT STORY ABOUT MACLEISH'S SPILL SUIT?
LOOKS LIKE I FOUND WHAT HAPPENED TO HIS OTHER SUIT. SAYS HE FISHED IT OUT OF A GARBAGE CAN DOWN THE BLOCK.

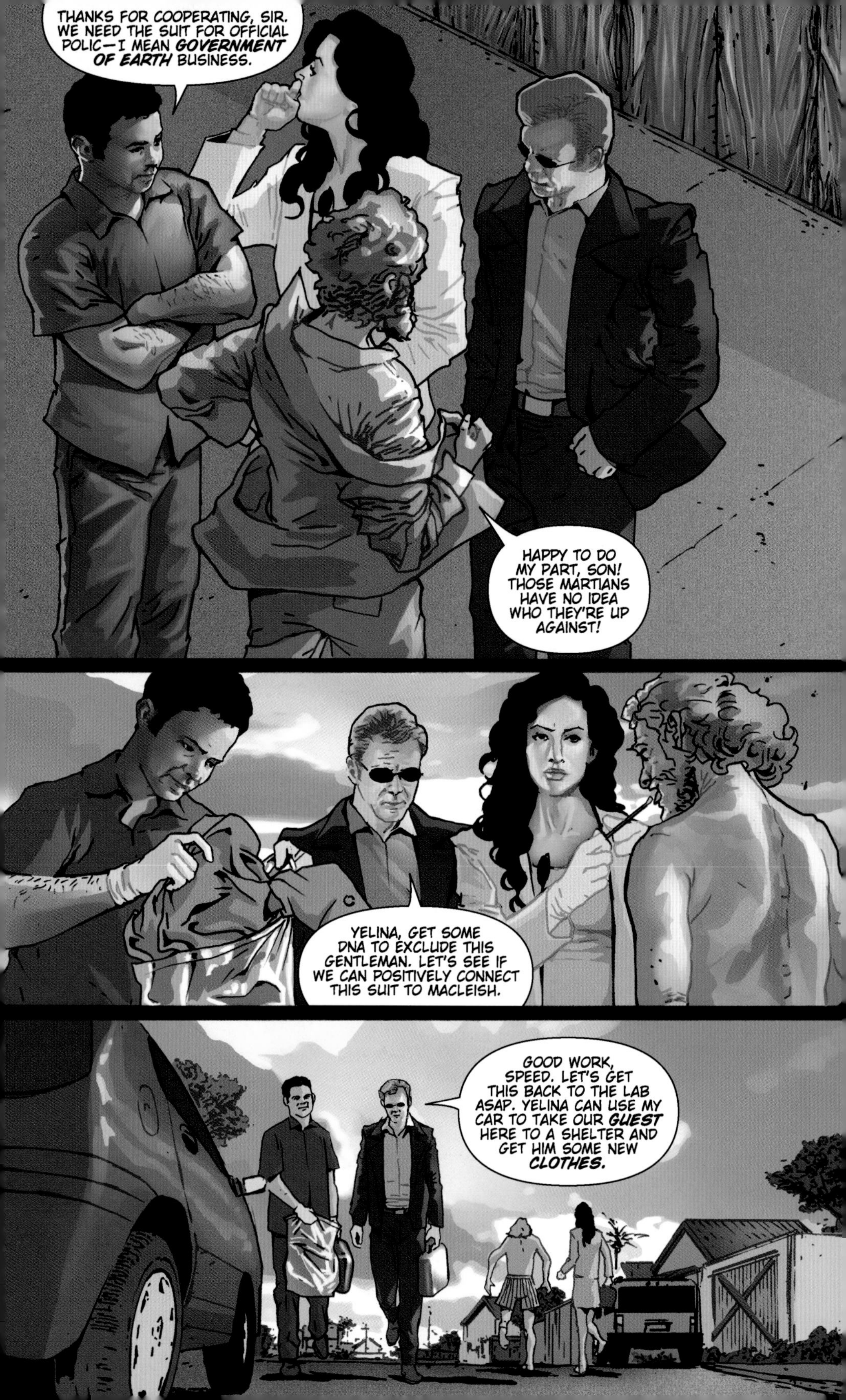
THANKS FOR COOPERATING, SIR. WE NEED THE SUIT FOR OFFICIAL POLIC—I MEAN ***GOVERNMENT OF EARTH*** BUSINESS.
HAPPY TO DO MY PART, SON! THOSE MARTIANS HAVE NO IDEA WHO THEY'RE UP AGAINST!
YELINA, GET SOME DNA TO EXCLUDE THIS GENTLEMAN. LET'S SEE IF WE CAN POSITIVELY CONNECT THIS SUIT TO MACLEISH.
GOOD WORK, SPEED. LET'S GET THIS BACK TO THE LAB ASAP. YELINA CAN USE MY CAR TO TAKE OUR ***GUEST*** HERE TO A SHELTER AND GET HIM SOME NEW ***CLOTHES.***

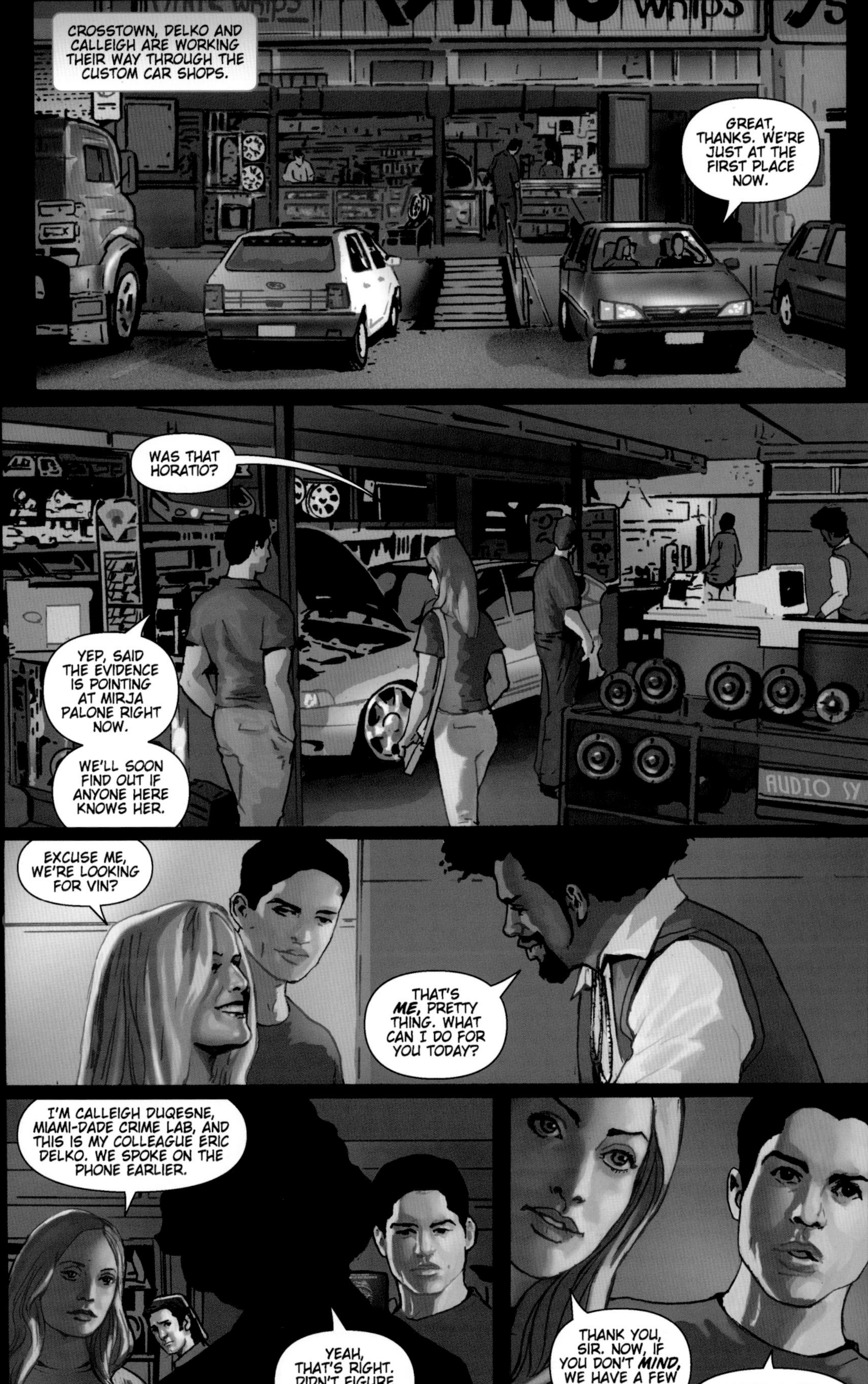
CROSSTOWN, DELKO AND CALLEIGH ARE WORKING THEIR WAY THROUGH THE CUSTOM CAR SHOPS.
GREAT, THANKS. WE'RE JUST AT THE FIRST PLACE NOW.
WAS THAT HORATIO?
YEP, SAID THE EVIDENCE IS POINTING AT MIRJA PALONE RIGHT NOW.
WE'LL SOON FIND OUT IF ANYONE HERE KNOWS HER.
AUDIO SY
EXCUSE ME, WE'RE LOOKING FOR VIN?
THAT'S *ME,* PRETTY THING. WHAT CAN I DO FOR YOU TODAY?
I'M CALLEIGH DUQESNE, MIAMI-DADE CRIME LAB, AND THIS IS MY COLLEAGUE ERIC DELKO. WE SPOKE ON THE PHONE EARLIER.
YEAH, THAT'S RIGHT. DIDN'T FIGURE YOU LOOKIN' LIKE *THIS!*
THANK YOU, SIR. NOW, IF YOU DON'T *MIND,* WE HAVE A FEW QUESTIONS.
NAMELY, YOU EVER DO ANY WORK FOR MIRJA PALONE?

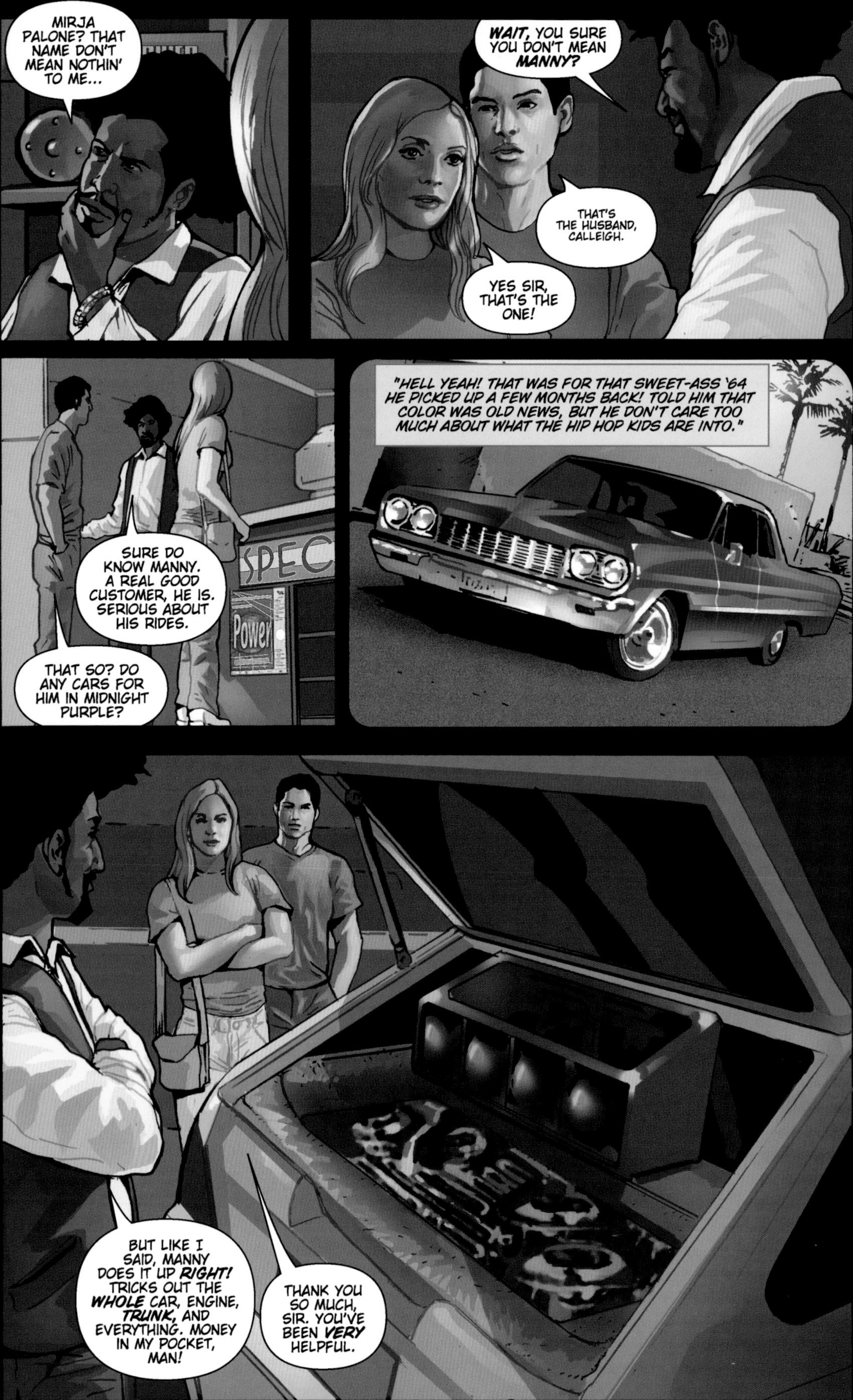
MIRJA PALONE? THAT NAME DON'T MEAN NOTHIN' TO ME...
WAIT, YOU SURE YOU DON'T MEAN MANNY?
THAT'S THE HUSBAND, CALLEIGH.
YES SIR, THAT'S THE ONE!
SPEC
Power
SURE DO KNOW MANNY. A REAL GOOD CUSTOMER, HE IS. SERIOUS ABOUT HIS RIDES.
THAT SO? DO ANY CARS FOR HIM IN MIDNIGHT PURPLE?
"HELL YEAH! THAT WAS FOR THAT SWEET-ASS '64 HE PICKED UP A FEW MONTHS BACK! TOLD HIM THAT COLOR WAS OLD NEWS, BUT HE DON'T CARE TOO MUCH ABOUT WHAT THE HIP HOP KIDS ARE INTO."
BUT LIKE I SAID, MANNY DOES IT UP RIGHT! TRICKS OUT THE WHOLE CAR, ENGINE, TRUNK, AND EVERYTHING. MONEY IN MY POCKET, MAN!
THANK YOU SO MUCH, SIR. YOU'VE BEEN VERY HELPFUL.

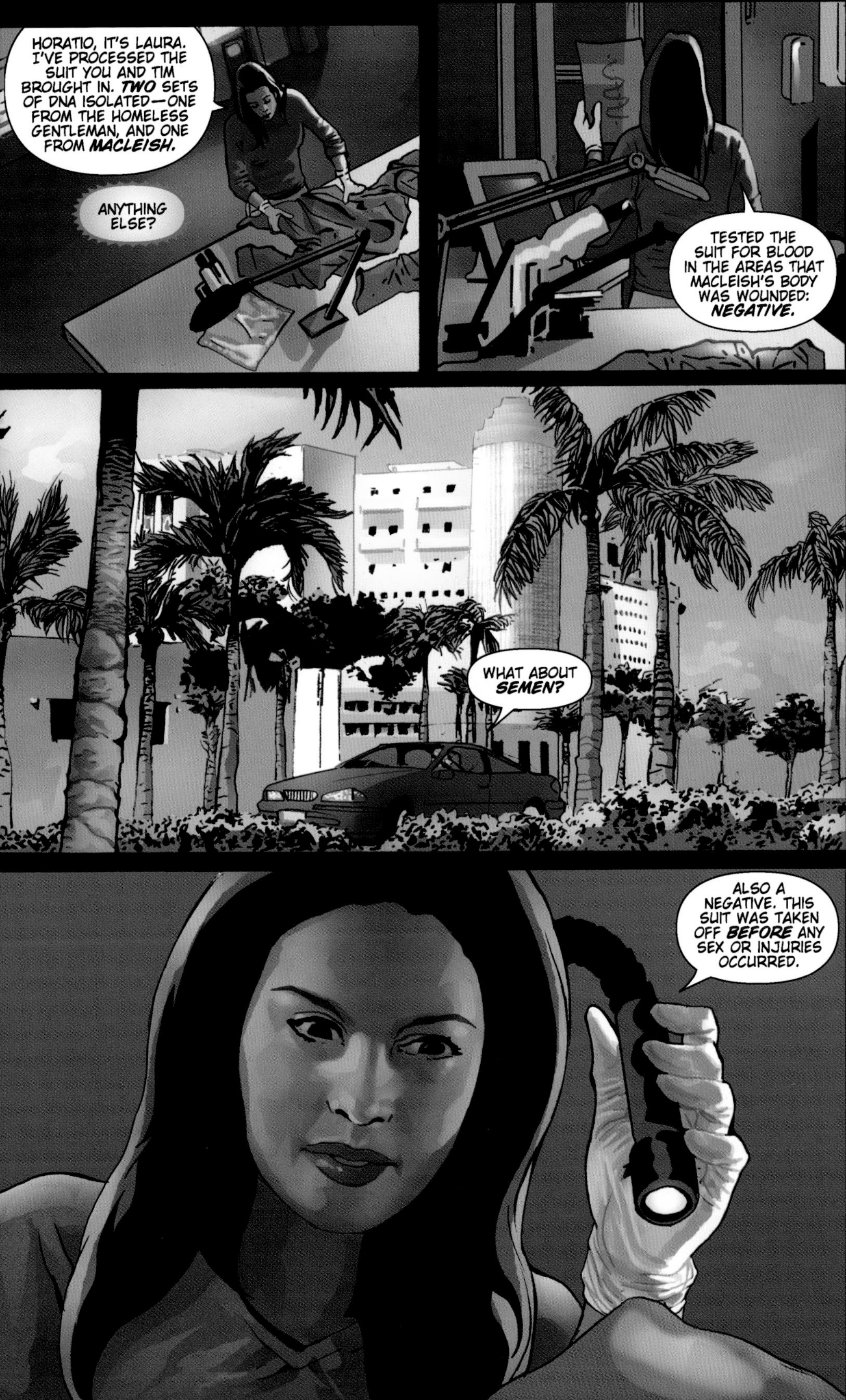
HORATIO, IT'S LAURA. I'VE PROCESSED THE SUIT YOU AND TIM BROUGHT IN. *TWO* SETS OF DNA ISOLATED—ONE FROM THE HOMELESS GENTLEMAN, AND ONE FROM *MACLEISH.*
ANYTHING ELSE?
TESTED THE SUIT FOR BLOOD IN THE AREAS THAT MACLEISH'S BODY WAS WOUNDED: *NEGATIVE.*
WHAT ABOUT *SEMEN?*
ALSO A NEGATIVE. THIS SUIT WAS TAKEN OFF *BEFORE* ANY SEX OR INJURIES OCCURRED.

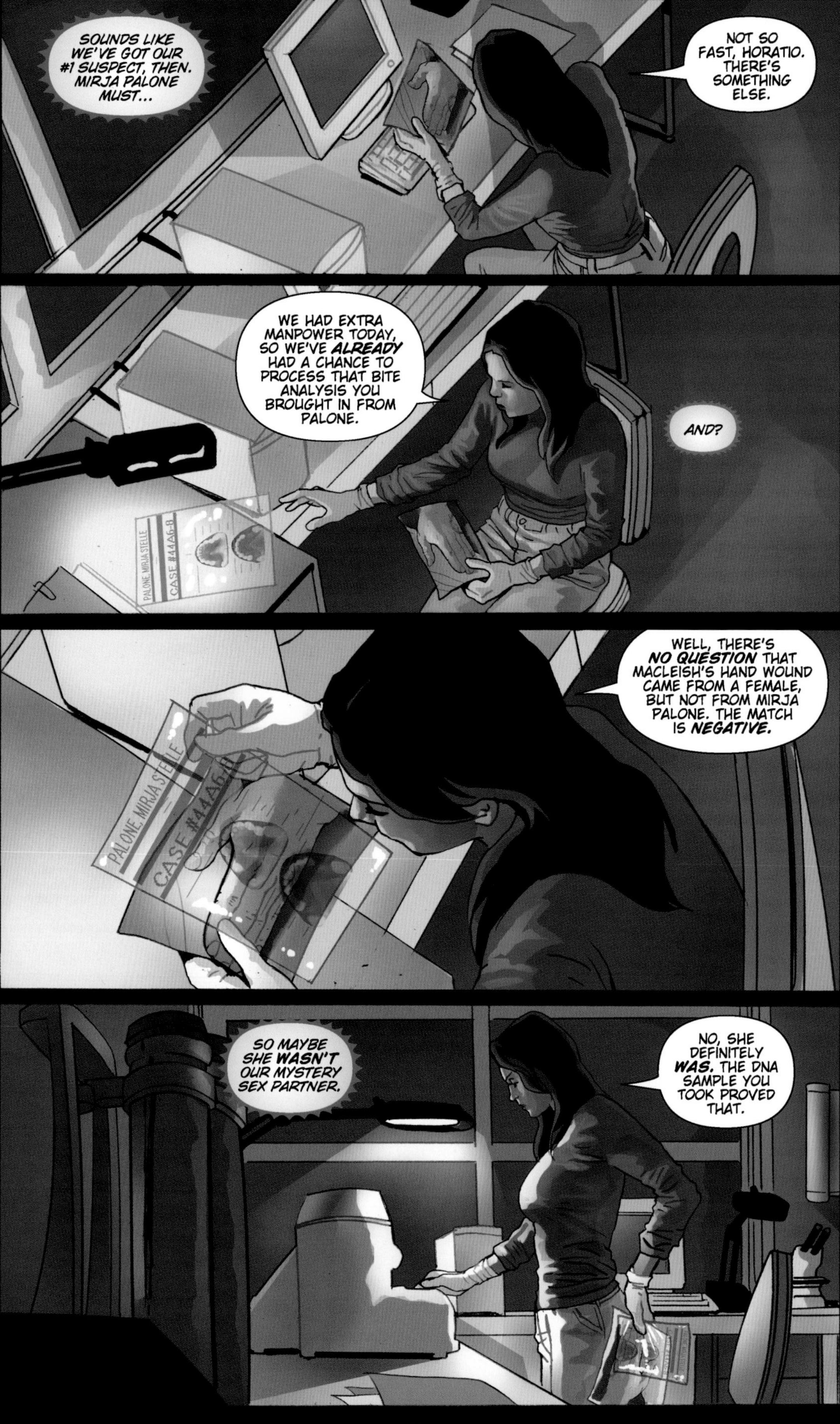
SOUNDS LIKE WE'VE GOT OUR #1 SUSPECT, THEN. MIRJA PALONE MUST...
NOT SO FAST, HORATIO. THERE'S SOMETHING ELSE.
WE HAD EXTRA MANPOWER TODAY, SO WE'VE ALREADY HAD A CHANCE TO PROCESS THAT BITE ANALYSIS YOU BROUGHT IN FROM PALONE.
AND?
PALONE, MIRJA STELLE
CASE #44A6-8
WELL, THERE'S NO QUESTION THAT MACLEISH'S HAND WOUND CAME FROM A FEMALE, BUT NOT FROM MIRJA PALONE. THE MATCH IS NEGATIVE.
SO MAYBE SHE WASN'T OUR MYSTERY SEX PARTNER.
NO, SHE DEFINITELY WAS. THE DNA SAMPLE YOU TOOK PROVED THAT.

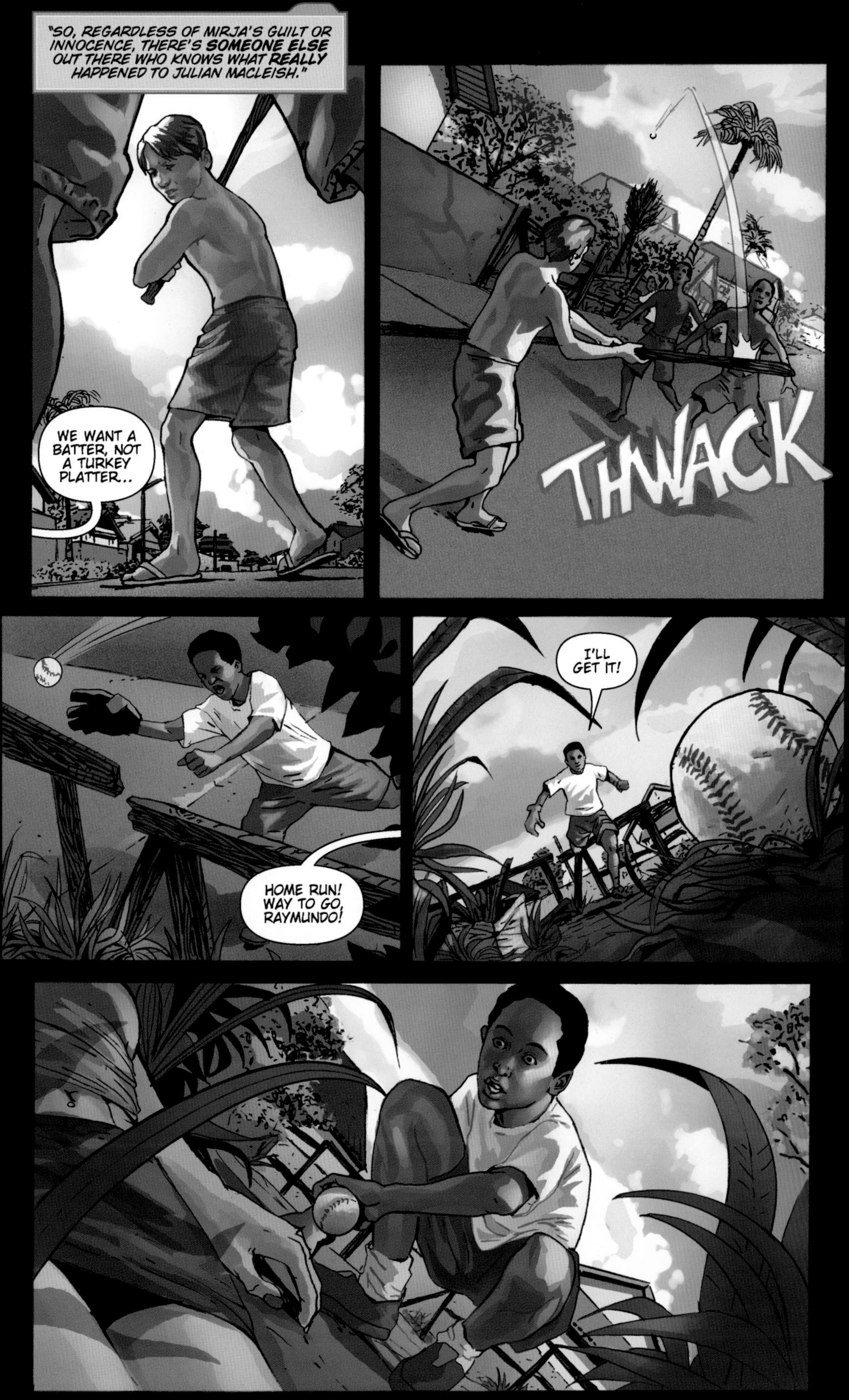
"SO, REGARDLESS OF MIRJA'S GUILT OR INNOCENCE, THERE'S SOMEONE ELSE OUT THERE WHO KNOWS WHAT REALLY HAPPENED TO JULIAN MACLEISH."
WE WANT A BATTER, NOT A TURKEY PLATTER...
THWACK
HOME RUN! WAY TO GO, RAYMUNDO!
I'LL GET IT!

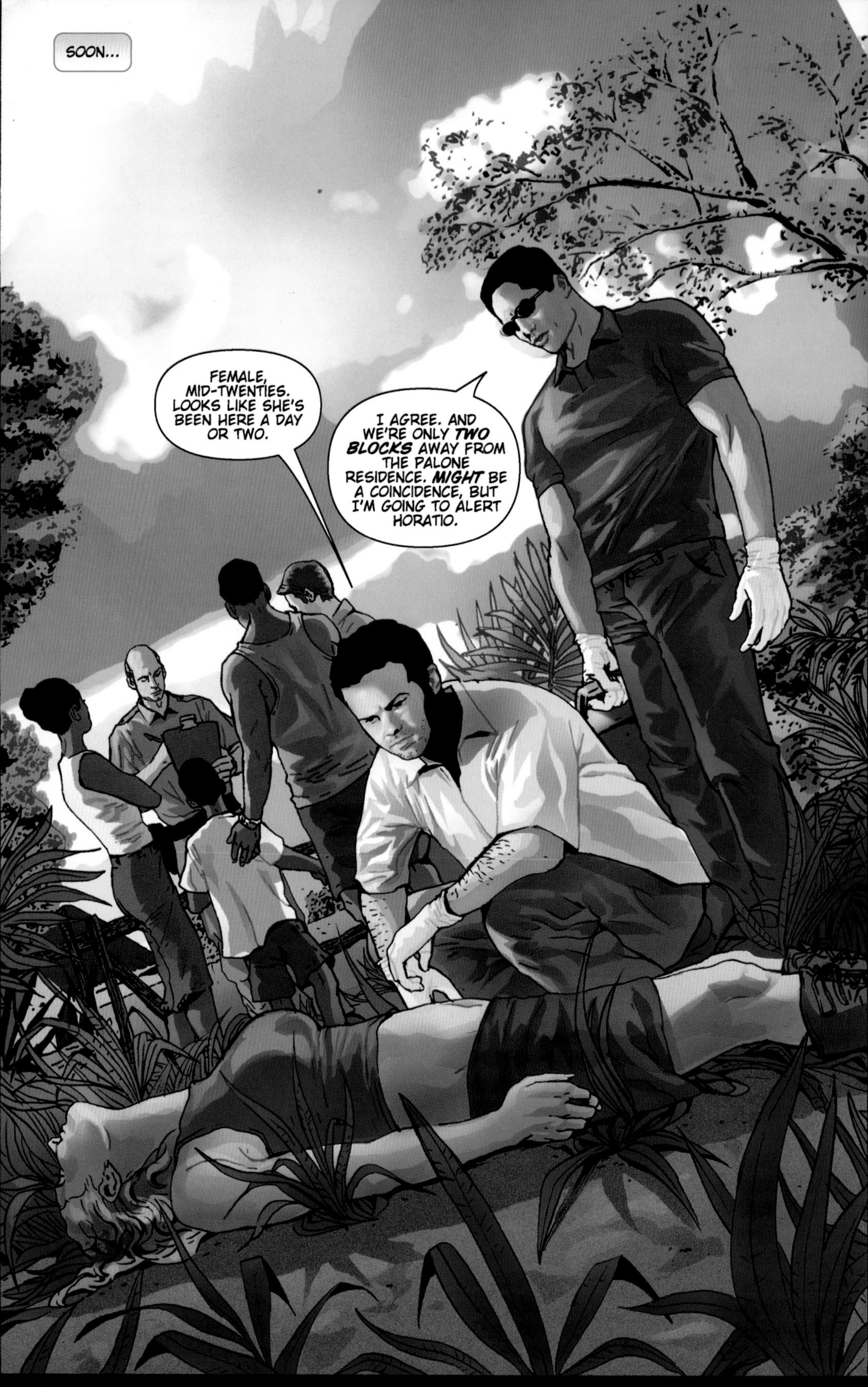
SOON...
FEMALE, MID-TWENTIES. LOOKS LIKE SHE'S BEEN HERE A DAY OR TWO.
I AGREE. AND WE'RE ONLY TWO BLOCKS AWAY FROM THE PALONE RESIDENCE. MIGHT BE A COINCIDENCE, BUT I'M GOING TO ALERT HORATIO.

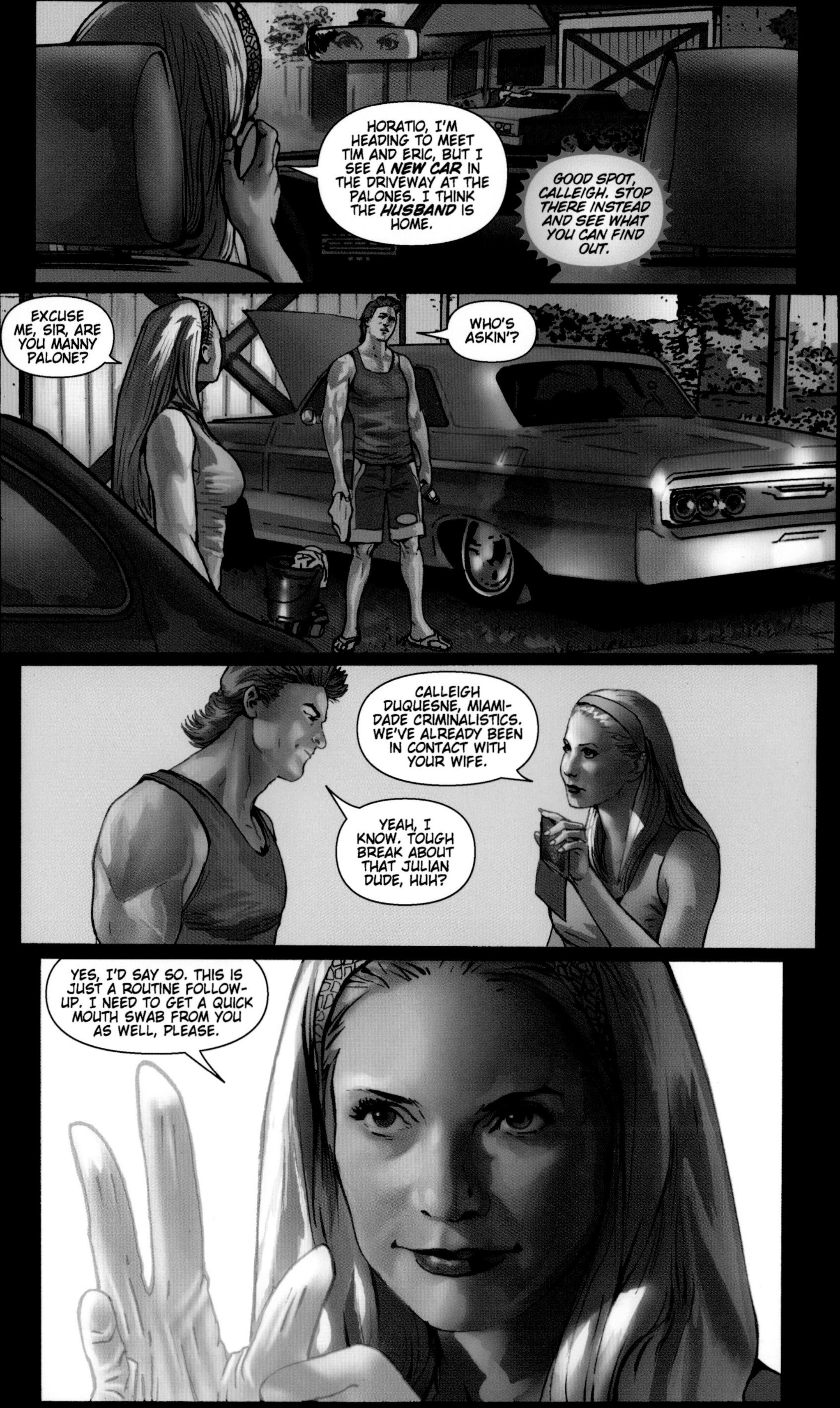
HORATIO, I'M HEADING TO MEET TIM AND ERIC, BUT I SEE A **NEW CAR** IN THE DRIVEWAY AT THE PALONES. I THINK THE **HUSBAND** IS HOME.
GOOD SPOT, CALLEIGH. STOP THERE INSTEAD AND SEE WHAT YOU CAN FIND OUT.
EXCUSE ME, SIR, ARE YOU MANNY PALONE?
WHO'S ASKIN'?
CALLEIGH DUQUESNE, MIAMI-DADE CRIMINALISTICS. WE'VE ALREADY BEEN IN CONTACT WITH YOUR WIFE.
YEAH, I KNOW. TOUGH BREAK ABOUT THAT JULIAN DUDE, HUH?
YES, I'D SAY SO. THIS IS JUST A ROUTINE FOLLOW-UP. I NEED TO GET A QUICK MOUTH SWAB FROM YOU AS WELL, PLEASE.

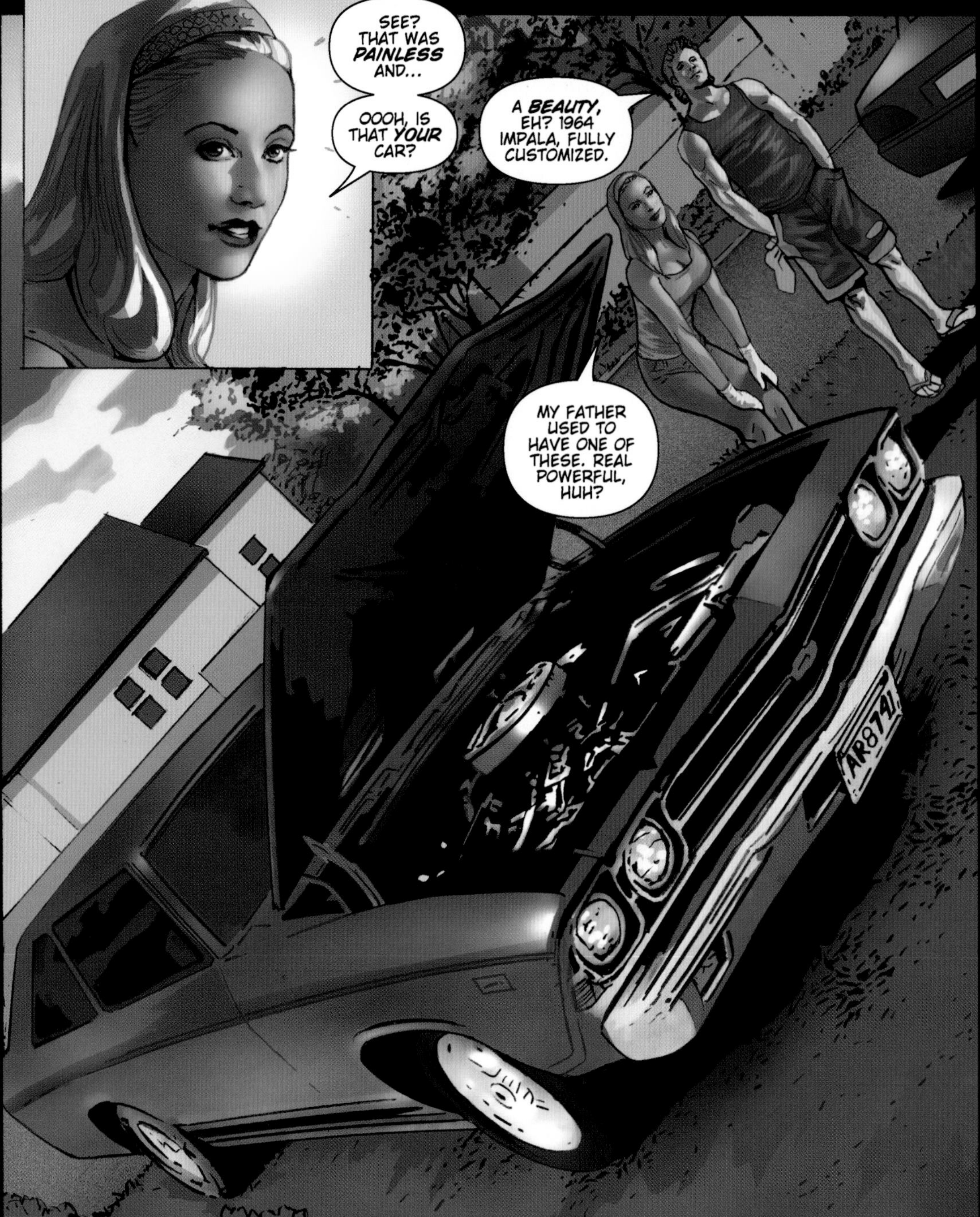
SEE? THAT WAS PAINLESS AND...
OOOH, IS THAT YOUR CAR?
A BEAUTY, EH? 1964 IMPALA, FULLY CUSTOMIZED.
MY FATHER USED TO HAVE ONE OF THESE. REAL POWERFUL, HUH?
AR8741

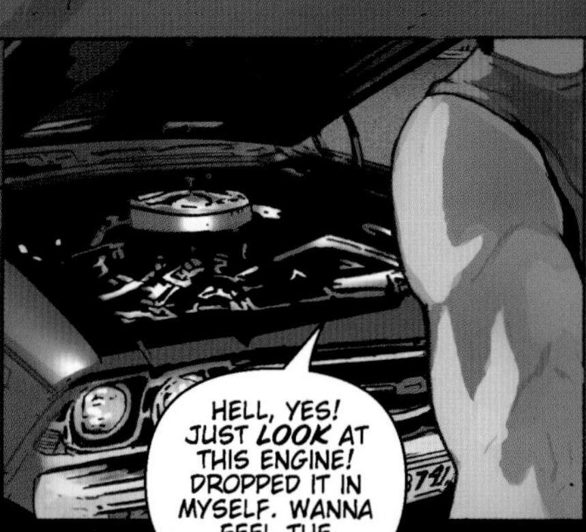
HELL, YES! JUST LOOK AT THIS ENGINE! DROPPED IT IN MYSELF. WANNA FEEL THE POWER?

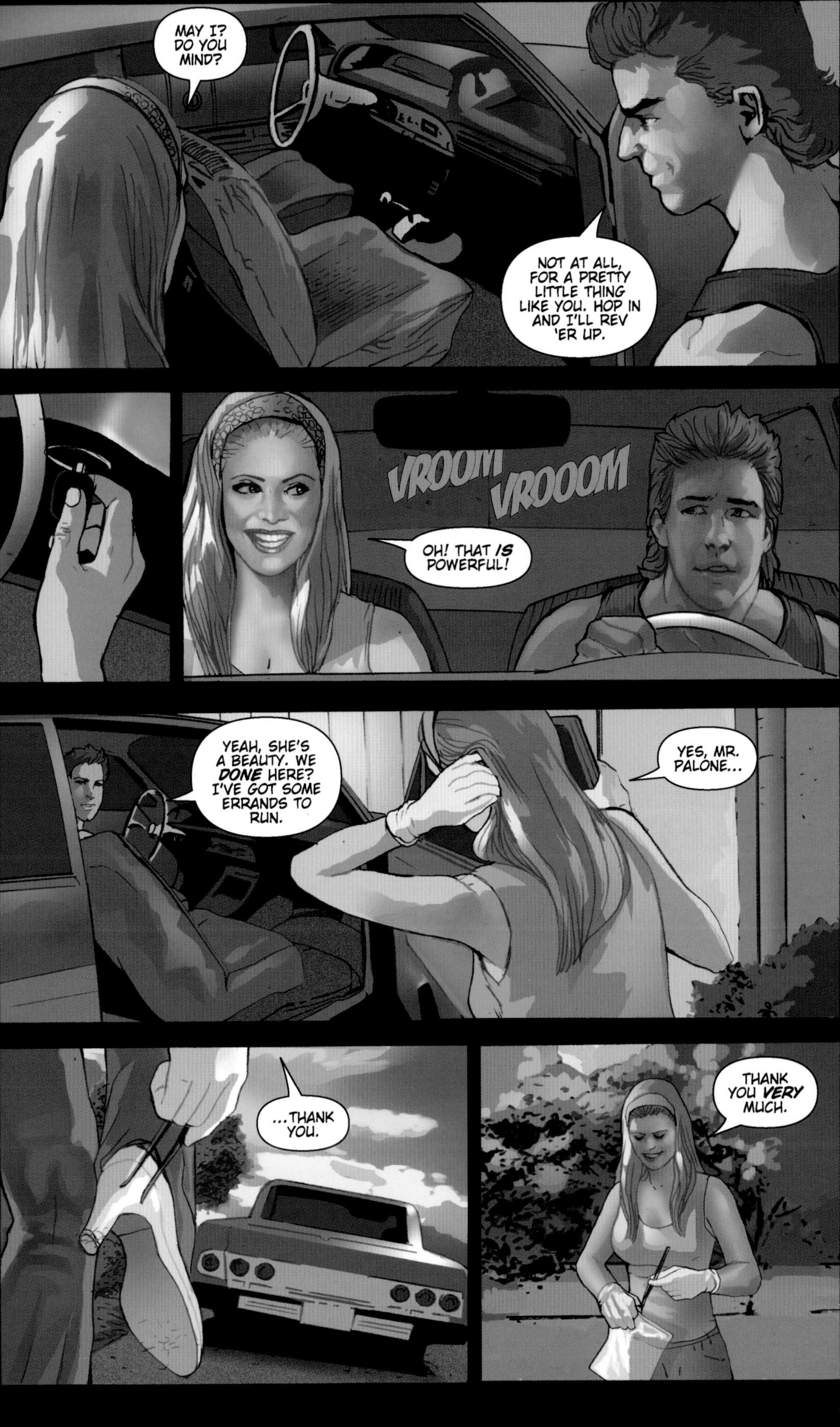
MAY I? DO YOU MIND?
NOT AT ALL, FOR A PRETTY LITTLE THING LIKE YOU. HOP IN AND I'LL REV 'ER UP.
VROOM
VROOOM
OH! THAT *IS* POWERFUL!
YEAH, SHE'S A BEAUTY. WE **DONE** HERE? I'VE GOT SOME ERRANDS TO RUN.
YES, MR. PALONE...
...THANK YOU.
THANK YOU **VERY** MUCH.

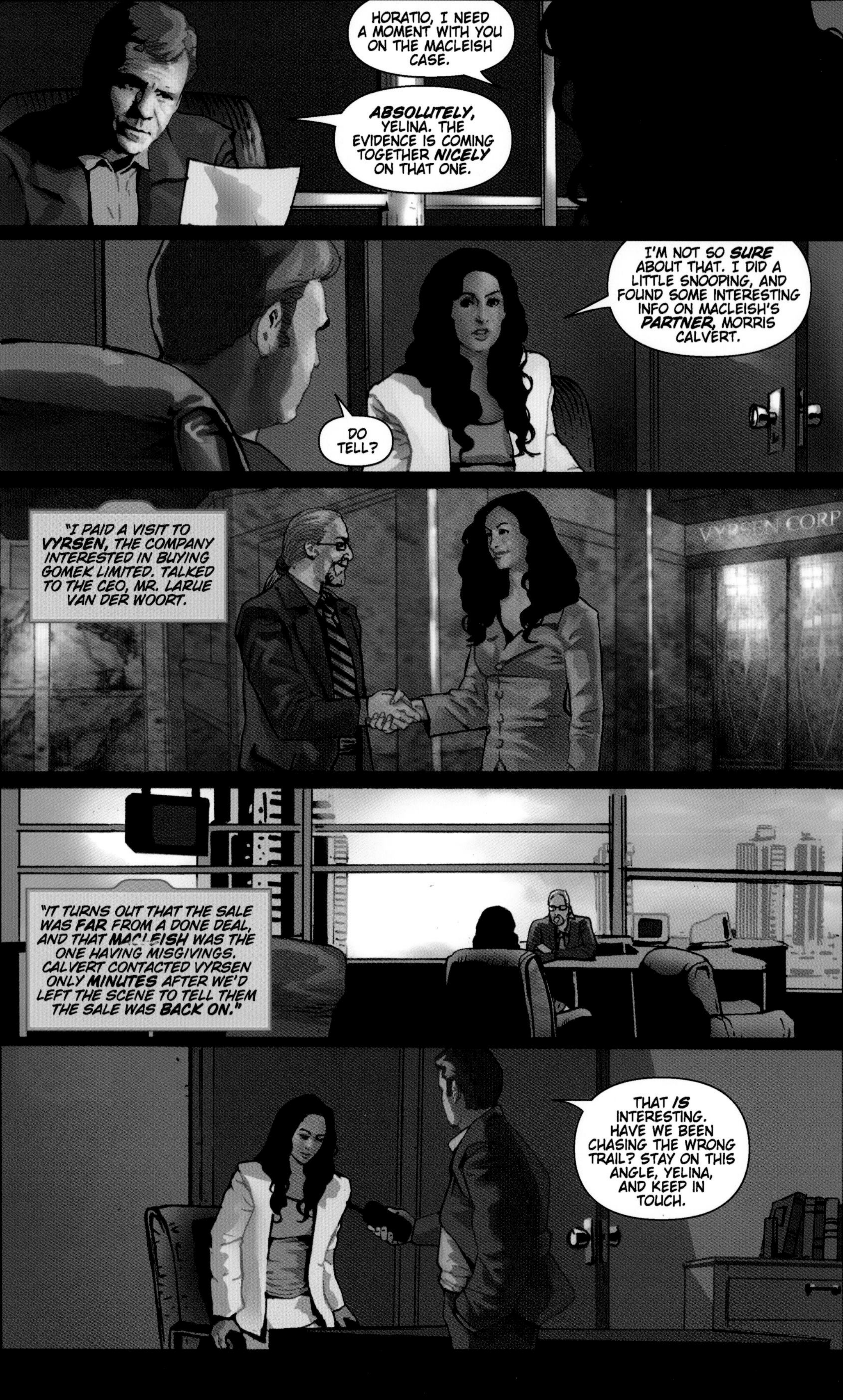
HORATIO, I NEED A MOMENT WITH YOU ON THE MACLEISH CASE.
ABSOLUTELY, YELINA. THE EVIDENCE IS COMING TOGETHER NICELY ON THAT ONE.
I'M NOT SO SURE ABOUT THAT. I DID A LITTLE SNOOPING, AND FOUND SOME INTERESTING INFO ON MACLEISH'S PARTNER, MORRIS CALVERT.
DO TELL?
"I PAID A VISIT TO VYRSEN, THE COMPANY INTERESTED IN BUYING GOMEK LIMITED. TALKED TO THE CEO, MR. LARUE VAN DER WOORT.
VYRSEN CORP
"IT TURNS OUT THAT THE SALE WAS FAR FROM A DONE DEAL, AND THAT MACLEISH WAS THE ONE HAVING MISGIVINGS. CALVERT CONTACTED VYRSEN ONLY MINUTES AFTER WE'D LEFT THE SCENE TO TELL THEM THE SALE WAS BACK ON."
THAT IS INTERESTING. HAVE WE BEEN CHASING THE WRONG TRAIL? STAY ON THIS ANGLE, YELINA, AND KEEP IN TOUCH.

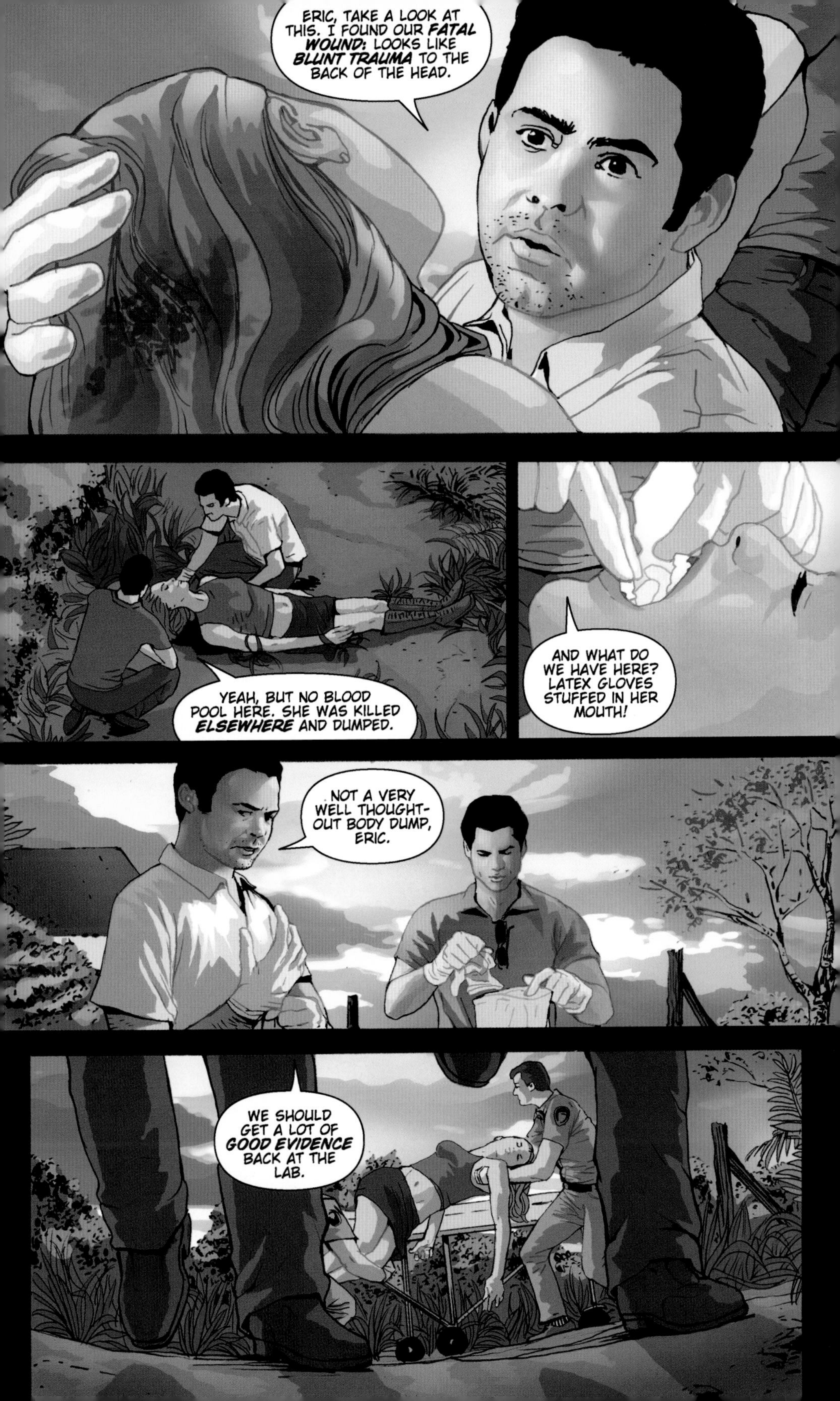
ERIC, TAKE A LOOK AT THIS. I FOUND OUR FATAL WOUND: LOOKS LIKE BLUNT TRAUMA TO THE BACK OF THE HEAD.
YEAH, BUT NO BLOOD POOL HERE. SHE WAS KILLED ELSEWHERE AND DUMPED.
AND WHAT DO WE HAVE HERE? LATEX GLOVES STUFFED IN HER MOUTH!
NOT A VERY WELL THOUGHT-OUT BODY DUMP, ERIC.
WE SHOULD GET A LOT OF GOOD EVIDENCE BACK AT THE LAB.

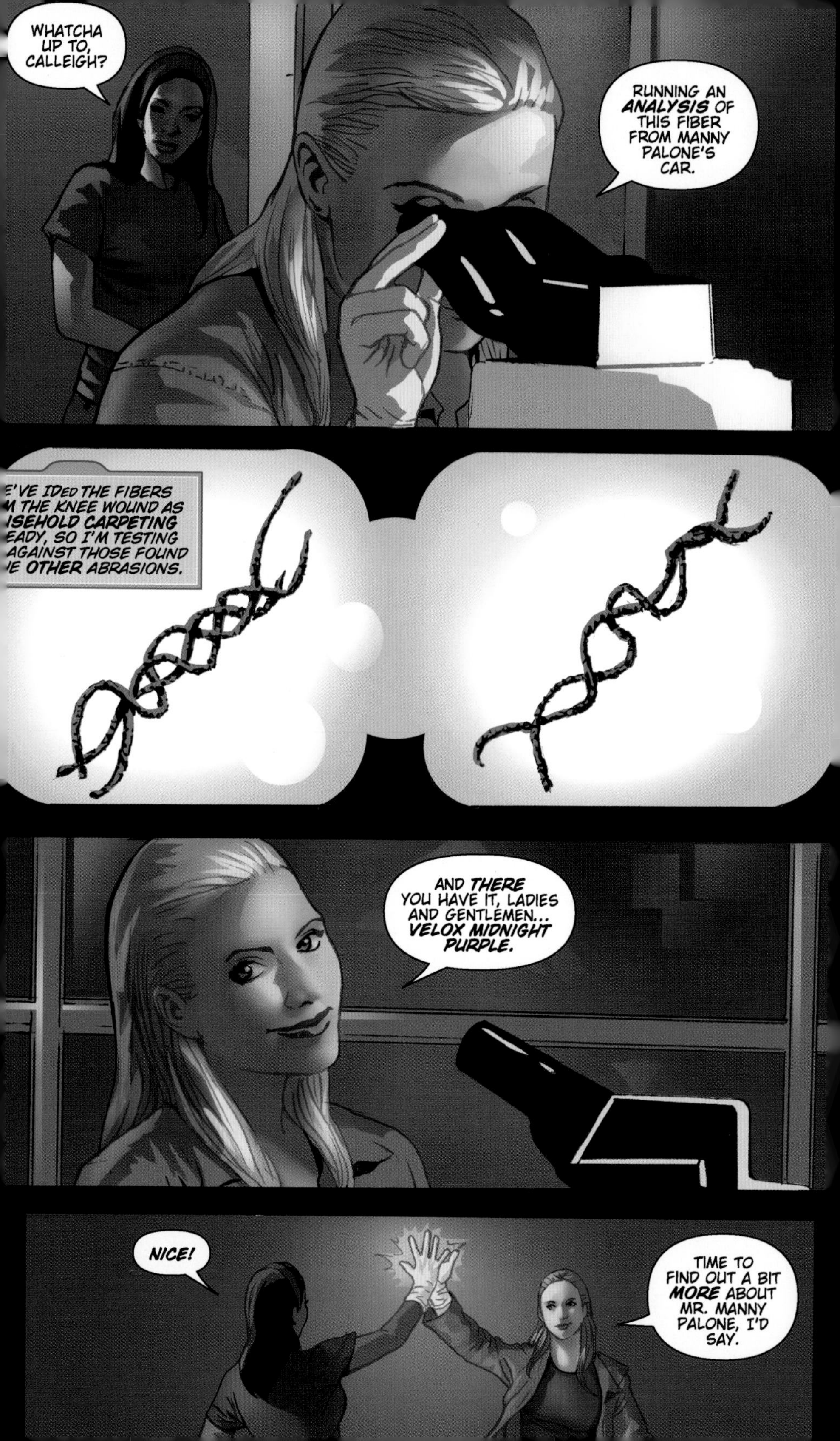

WHATCHA UP TO, CALLEIGH?
RUNNING AN ANALYSIS OF THIS FIBER FROM MANNY PALONE'S CAR.
E'VE IDed THE FIBERS M THE KNEE WOUND AS ISEHOLD CARPETING EADY, SO I'M TESTING AGAINST THOSE FOUND E OTHER ABRASIONS.
AND THERE YOU HAVE IT, LADIES AND GENTLEMEN... VELOX MIDNIGHT PURPLE.
NICE!
TIME TO FIND OUT A BIT MORE ABOUT MR. MANNY PALONE, I'D SAY.

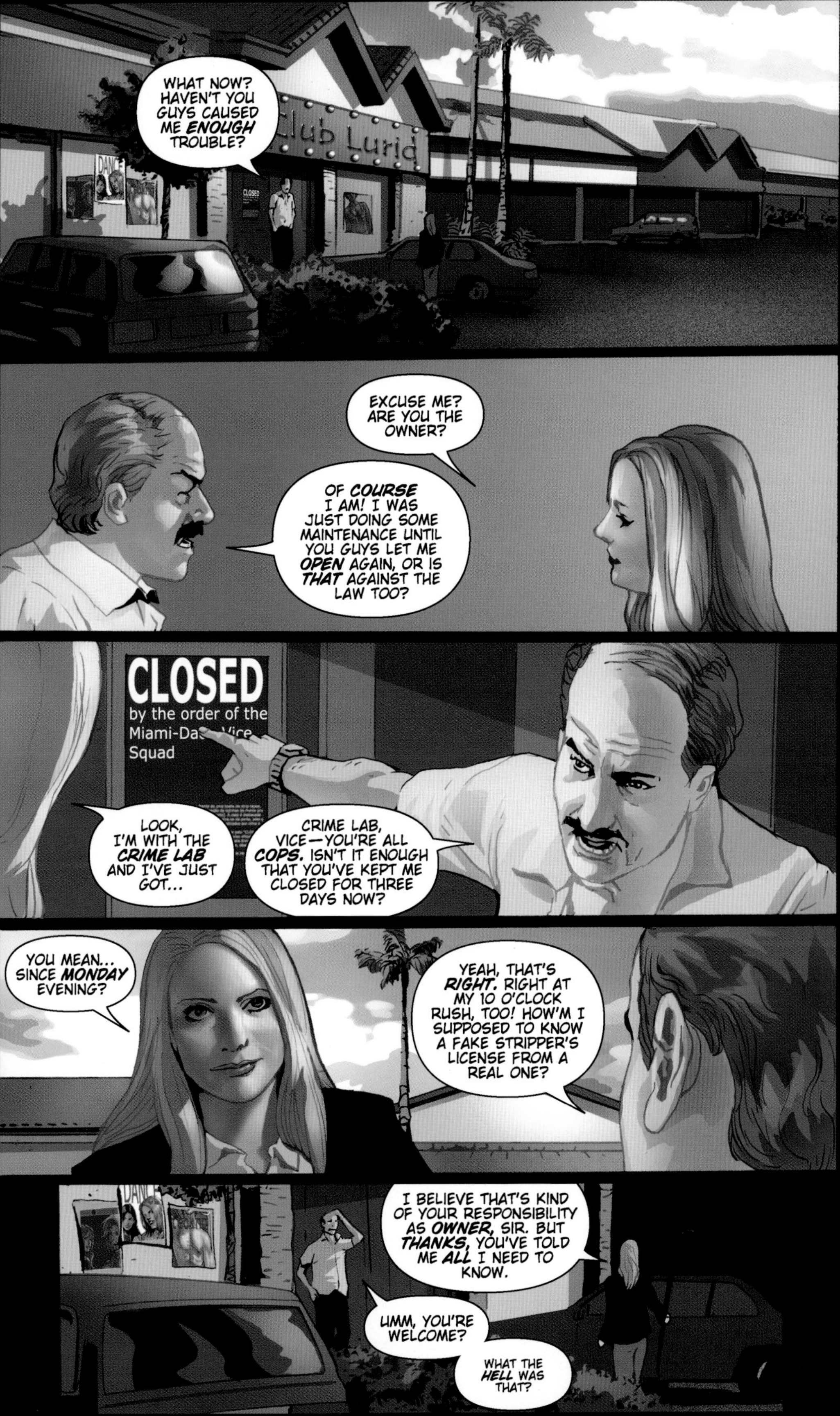
WHAT NOW? HAVEN'T YOU GUYS CAUSED ME ENOUGH TROUBLE?
Club Lurid
DANCE
CLOSED
EXCUSE ME? ARE YOU THE OWNER?
OF COURSE I AM! I WAS JUST DOING SOME MAINTENANCE UNTIL YOU GUYS LET ME OPEN AGAIN, OR IS THAT AGAINST THE LAW TOO?
CLOSED
by the order of the
Miami-Dade Vice
Squad
LOOK, I'M WITH THE CRIME LAB AND I'VE JUST GOT...
CRIME LAB, VICE—YOU'RE ALL COPS. ISN'T IT ENOUGH THAT YOU'VE KEPT ME CLOSED FOR THREE DAYS NOW?
YOU MEAN... SINCE MONDAY EVENING?
YEAH, THAT'S RIGHT. RIGHT AT MY 10 O'CLOCK RUSH, TOO! HOW'M I SUPPOSED TO KNOW A FAKE STRIPPER'S LICENSE FROM A REAL ONE?
I BELIEVE THAT'S KIND OF YOUR RESPONSIBILITY AS OWNER, SIR. BUT THANKS, YOU'VE TOLD ME ALL I NEED TO KNOW.
UMM, YOU'RE WELCOME?
WHAT THE HELL WAS THAT?

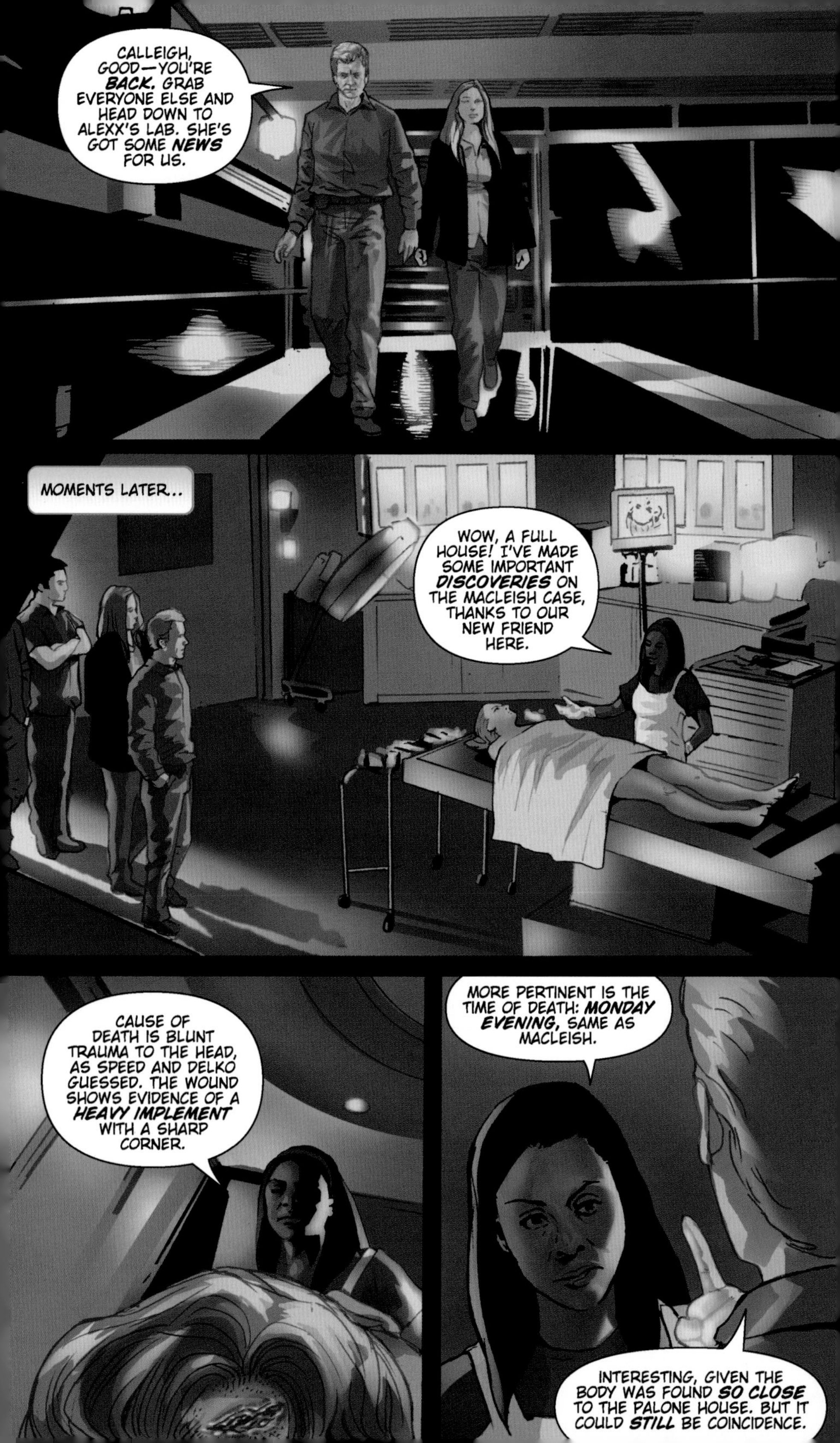
CALLEIGH, GOOD—YOU'RE BACK. GRAB EVERYONE ELSE AND HEAD DOWN TO ALEXX'S LAB. SHE'S GOT SOME NEWS FOR US.
MOMENTS LATER...
WOW, A FULL HOUSE! I'VE MADE SOME IMPORTANT DISCOVERIES ON THE MACLEISH CASE, THANKS TO OUR NEW FRIEND HERE.
CAUSE OF DEATH IS BLUNT TRAUMA TO THE HEAD, AS SPEED AND DELKO GUESSED. THE WOUND SHOWS EVIDENCE OF A HEAVY IMPLEMENT WITH A SHARP CORNER.
MORE PERTINENT IS THE TIME OF DEATH: MONDAY EVENING, SAME AS MACLEISH.
INTERESTING, GIVEN THE BODY WAS FOUND SO CLOSE TO THE PALONE HOUSE. BUT IT COULD STILL BE COINCIDENCE.

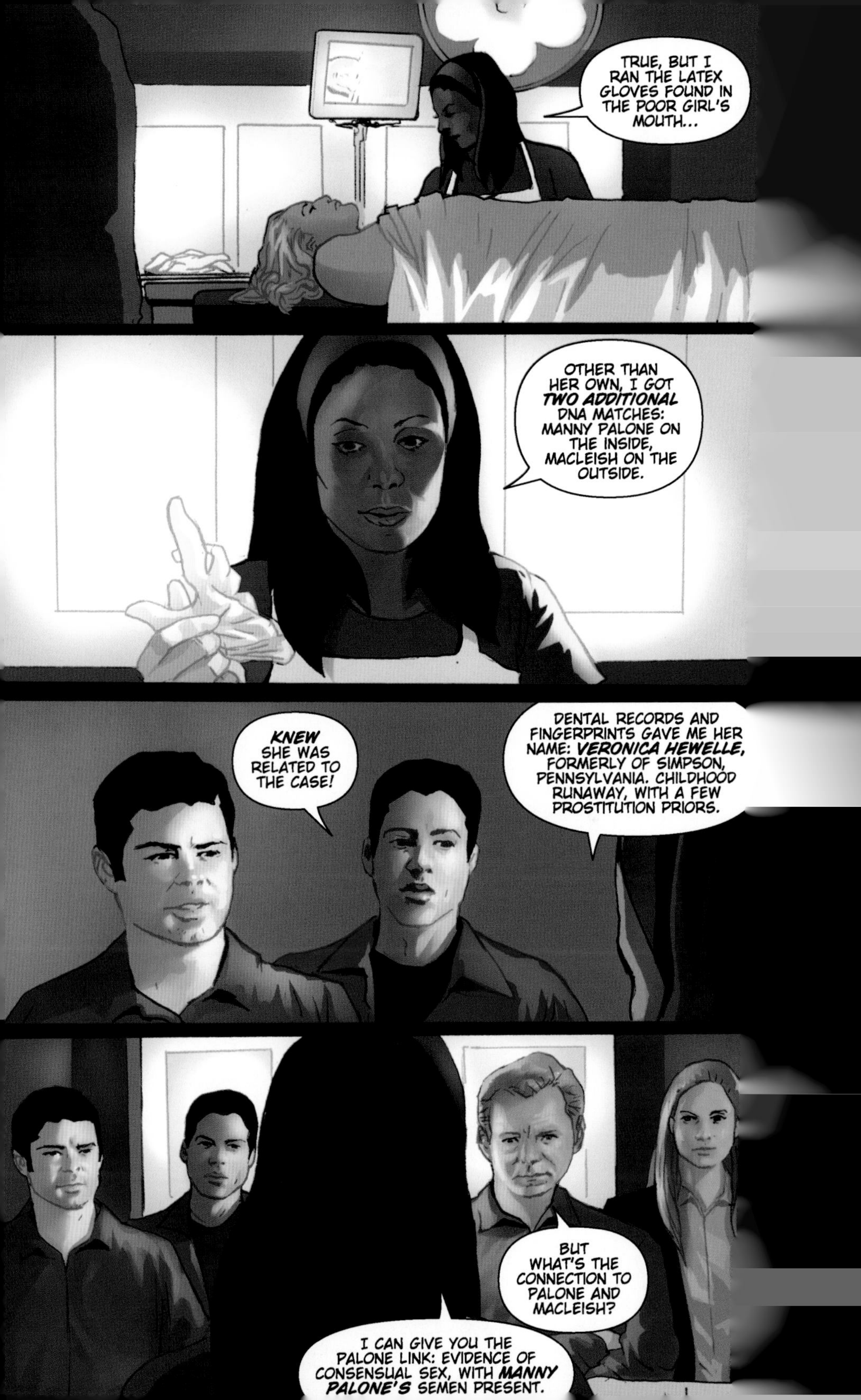
TRUE, BUT I RAN THE LATEX GLOVES FOUND IN THE POOR GIRL'S MOUTH...
OTHER THAN HER OWN, I GOT **TWO ADDITIONAL** DNA MATCHES: MANNY PALONE ON THE INSIDE, MACLEISH ON THE OUTSIDE.
**KNEW** SHE WAS RELATED TO THE CASE!
DENTAL RECORDS AND FINGERPRINTS GAVE ME HER NAME: **VERONICA HEWELLE,** FORMERLY OF SIMPSON, PENNSYLVANIA. CHILDHOOD RUNAWAY, WITH A FEW PROSTITUTION PRIORS.
BUT WHAT'S THE CONNECTION TO PALONE AND MACLEISH?
I CAN GIVE YOU THE PALONE LINK: EVIDENCE OF CONSENSUAL SEX, WITH **MANNY PALONE'S** SEMEN PRESENT.

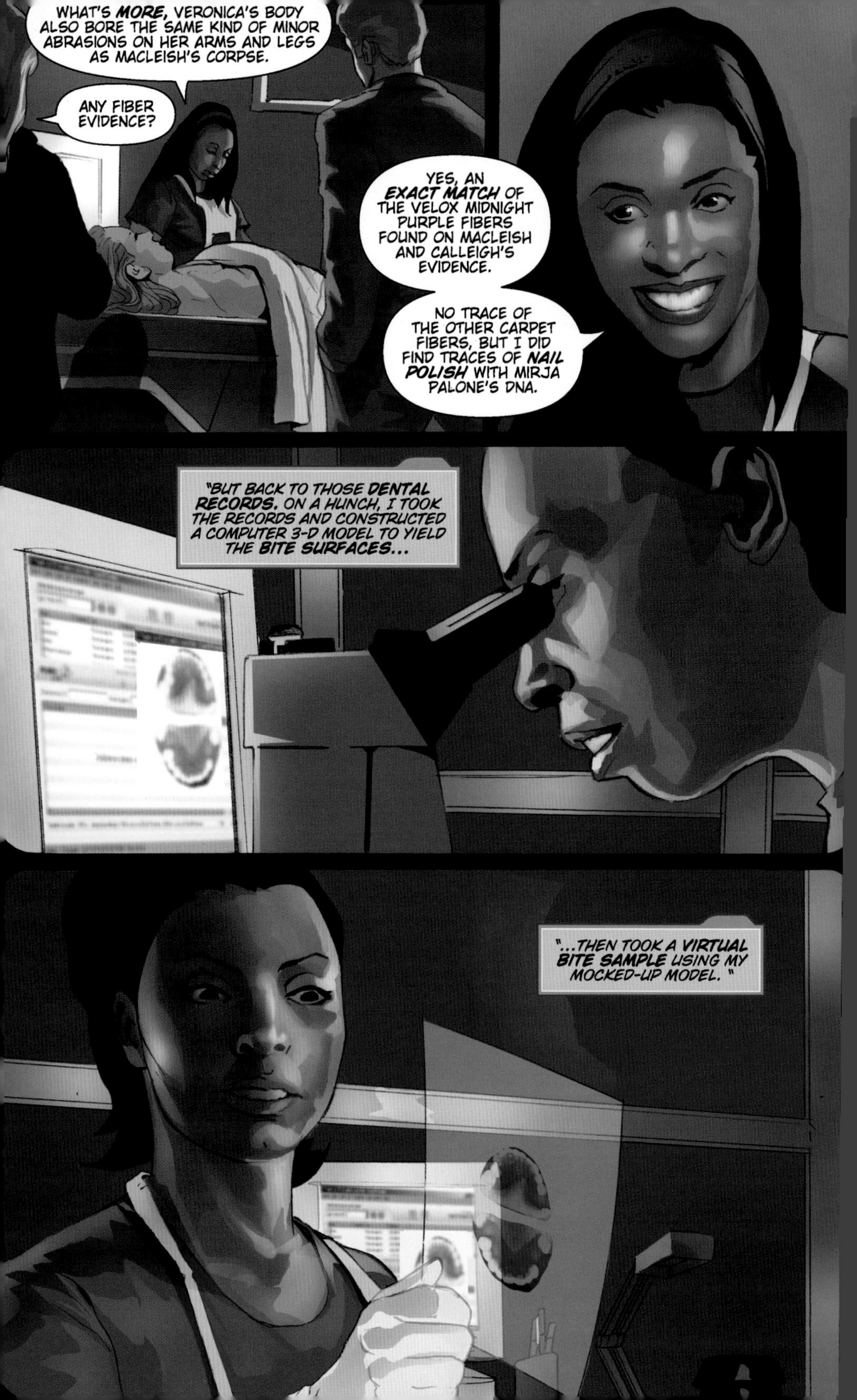
WHAT'S MORE, VERONICA'S BODY ALSO BORE THE SAME KIND OF MINOR ABRASIONS ON HER ARMS AND LEGS AS MACLEISH'S CORPSE.
ANY FIBER EVIDENCE?
YES, AN EXACT MATCH OF THE VELOX MIDNIGHT PURPLE FIBERS FOUND ON MACLEISH AND CALLEIGH'S EVIDENCE.
NO TRACE OF THE OTHER CARPET FIBERS, BUT I DID FIND TRACES OF NAIL POLISH WITH MIRJA PALONE'S DNA.
"BUT BACK TO THOSE DENTAL RECORDS. ON A HUNCH, I TOOK THE RECORDS AND CONSTRUCTED A COMPUTER 3-D MODEL TO YIELD THE BITE SURFACES...
"...THEN TOOK A VIRTUAL BITE SAMPLE USING MY MOCKED-UP MODEL."

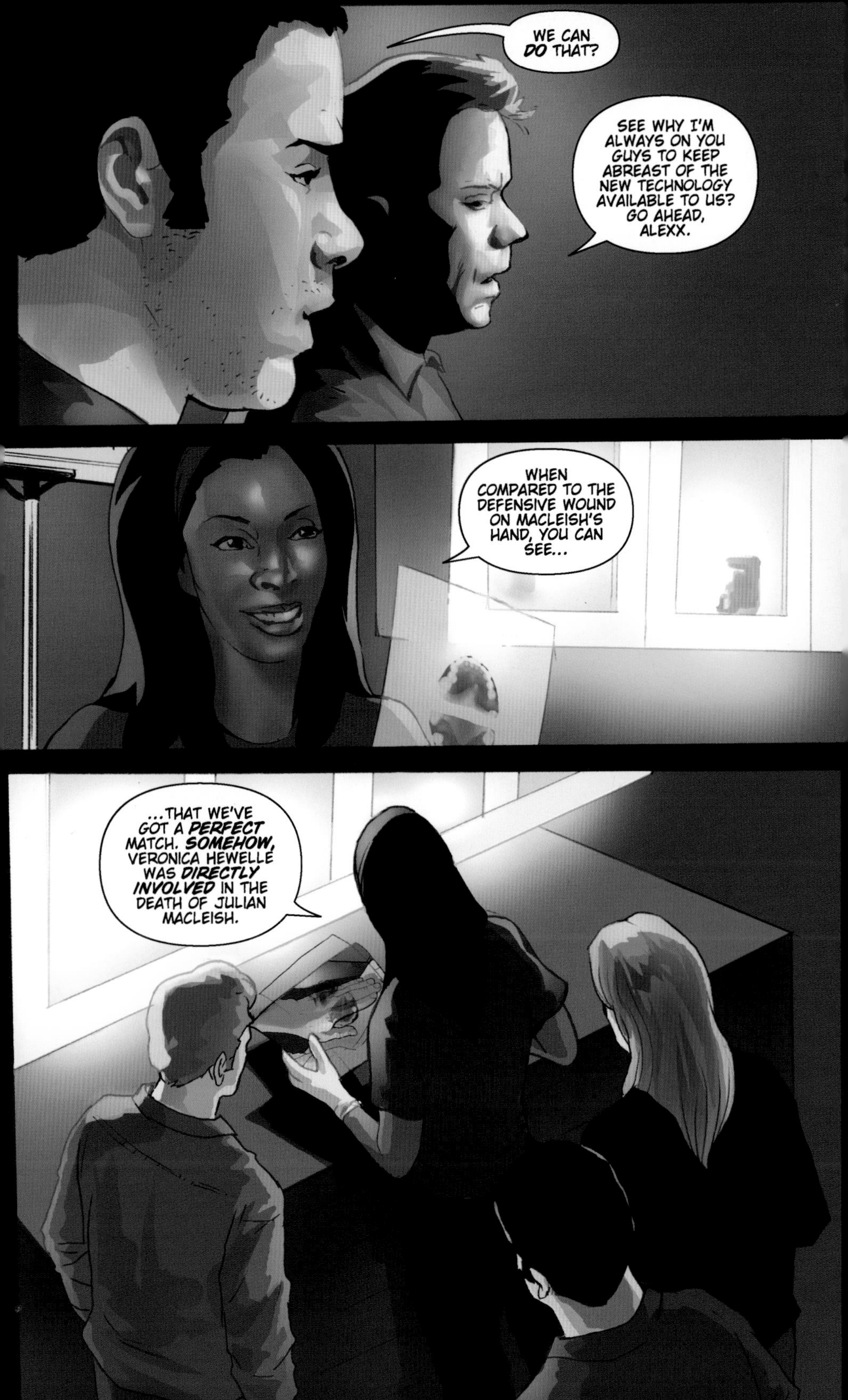
WE CAN DO THAT?
SEE WHY I'M ALWAYS ON YOU GUYS TO KEEP ABREAST OF THE NEW TECHNOLOGY AVAILABLE TO US? GO AHEAD, ALEXX.
WHEN COMPARED TO THE DEFENSIVE WOUND ON MACLEISH'S HAND, YOU CAN SEE...
...THAT WE'VE GOT A PERFECT MATCH. SOMEHOW, VERONICA HEWELLE WAS DIRECTLY INVOLVED IN THE DEATH OF JULIAN MACLEISH.

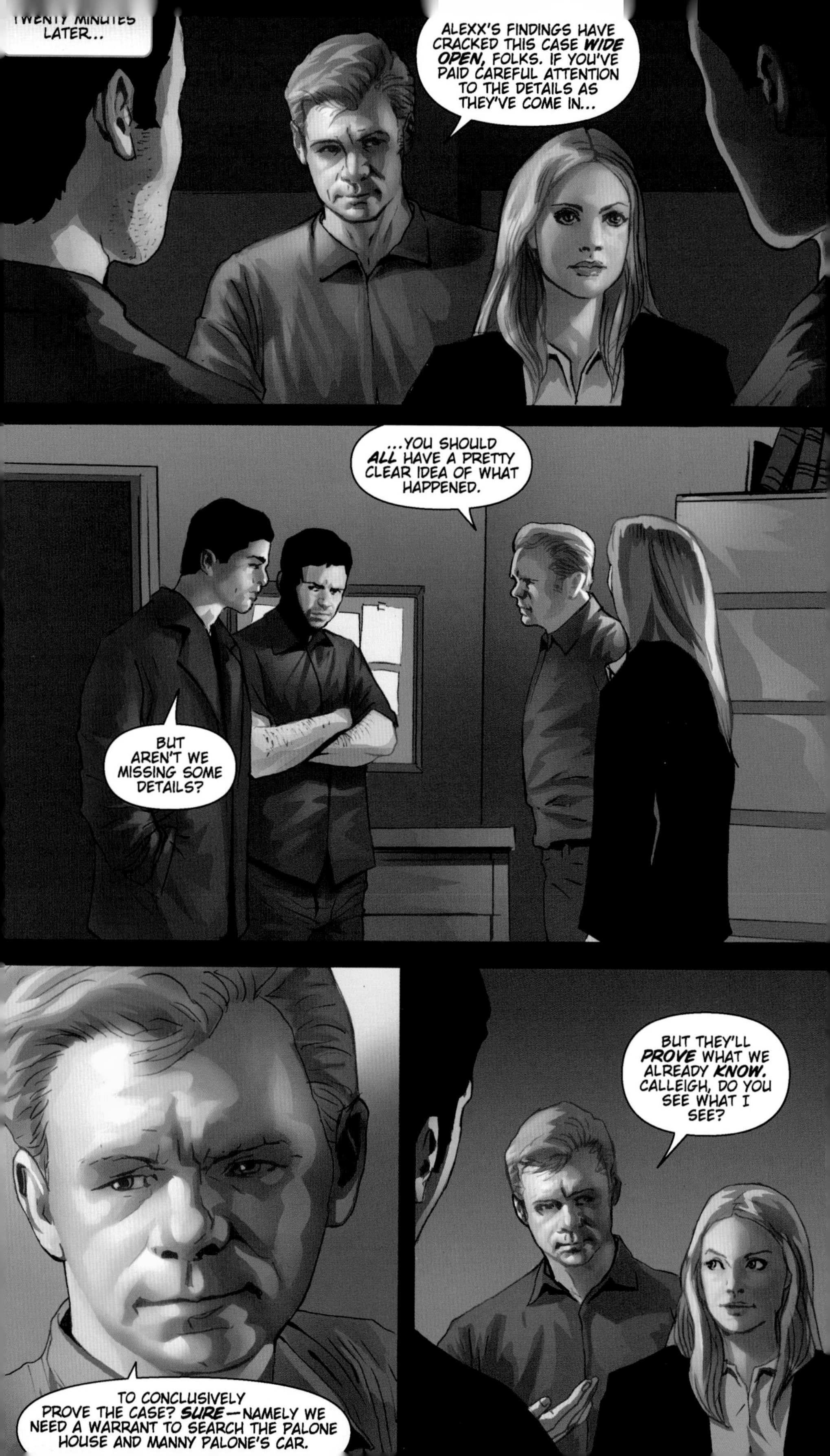
TWENTY MINUTES LATER...
ALEXX'S FINDINGS HAVE CRACKED THIS CASE WIDE OPEN, FOLKS. IF YOU'VE PAID CAREFUL ATTENTION TO THE DETAILS AS THEY'VE COME IN...
...YOU SHOULD ALL HAVE A PRETTY CLEAR IDEA OF WHAT HAPPENED.
BUT AREN'T WE MISSING SOME DETAILS?
TO CONCLUSIVELY PROVE THE CASE? SURE—NAMELY WE NEED A WARRANT TO SEARCH THE PALONE HOUSE AND MANNY PALONE'S CAR.
BUT THEY'LL PROVE WHAT WE ALREADY KNOW. CALLEIGH, DO YOU SEE WHAT I SEE?

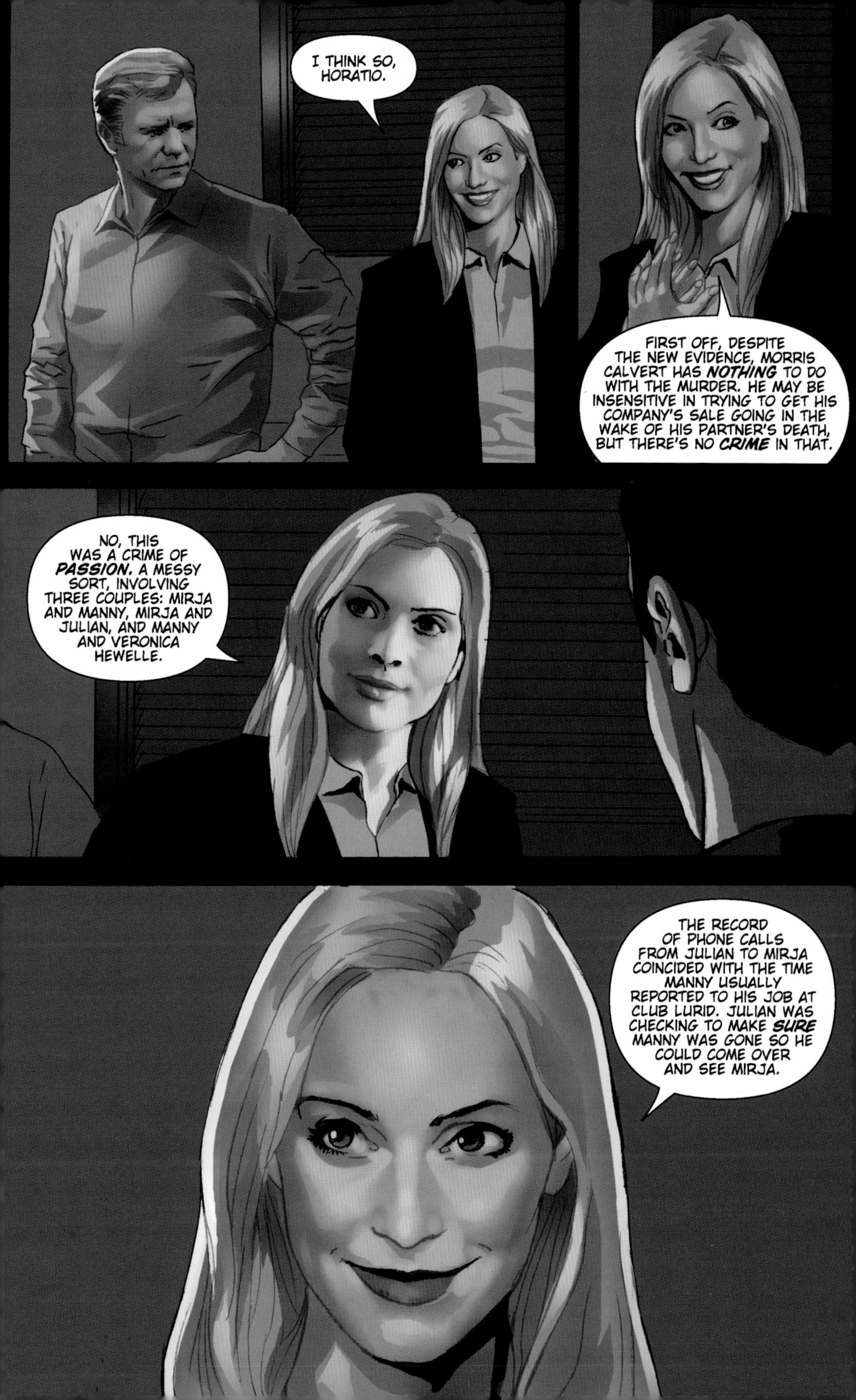
I THINK SO, HORATIO.
FIRST OFF, DESPITE THE NEW EVIDENCE, MORRIS CALVERT HAS NOTHING TO DO WITH THE MURDER. HE MAY BE INSENSITIVE IN TRYING TO GET HIS COMPANY'S SALE GOING IN THE WAKE OF HIS PARTNER'S DEATH, BUT THERE'S NO CRIME IN THAT.
NO, THIS WAS A CRIME OF PASSION. A MESSY SORT, INVOLVING THREE COUPLES: MIRJA AND MANNY, MIRJA AND JULIAN, AND MANNY AND VERONICA HEWELLE.
THE RECORD OF PHONE CALLS FROM JULIAN TO MIRJA COINCIDED WITH THE TIME MANNY USUALLY REPORTED TO HIS JOB AT CLUB LURID. JULIAN WAS CHECKING TO MAKE SURE MANNY WAS GONE SO HE COULD COME OVER AND SEE MIRJA.

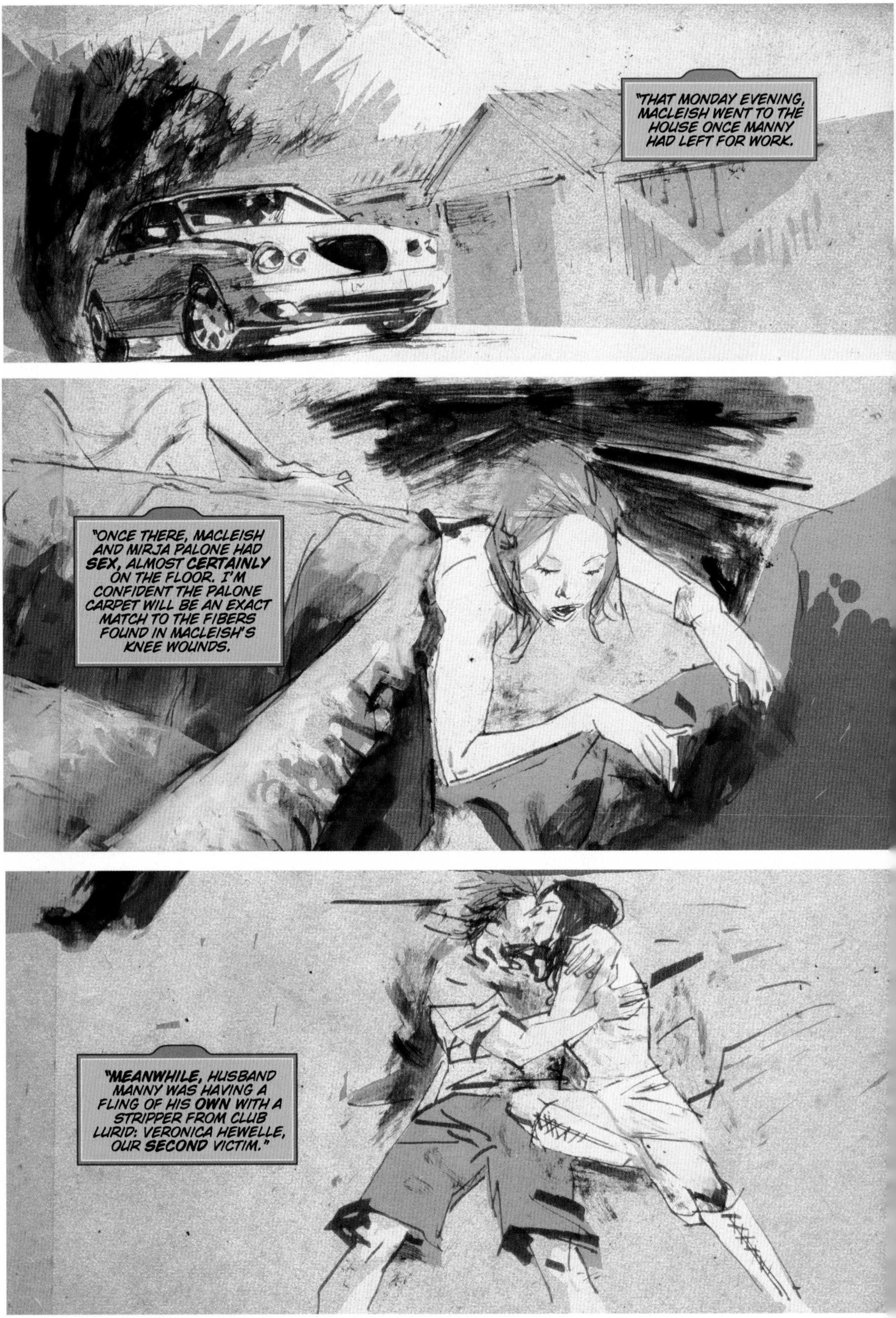
"THAT MONDAY EVENING, MACLEISH WENT TO THE HOUSE ONCE MANNY HAD LEFT FOR WORK.
"ONCE THERE, MACLEISH AND MIRJA PALONE HAD **SEX**, ALMOST **CERTAINLY** ON THE FLOOR. I'M CONFIDENT THE PALONE CARPET WILL BE AN EXACT MATCH TO THE FIBERS FOUND IN MACLEISH'S KNEE WOUNDS.
"**MEANWHILE**, HUSBAND MANNY WAS HAVING A FLING OF HIS **OWN** WITH A STRIPPER FROM CLUB LURID: VERONICA HEWELLE, OUR **SECOND** VICTIM."

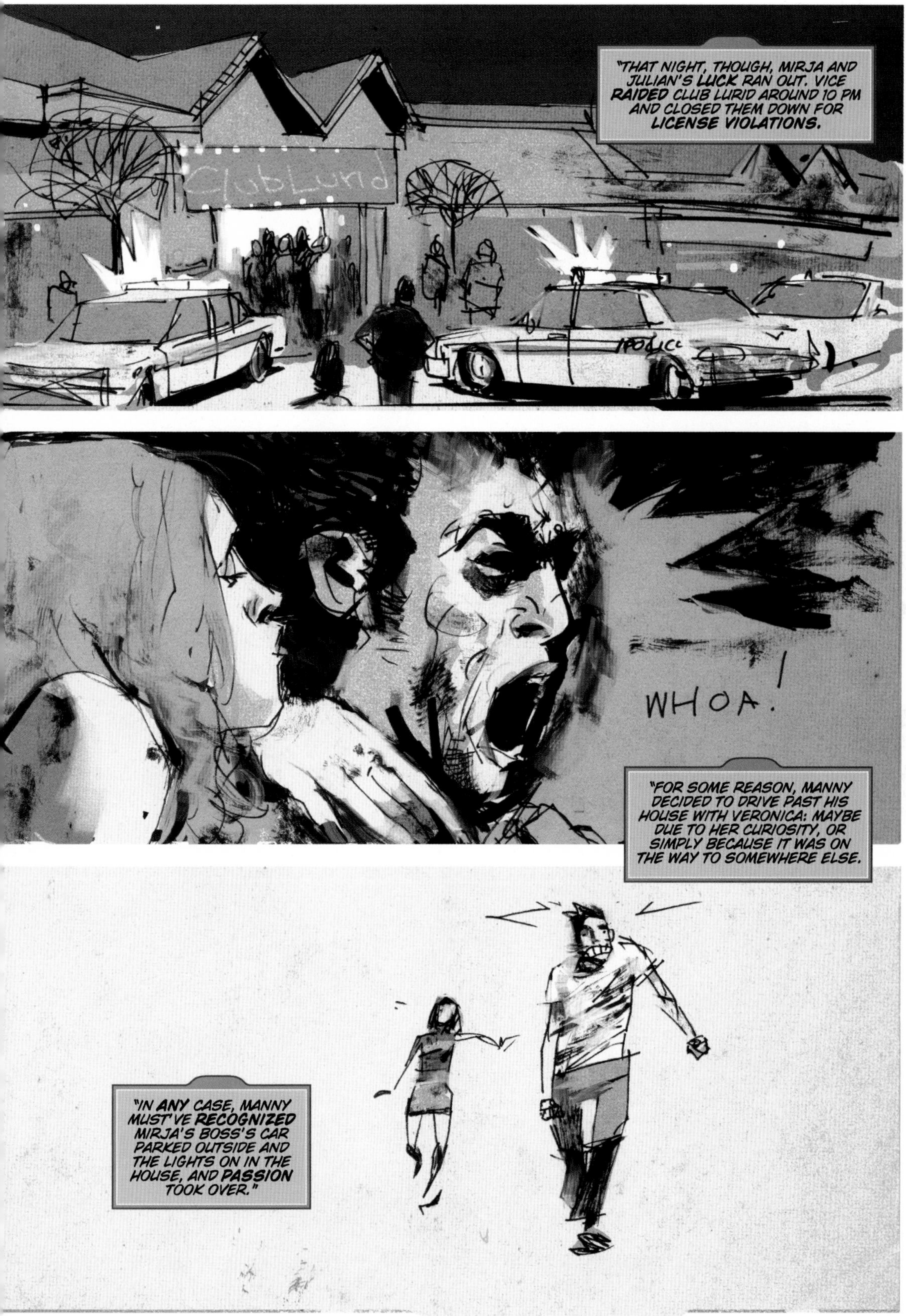
"THAT NIGHT, THOUGH, MIRJA AND JULIAN'S LUCK RAN OUT. VICE RAIDED CLUB LURID AROUND 10 PM AND CLOSED THEM DOWN FOR LICENSE VIOLATIONS.
WHOA!
"FOR SOME REASON, MANNY DECIDED TO DRIVE PAST HIS HOUSE WITH VERONICA: MAYBE DUE TO HER CURIOSITY, OR SIMPLY BECAUSE IT WAS ON THE WAY TO SOMEWHERE ELSE.
"IN ANY CASE, MANNY MUST'VE RECOGNIZED MIRJA'S BOSS'S CAR PARKED OUTSIDE AND THE LIGHTS ON IN THE HOUSE, AND PASSION TOOK OVER."

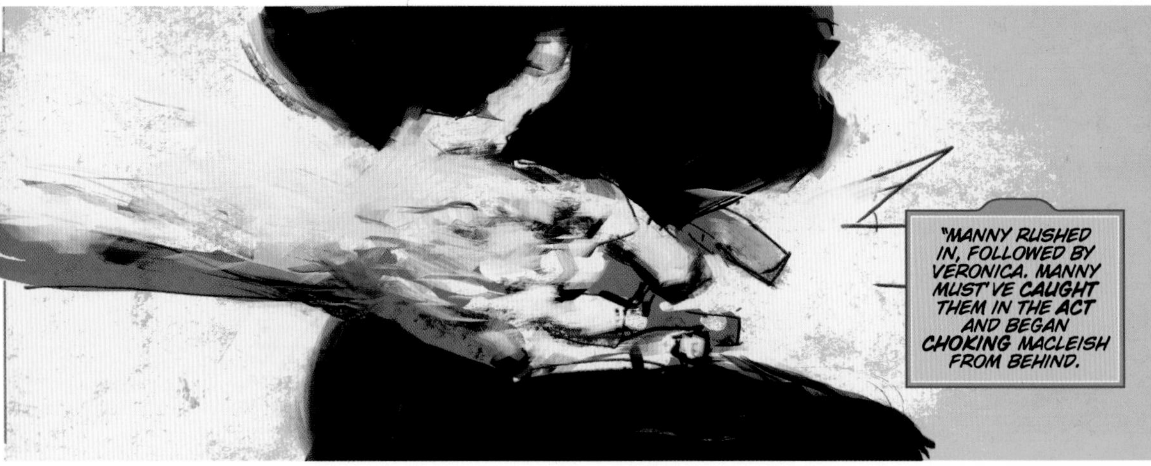
"MANNY RUSHED IN, FOLLOWED BY VERONICA. MANNY MUST'VE CAUGHT THEM IN THE ACT AND BEGAN CHOKING MACLEISH FROM BEHIND.

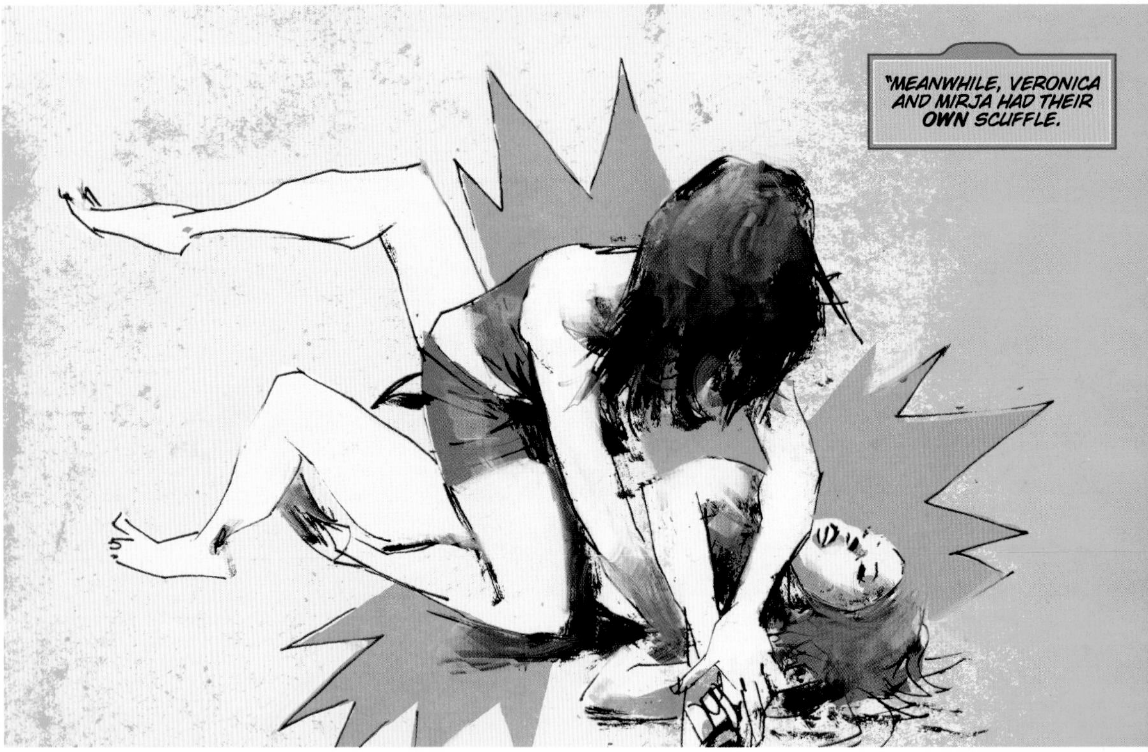
"MEANWHILE, VERONICA AND MIRJA HAD THEIR OWN SCUFFLE.

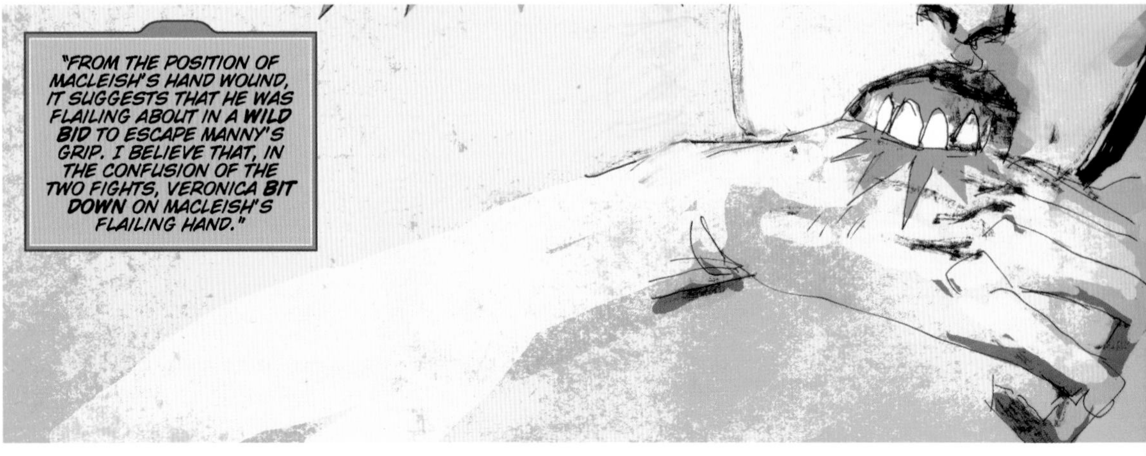
"FROM THE POSITION OF MACLEISH'S HAND WOUND, IT SUGGESTS THAT HE WAS FLAILING ABOUT IN A WILD BID TO ESCAPE MANNY'S GRIP. I BELIEVE THAT, IN THE CONFUSION OF THE TWO FIGHTS, VERONICA BIT DOWN ON MACLEISH'S FLAILING HAND."

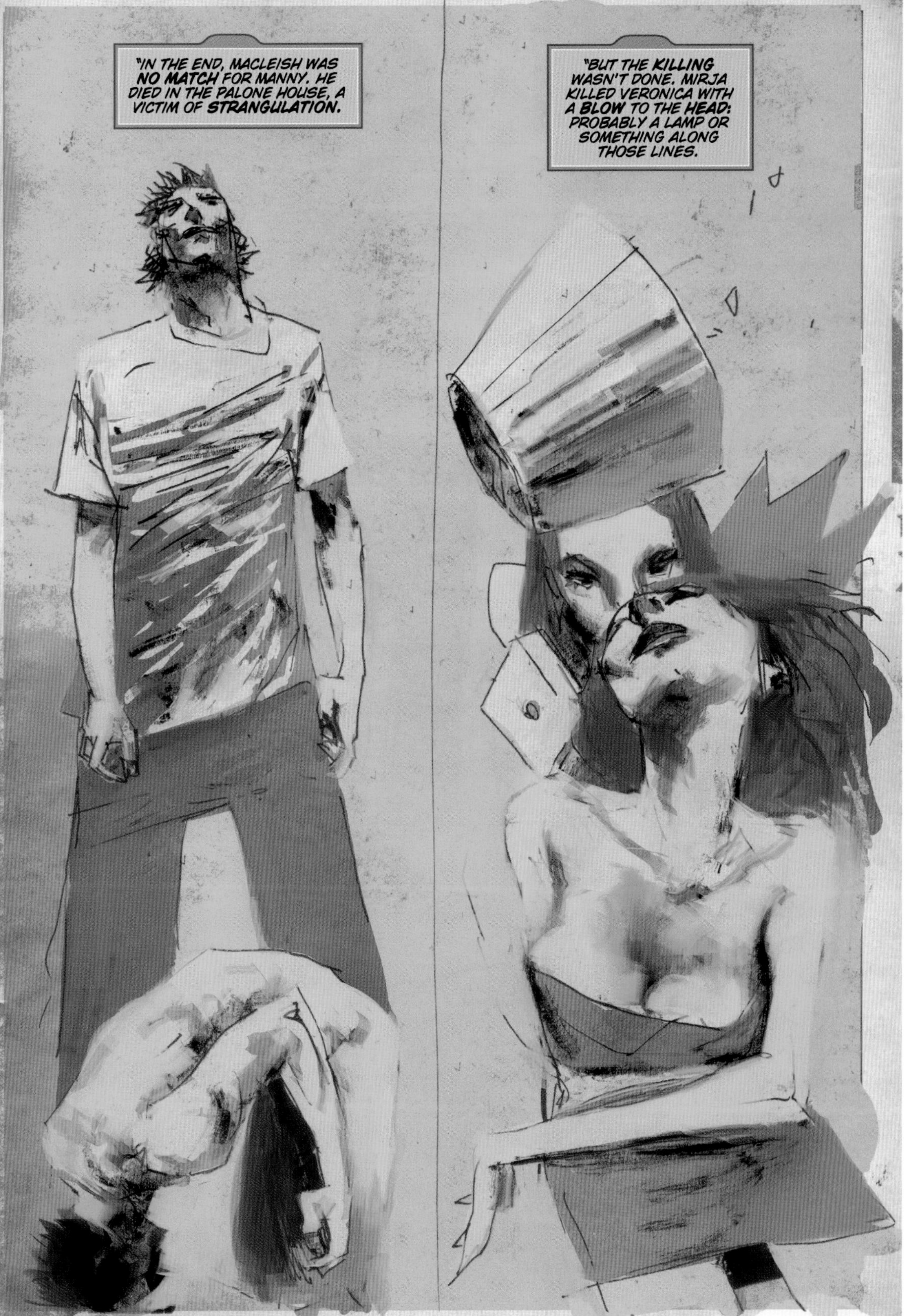
"IN THE END, MACLEISH WAS NO MATCH FOR MANNY. HE DIED IN THE PALONE HOUSE, A VICTIM OF STRANGULATION.
"BUT THE KILLING WASN'T DONE. MIRJA KILLED VERONICA WITH A BLOW TO THE HEAD: PROBABLY A LAMP OR SOMETHING ALONG THOSE LINES.

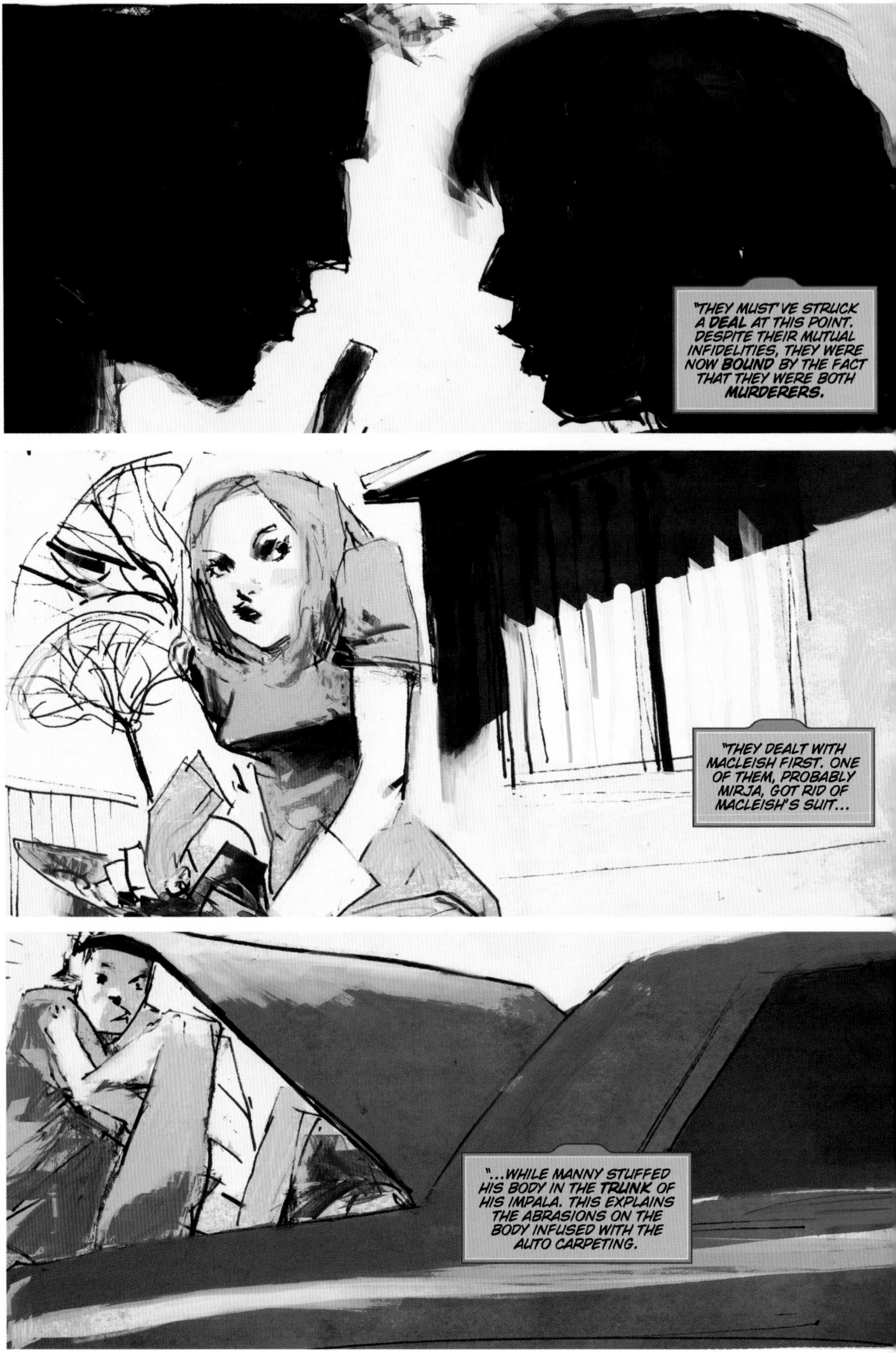
"THEY MUST'VE STRUCK A DEAL AT THIS POINT. DESPITE THEIR MUTUAL INFIDELITIES, THEY WERE NOW BOUND BY THE FACT THAT THEY WERE BOTH MURDERERS.
"THEY DEALT WITH MACLEISH FIRST. ONE OF THEM, PROBABLY MIRJA, GOT RID OF MACLEISH'S SUIT...
"...WHILE MANNY STUFFED HIS BODY IN THE TRUNK OF HIS IMPALA. THIS EXPLAINS THE ABRASIONS ON THE BODY INFUSED WITH THE AUTO CARPETING.

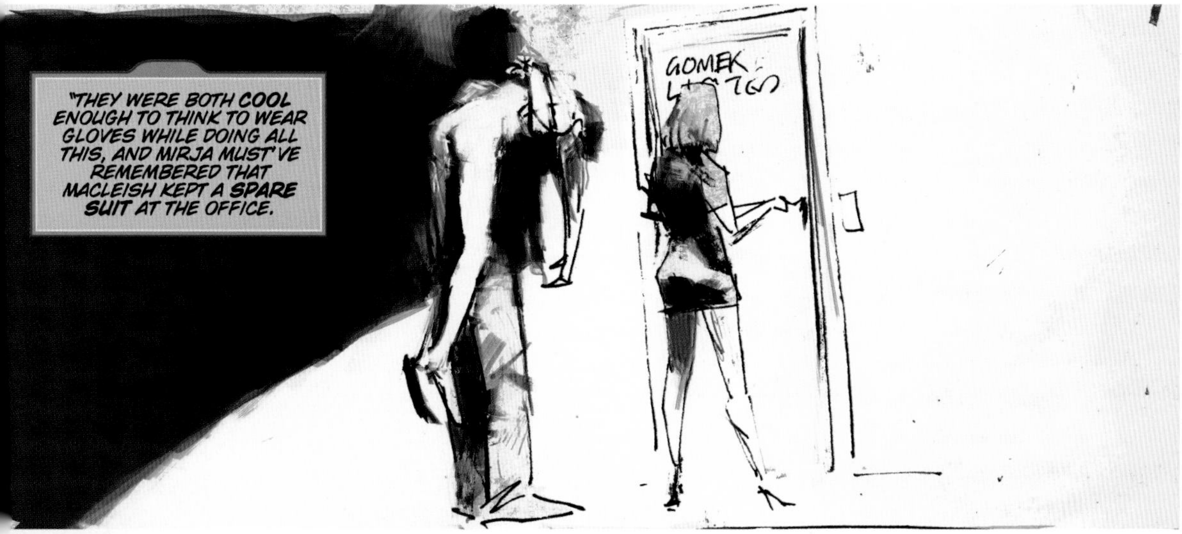
"THEY WERE BOTH COOL ENOUGH TO THINK TO WEAR GLOVES WHILE DOING ALL THIS, AND MIRJA MUST'VE REMEMBERED THAT MACLEISH KEPT A SPARE SUIT AT THE OFFICE.
GOMEK

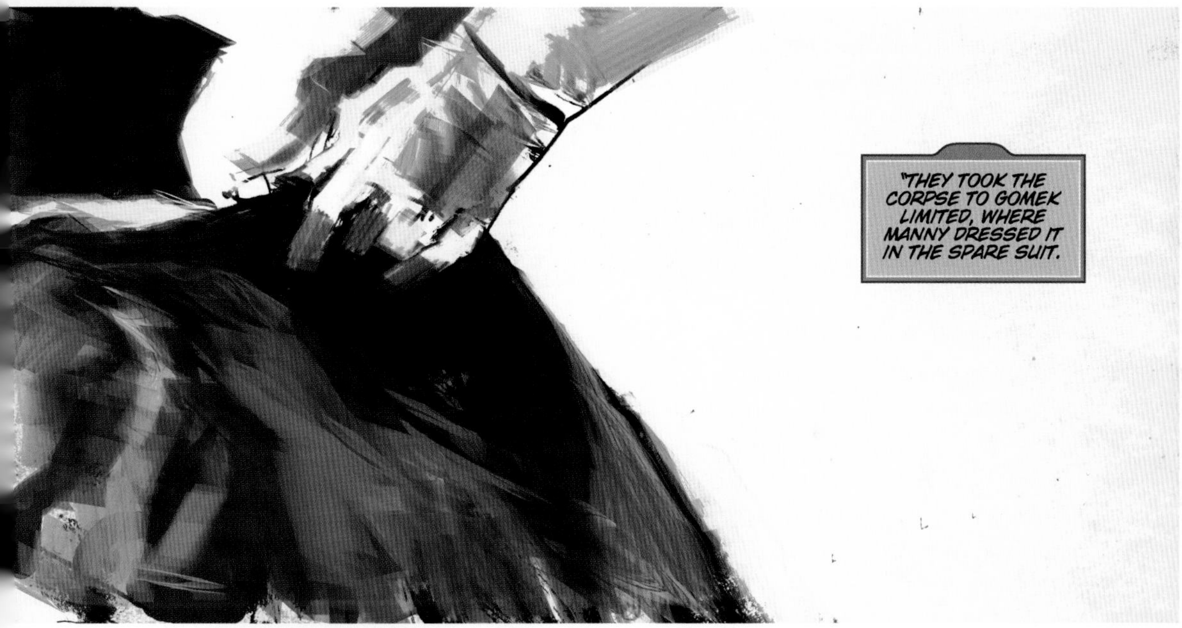
"THEY TOOK THE CORPSE TO GOMEK LIMITED, WHERE MANNY DRESSED IT IN THE SPARE SUIT.

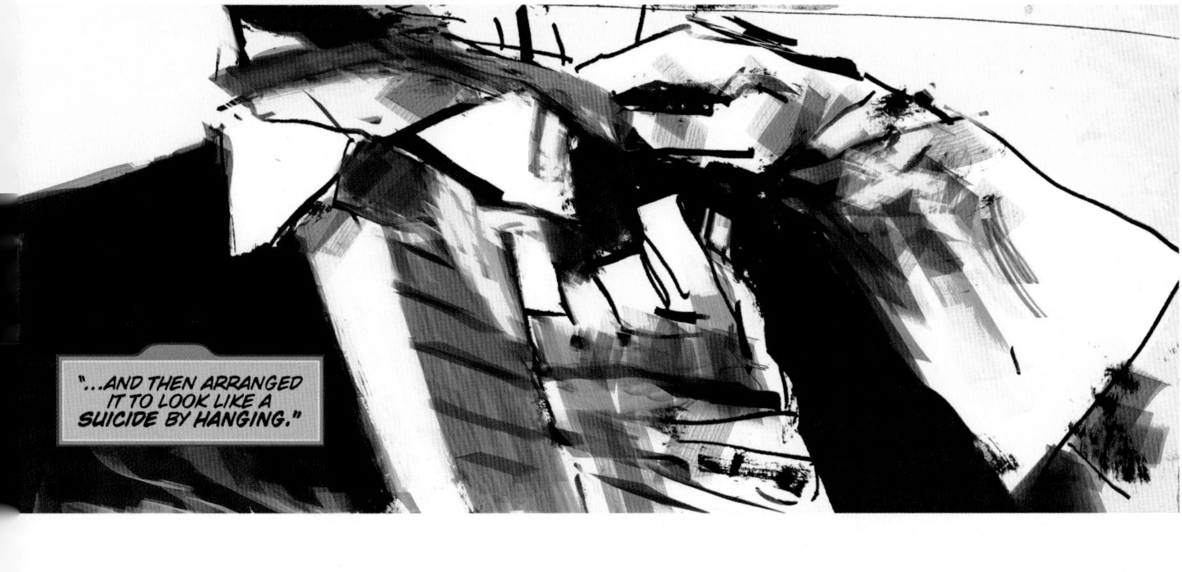
"...AND THEN ARRANGED IT TO LOOK LIKE A SUICIDE BY HANGING."

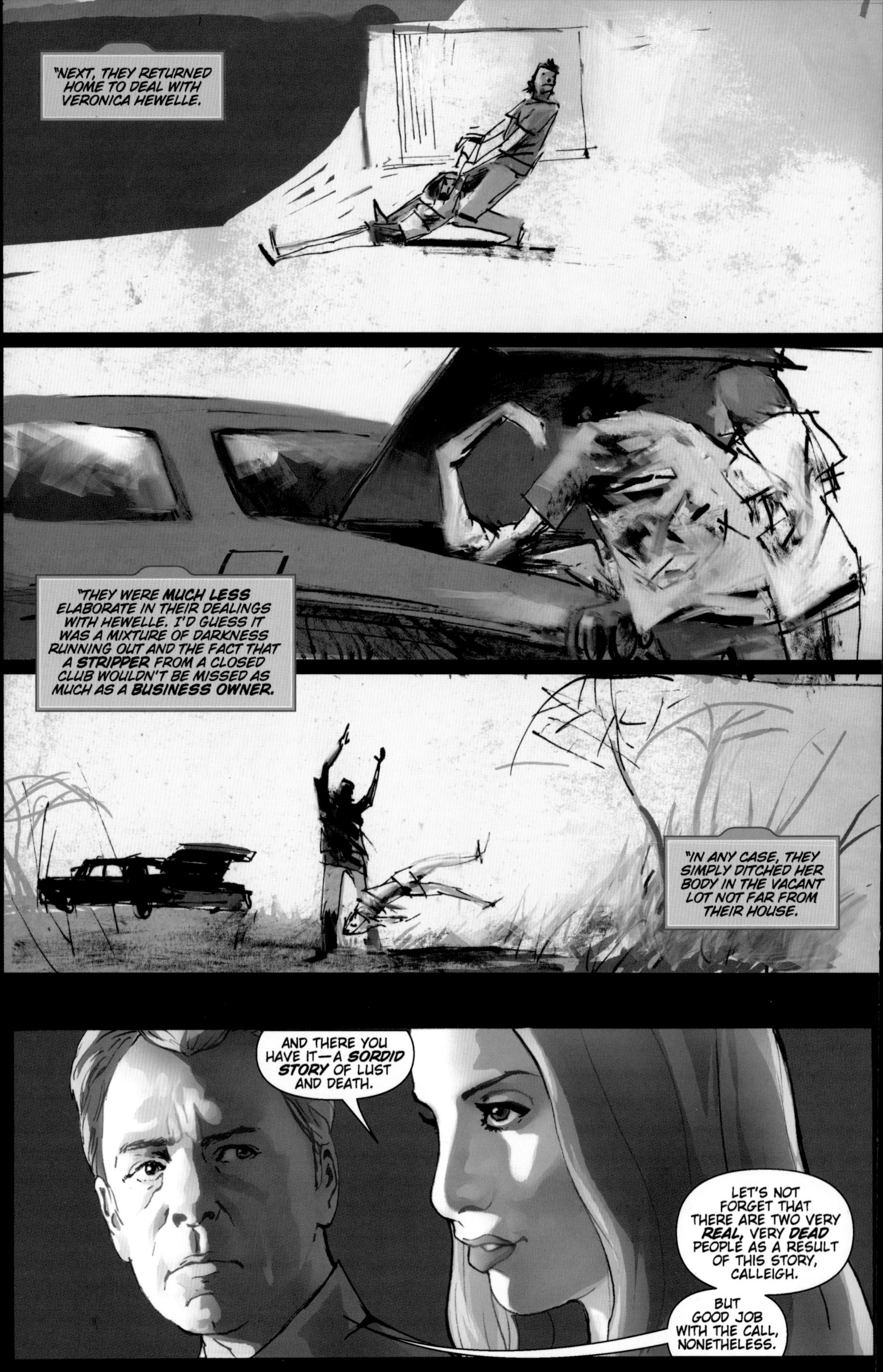
"NEXT, THEY RETURNED HOME TO DEAL WITH VERONICA HEWELLE.
"THEY WERE MUCH LESS ELABORATE IN THEIR DEALINGS WITH HEWELLE. I'D GUESS IT WAS A MIXTURE OF DARKNESS RUNNING OUT AND THE FACT THAT A STRIPPER FROM A CLOSED CLUB WOULDN'T BE MISSED AS MUCH AS A BUSINESS OWNER.
"IN ANY CASE, THEY SIMPLY DITCHED HER BODY IN THE VACANT LOT NOT FAR FROM THEIR HOUSE.
AND THERE YOU HAVE IT—A SORDID STORY OF LUST AND DEATH.
LET'S NOT FORGET THAT THERE ARE TWO VERY REAL, VERY DEAD PEOPLE AS A RESULT OF THIS STORY, CALLEIGH.
BUT GOOD JOB WITH THE CALL, NONETHELESS.

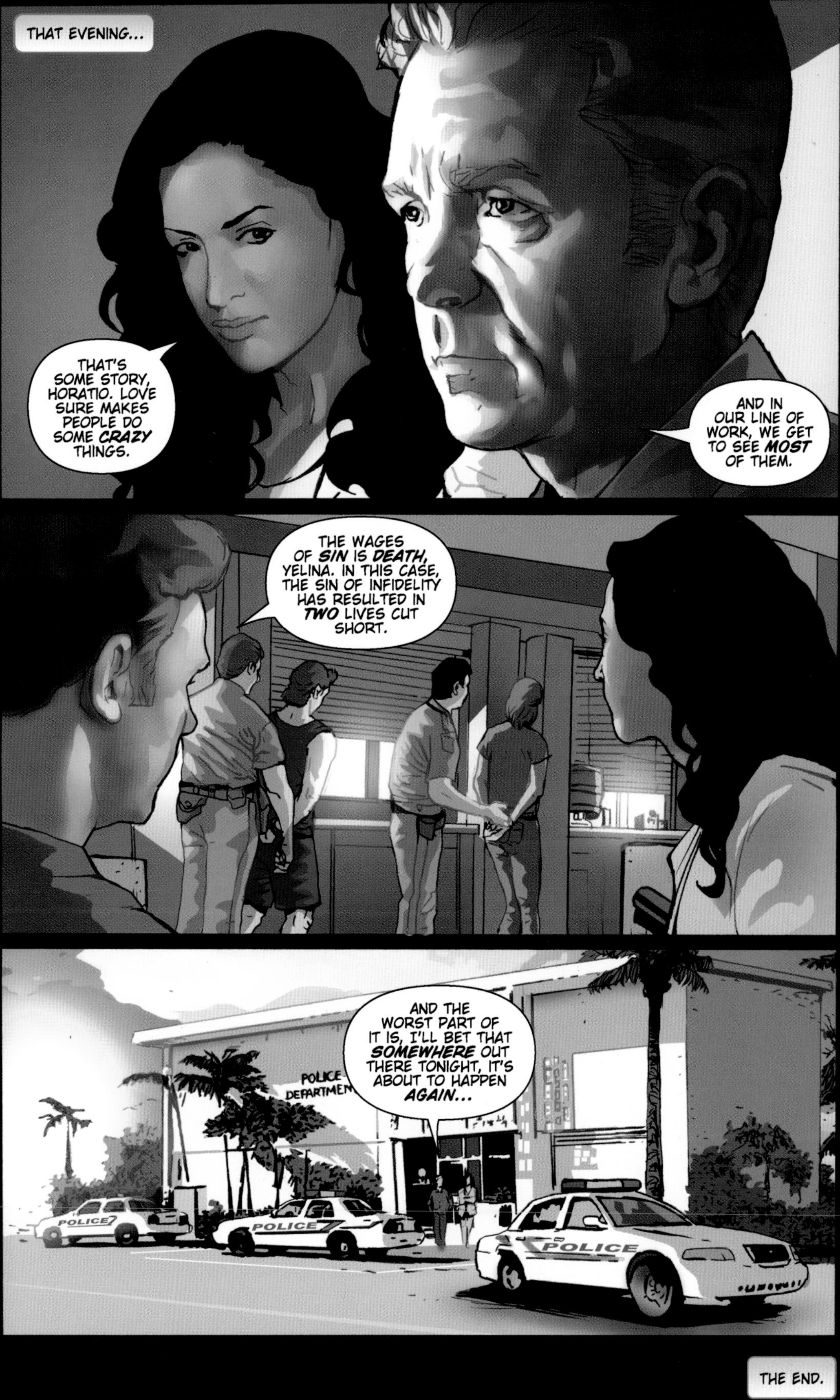

THAT EVENING...
THAT'S SOME STORY, HORATIO. LOVE SURE MAKES PEOPLE DO SOME CRAZY THINGS.
AND IN OUR LINE OF WORK, WE GET TO SEE MOST OF THEM.
THE WAGES OF SIN IS DEATH, YELINA. IN THIS CASE, THE SIN OF INFIDELITY HAS RESULTED IN TWO LIVES CUT SHORT.
POLICE DEPARTMEN
AND THE WORST PART OF IT IS, I'LL BET THAT SOMEWHERE OUT THERE TONIGHT, IT'S ABOUT TO HAPPEN AGAIN...
POLICE
POLICE
POLICE
THE END.

# CSI: MIAMI

## BLOOD/MONEY

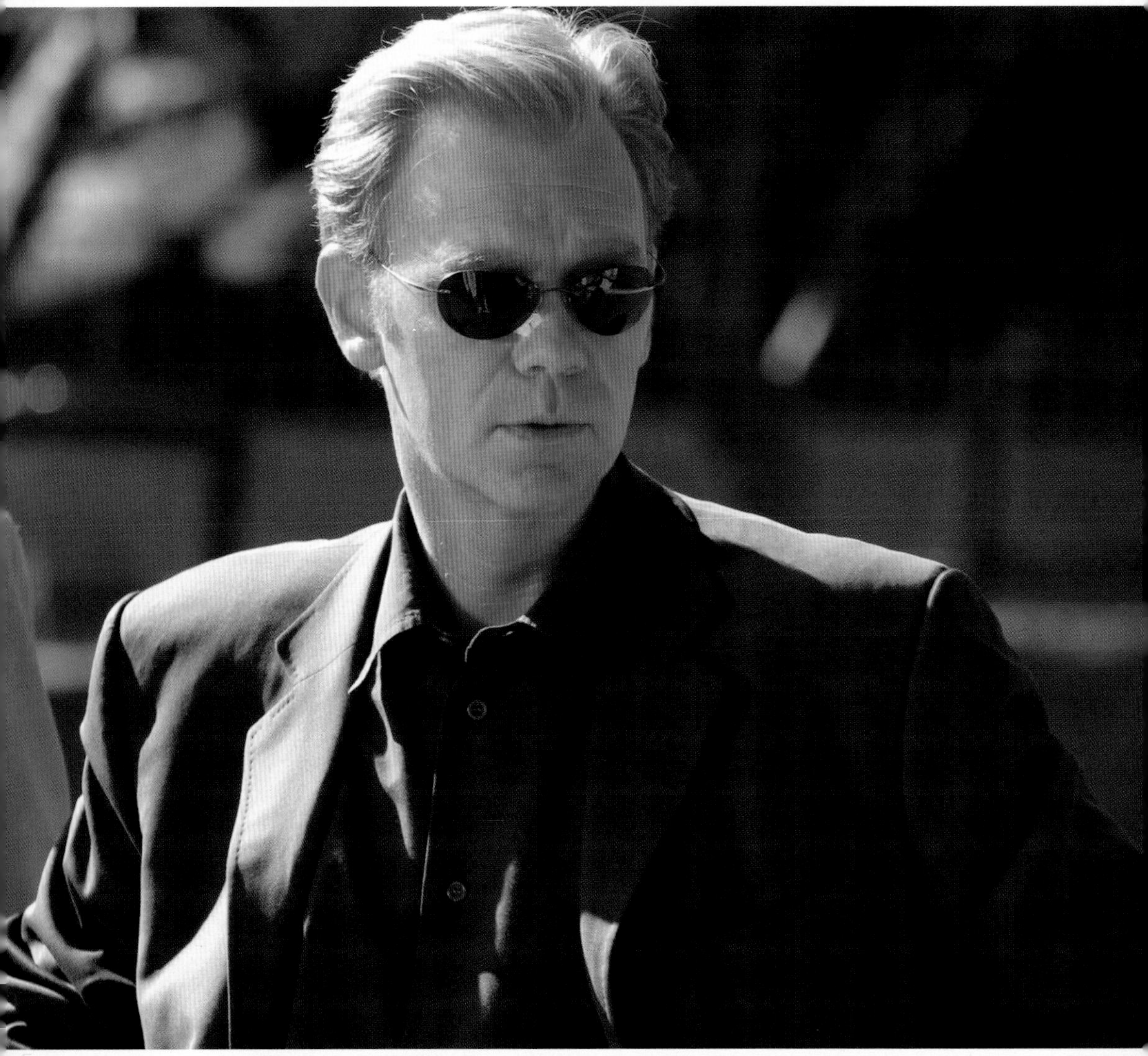

OPRISKO • GUEDES • PERKINS

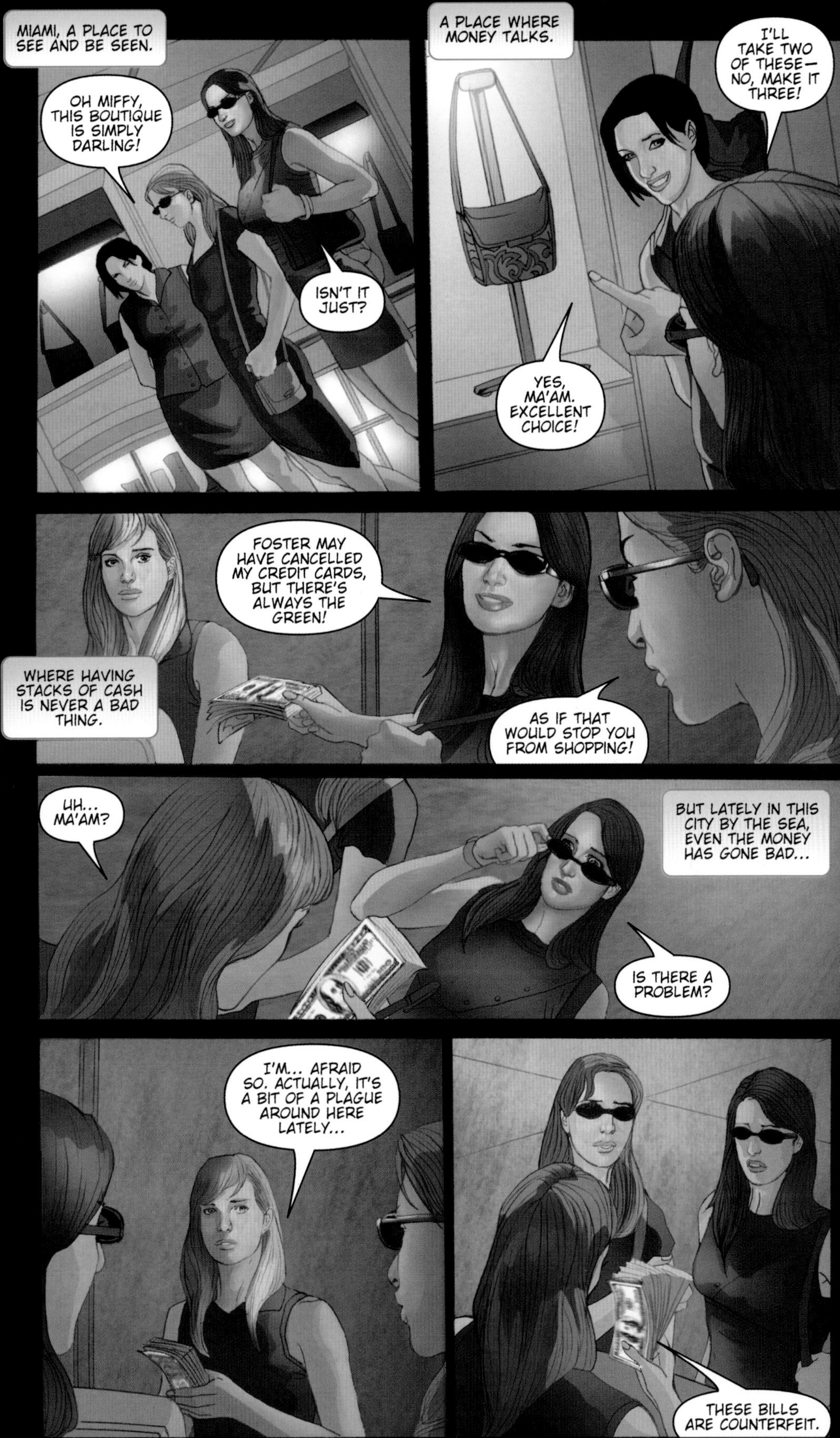

MIAMI, A PLACE TO SEE AND BE SEEN.
OH MIFFY, THIS BOUTIQUE IS SIMPLY DARLING!
ISN'T IT JUST?
A PLACE WHERE MONEY TALKS.
I'LL TAKE TWO OF THESE— NO, MAKE IT THREE!
YES, MA'AM. EXCELLENT CHOICE!
FOSTER MAY HAVE CANCELLED MY CREDIT CARDS, BUT THERE'S ALWAYS THE GREEN!
WHERE HAVING STACKS OF CASH IS NEVER A BAD THING.
AS IF THAT WOULD STOP YOU FROM SHOPPING!
UH... MA'AM?
BUT LATELY IN THIS CITY BY THE SEA, EVEN THE MONEY HAS GONE BAD...
IS THERE A PROBLEM?
I'M... AFRAID SO. ACTUALLY, IT'S A BIT OF A PLAGUE AROUND HERE LATELY...
THESE BILLS ARE COUNTERFEIT.

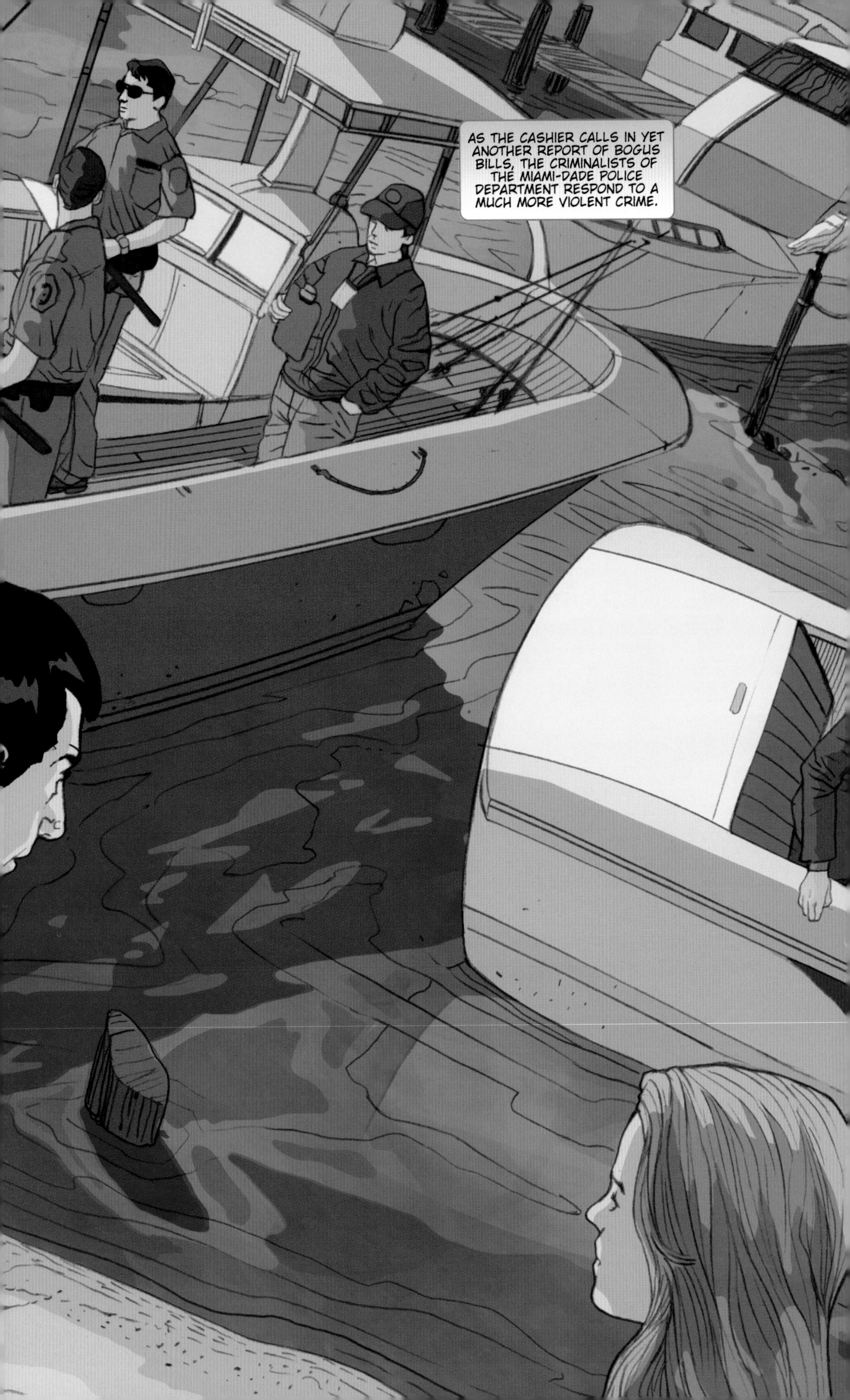
AS THE CASHIER CALLS IN YET ANOTHER REPORT OF BOGUS BILLS, THE CRIMINALISTS OF THE MIAMI-DADE POLICE DEPARTMENT RESPOND TO A MUCH MORE VIOLENT CRIME.

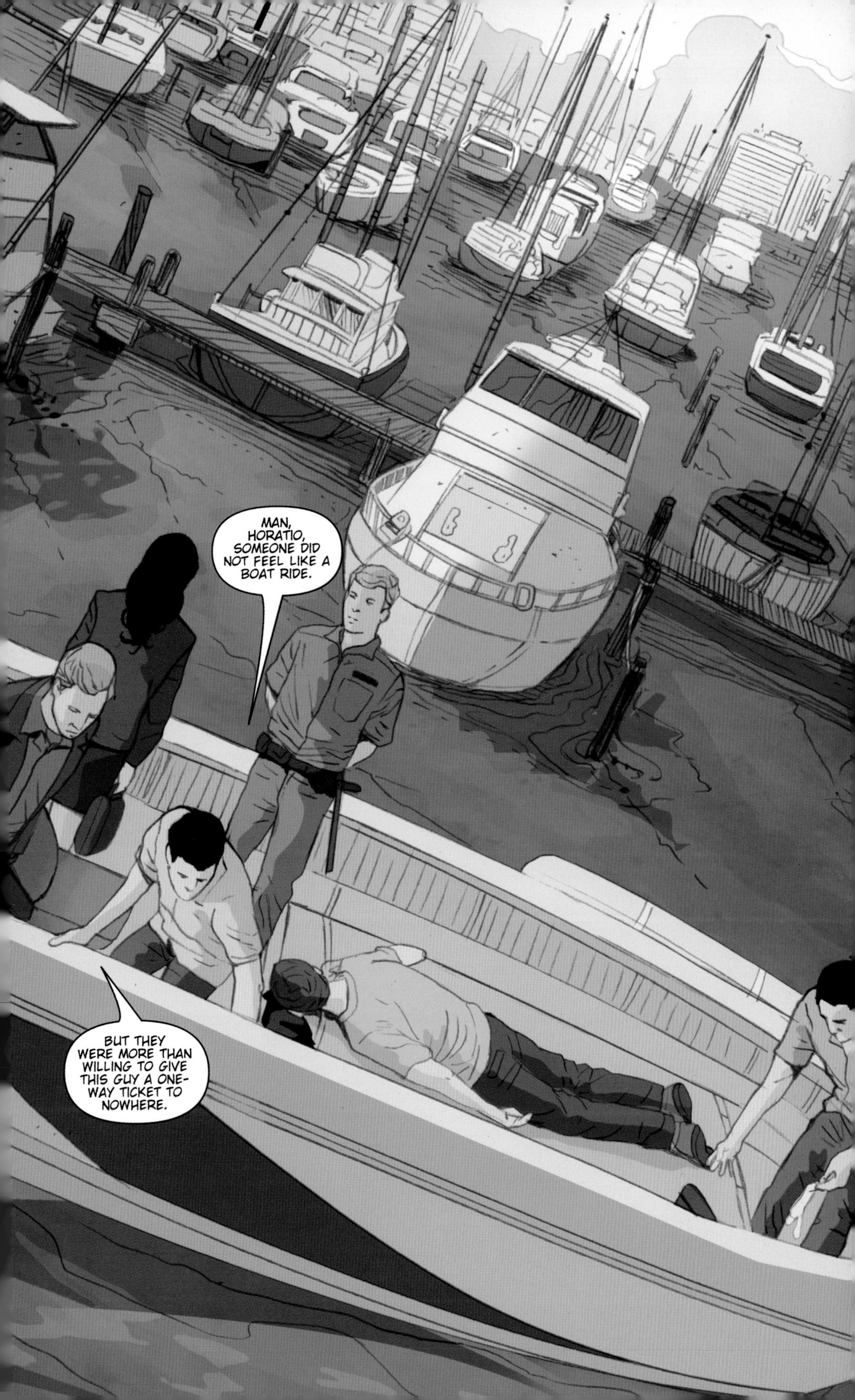
MAN, HORATIO, SOMEONE DID NOT FEEL LIKE A BOAT RIDE.
BUT THEY WERE MORE THAN WILLING TO GIVE THIS GUY A ONE-WAY TICKET TO NOWHERE.

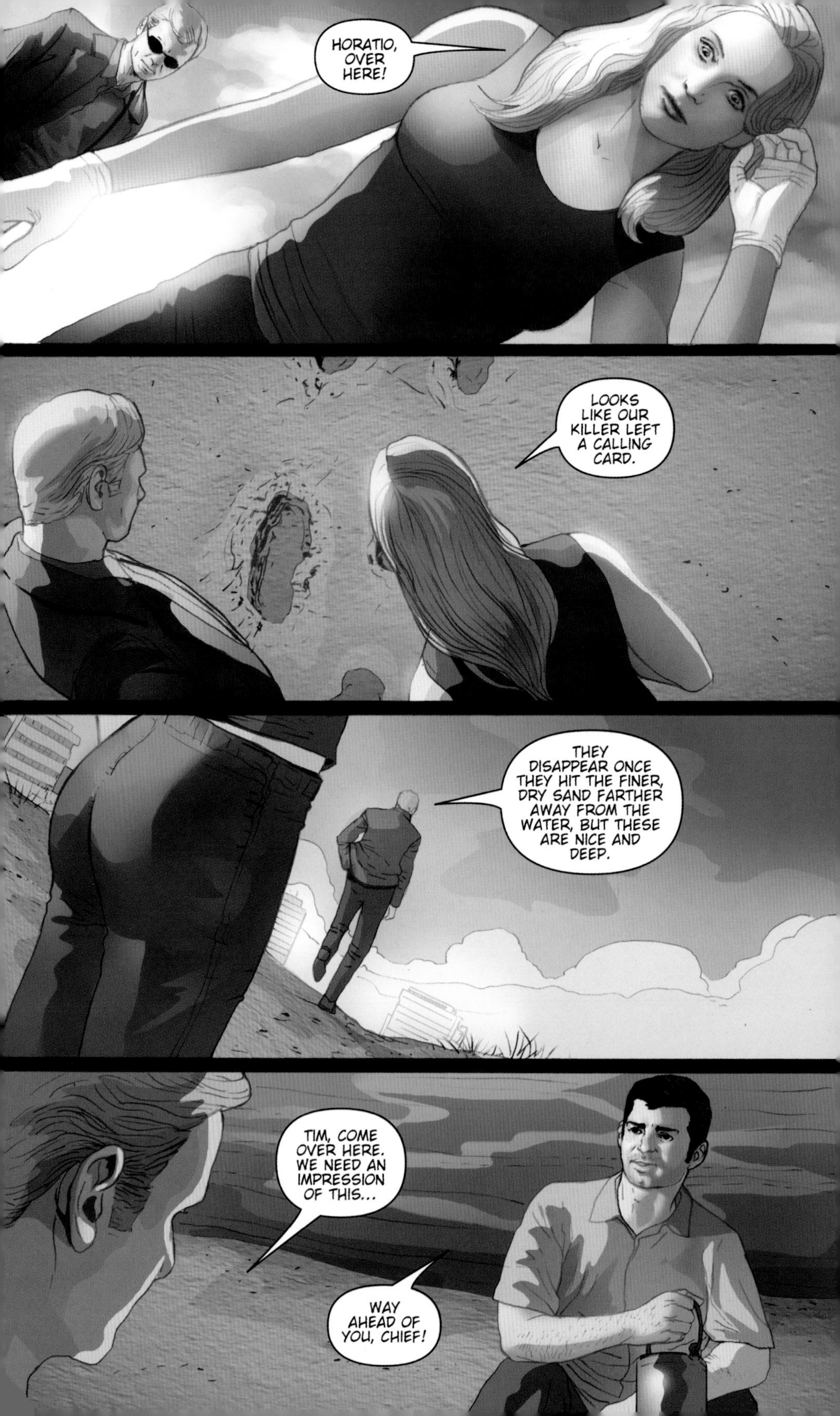
HORATIO, OVER HERE!
LOOKS LIKE OUR KILLER LEFT A CALLING CARD.
THEY DISAPPEAR ONCE THEY HIT THE FINER, DRY SAND FARTHER AWAY FROM THE WATER, BUT THESE ARE NICE AND DEEP.
TIM, COME OVER HERE. WE NEED AN IMPRESSION OF THIS...
WAY AHEAD OF YOU, CHIEF!

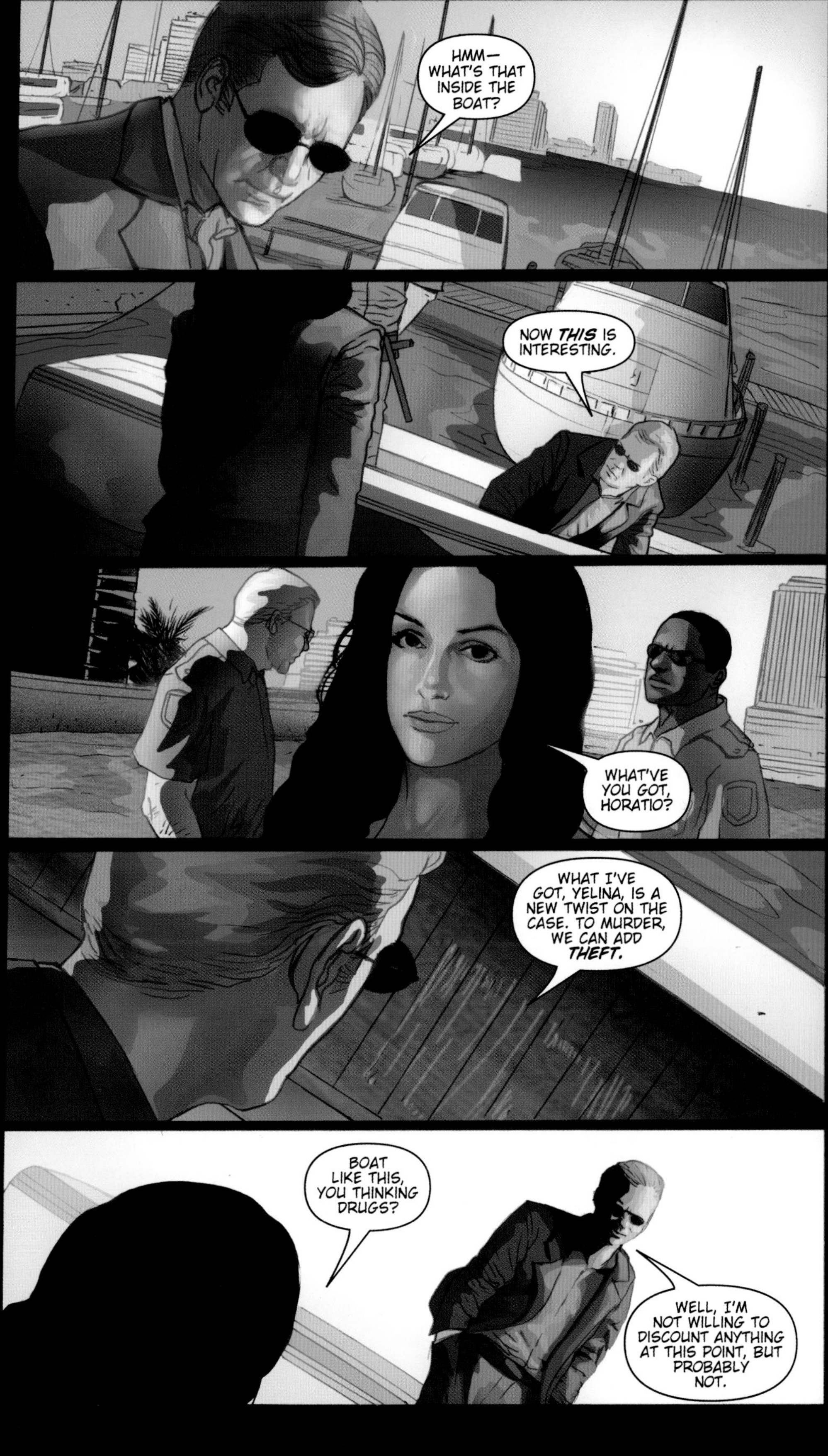
HMM— WHAT'S THAT INSIDE THE BOAT?
NOW THIS IS INTERESTING.
WHAT'VE YOU GOT, HORATIO?
WHAT I'VE GOT, YELINA, IS A NEW TWIST ON THE CASE. TO MURDER, WE CAN ADD THEFT.
BOAT LIKE THIS, YOU THINKING DRUGS?
WELL, I'M NOT WILLING TO DISCOUNT ANYTHING AT THIS POINT, BUT PROBABLY NOT.

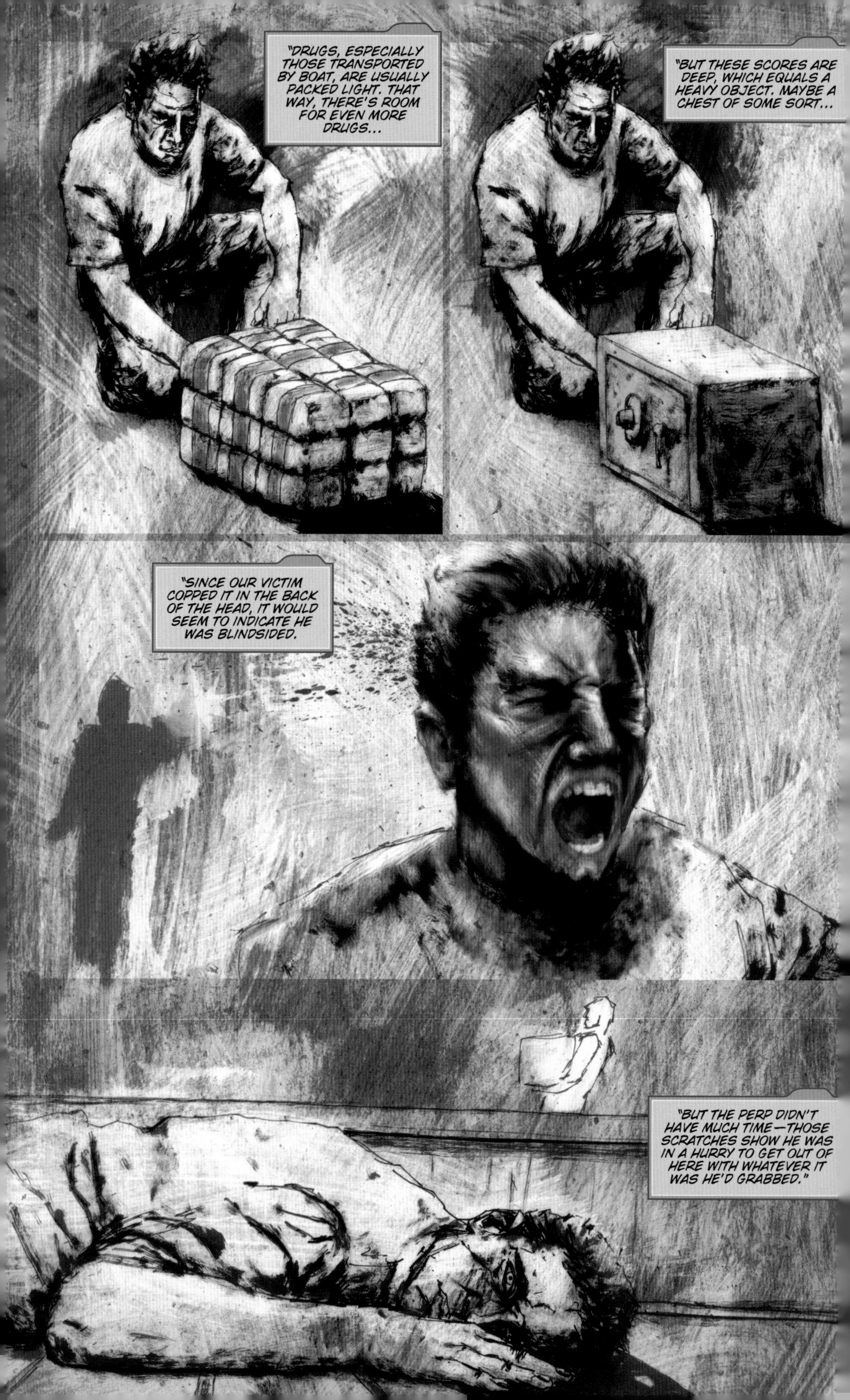
"DRUGS, ESPECIALLY THOSE TRANSPORTED BY BOAT, ARE USUALLY PACKED LIGHT. THAT WAY, THERE'S ROOM FOR EVEN MORE DRUGS...
"BUT THESE SCORES ARE DEEP, WHICH EQUALS A HEAVY OBJECT. MAYBE A CHEST OF SOME SORT...
"SINCE OUR VICTIM COPPED IT IN THE BACK OF THE HEAD, IT WOULD SEEM TO INDICATE HE WAS BLINDSIDED.
"BUT THE PERP DIDN'T HAVE MUCH TIME—THOSE SCRATCHES SHOW HE WAS IN A HURRY TO GET OUT OF HERE WITH WHATEVER IT WAS HE'D GRABBED."

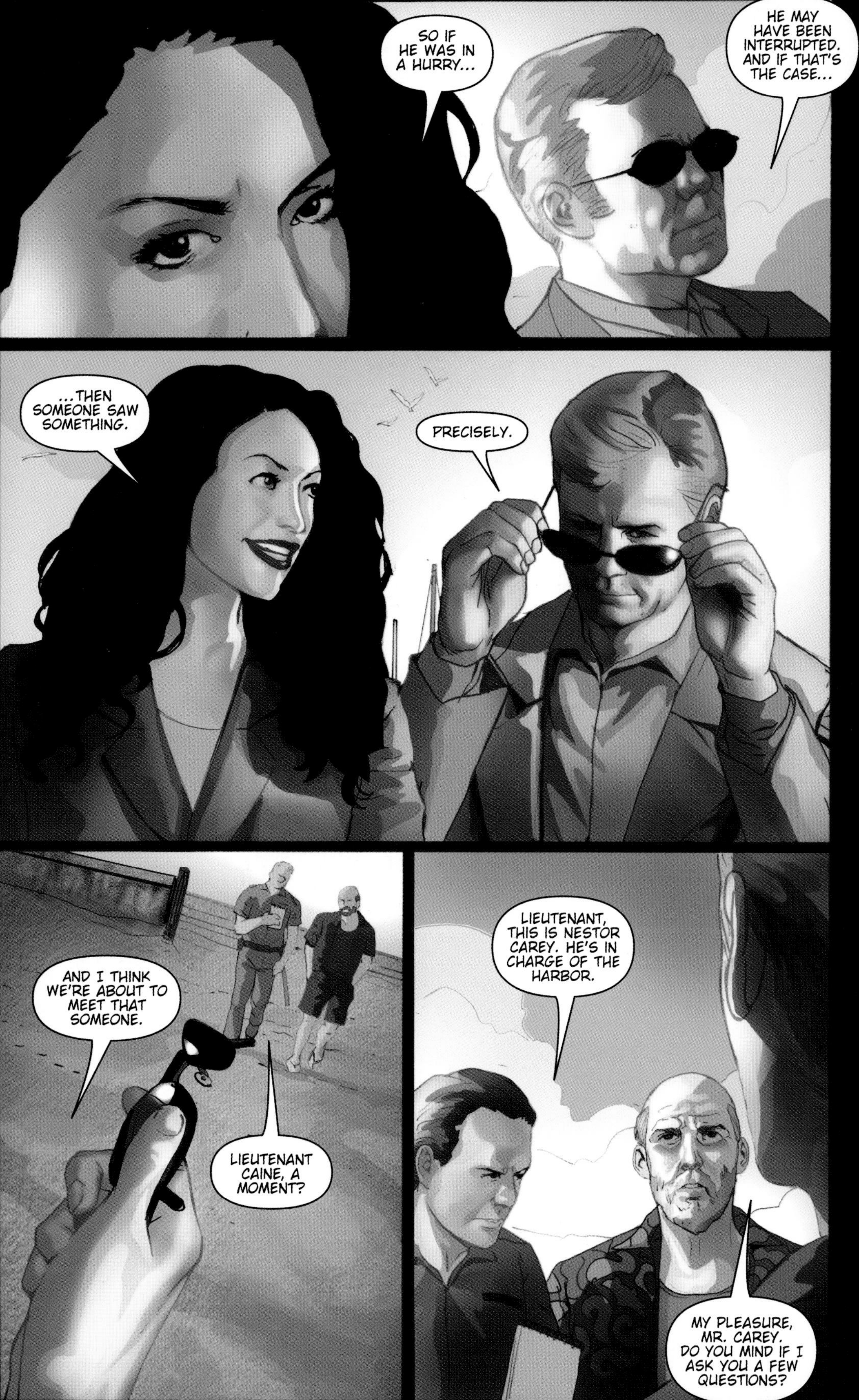
SO IF HE WAS IN A HURRY...
HE MAY HAVE BEEN INTERRUPTED. AND IF THAT'S THE CASE...
...THEN SOMEONE SAW SOMETHING.
PRECISELY.
AND I THINK WE'RE ABOUT TO MEET THAT SOMEONE.
LIEUTENANT CAINE, A MOMENT?
LIEUTENANT, THIS IS NESTOR CAREY. HE'S IN CHARGE OF THE HARBOR.
MY PLEASURE, MR. CAREY. DO YOU MIND IF I ASK YOU A FEW QUESTIONS?

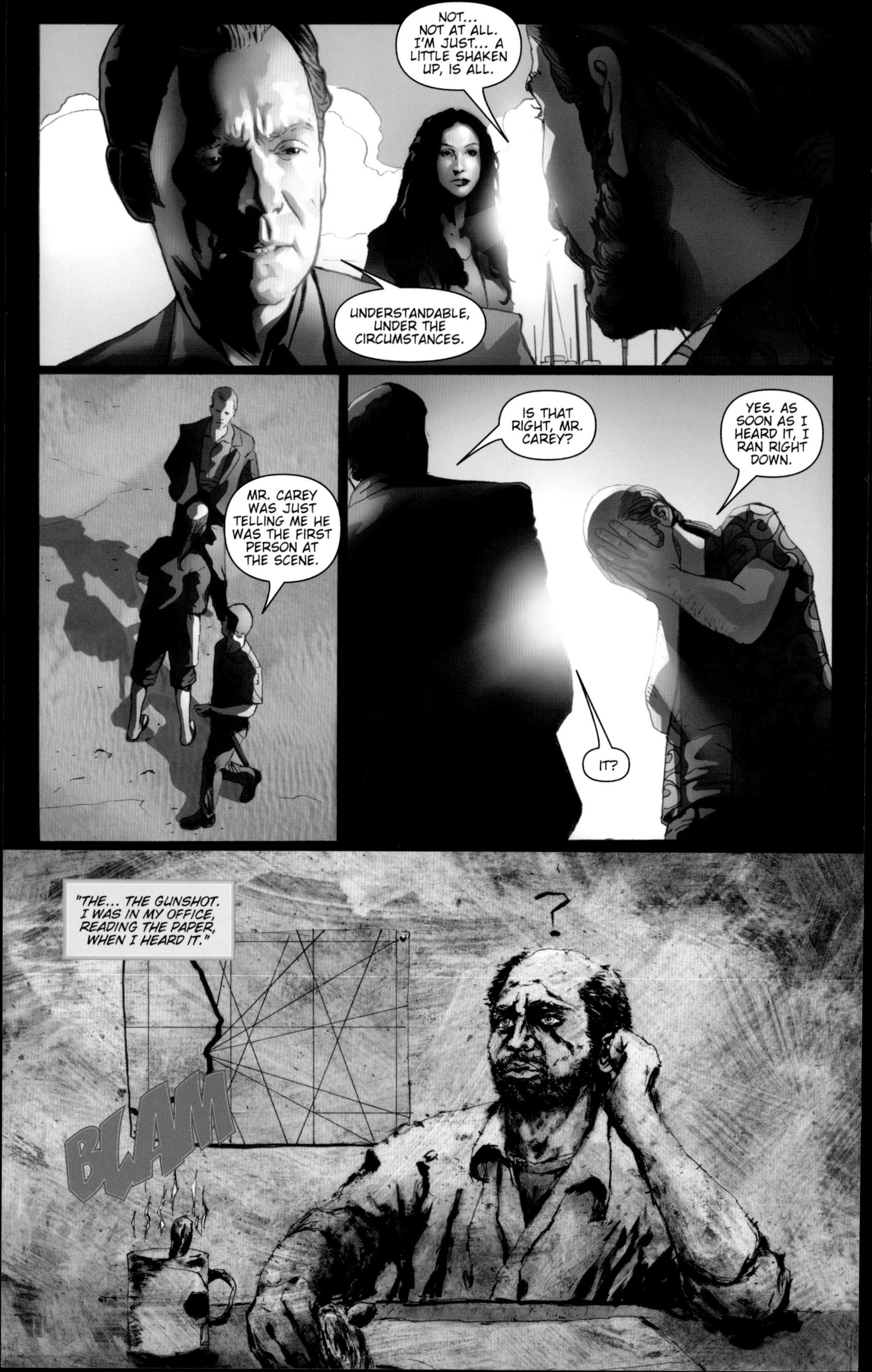
NOT... NOT AT ALL. I'M JUST... A LITTLE SHAKEN UP, IS ALL.
UNDERSTANDABLE, UNDER THE CIRCUMSTANCES.
MR. CAREY WAS JUST TELLING ME HE WAS THE FIRST PERSON AT THE SCENE.
IS THAT RIGHT, MR. CAREY?
YES. AS SOON AS I HEARD IT, I RAN RIGHT DOWN.
IT?
"THE... THE GUNSHOT. I WAS IN MY OFFICE, READING THE PAPER, WHEN I HEARD IT."
?
BLAM

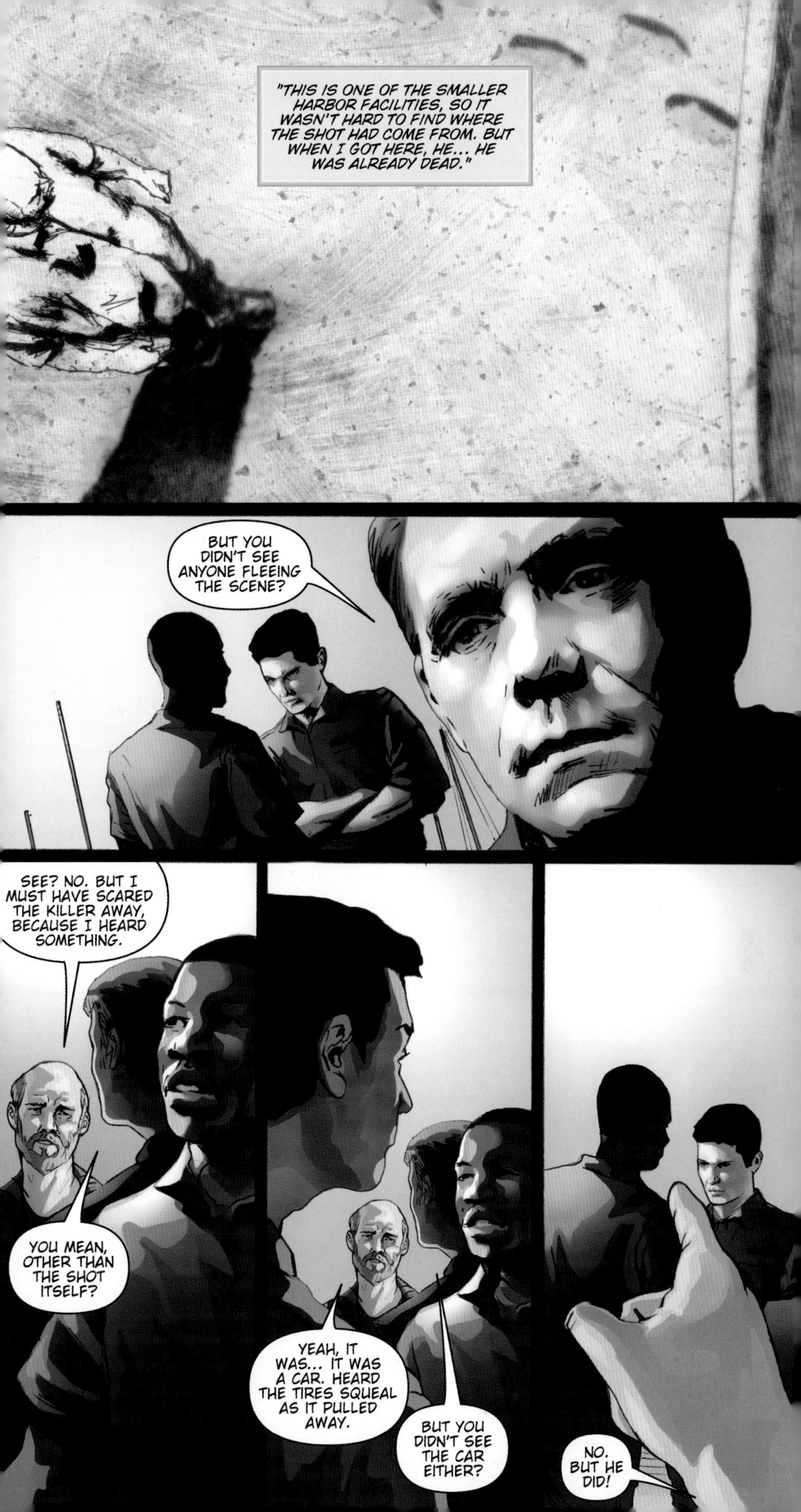
"THIS IS ONE OF THE SMALLER HARBOR FACILITIES, SO IT WASN'T HARD TO FIND WHERE THE SHOT HAD COME FROM. BUT WHEN I GOT HERE, HE... HE WAS ALREADY DEAD."
BUT YOU DIDN'T SEE ANYONE FLEEING THE SCENE?
SEE? NO. BUT I MUST HAVE SCARED THE KILLER AWAY, BECAUSE I HEARD SOMETHING.
YOU MEAN, OTHER THAN THE SHOT ITSELF?
YEAH, IT WAS... IT WAS A CAR. HEARD THE TIRES SQUEAL AS IT PULLED AWAY.
BUT YOU DIDN'T SEE THE CAR EITHER?
NO. BUT HE DID!

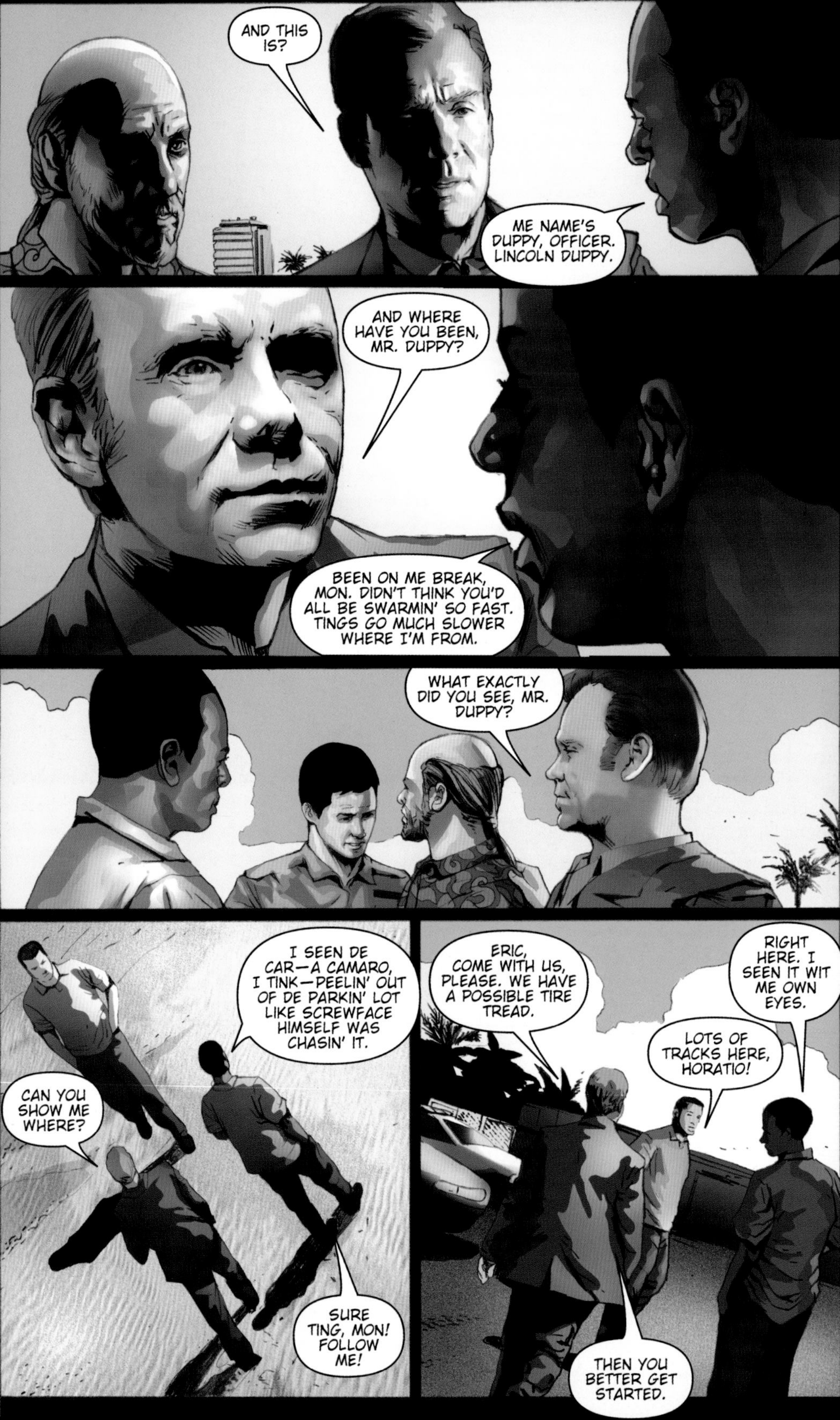
AND THIS IS?
ME NAME'S DUPPY, OFFICER. LINCOLN DUPPY.
AND WHERE HAVE YOU BEEN, MR. DUPPY?
BEEN ON ME BREAK, MON. DIDN'T THINK YOU'D ALL BE SWARMIN' SO FAST. TINGS GO MUCH SLOWER WHERE I'M FROM.
WHAT EXACTLY DID YOU SEE, MR. DUPPY?
I SEEN DE CAR—A CAMARO, I TINK—PEELIN' OUT OF DE PARKIN' LOT LIKE SCREWFACE HIMSELF WAS CHASIN' IT.
CAN YOU SHOW ME WHERE?
SURE TING, MON! FOLLOW ME!
ERIC, COME WITH US, PLEASE. WE HAVE A POSSIBLE TIRE TREAD.
RIGHT HERE. I SEEN IT WIT ME OWN EYES.
LOTS OF TRACKS HERE, HORATIO!
THEN YOU BETTER GET STARTED.

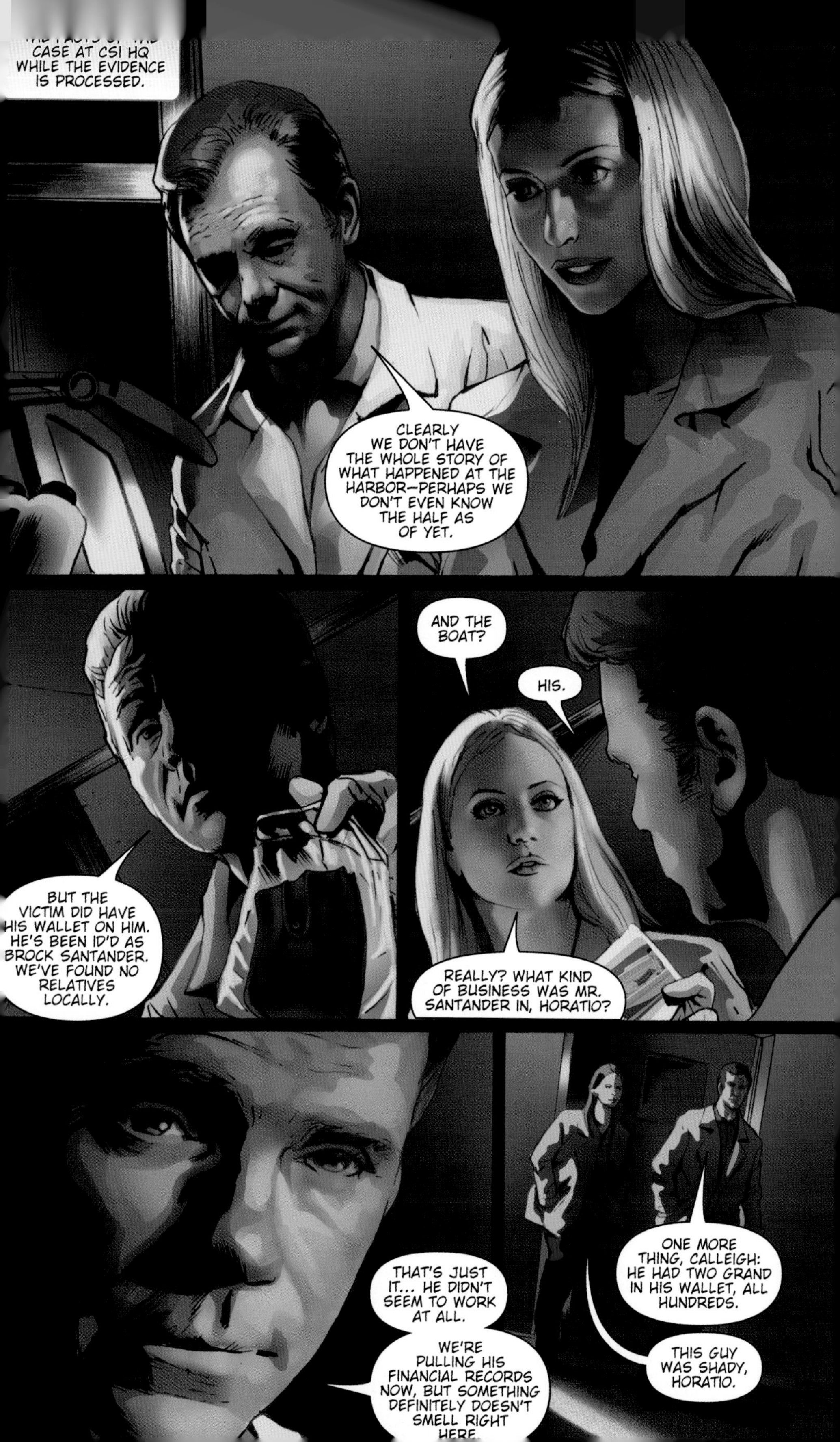
CASE AT CSI HQ WHILE THE EVIDENCE IS PROCESSED.
CLEARLY WE DON'T HAVE THE WHOLE STORY OF WHAT HAPPENED AT THE HARBOR—PERHAPS WE DON'T EVEN KNOW THE HALF AS OF YET.
BUT THE VICTIM DID HAVE HIS WALLET ON HIM. HE'S BEEN ID'D AS BROCK SANTANDER. WE'VE FOUND NO RELATIVES LOCALLY.
AND THE BOAT?
HIS.
REALLY? WHAT KIND OF BUSINESS WAS MR. SANTANDER IN, HORATIO?
THAT'S JUST IT... HE DIDN'T SEEM TO WORK AT ALL.
WE'RE PULLING HIS FINANCIAL RECORDS NOW, BUT SOMETHING DEFINITELY DOESN'T SMELL RIGHT HERE.
ONE MORE THING, CALLEIGH: HE HAD TWO GRAND IN HIS WALLET, ALL HUNDREDS.
THIS GUY WAS SHADY, HORATIO.

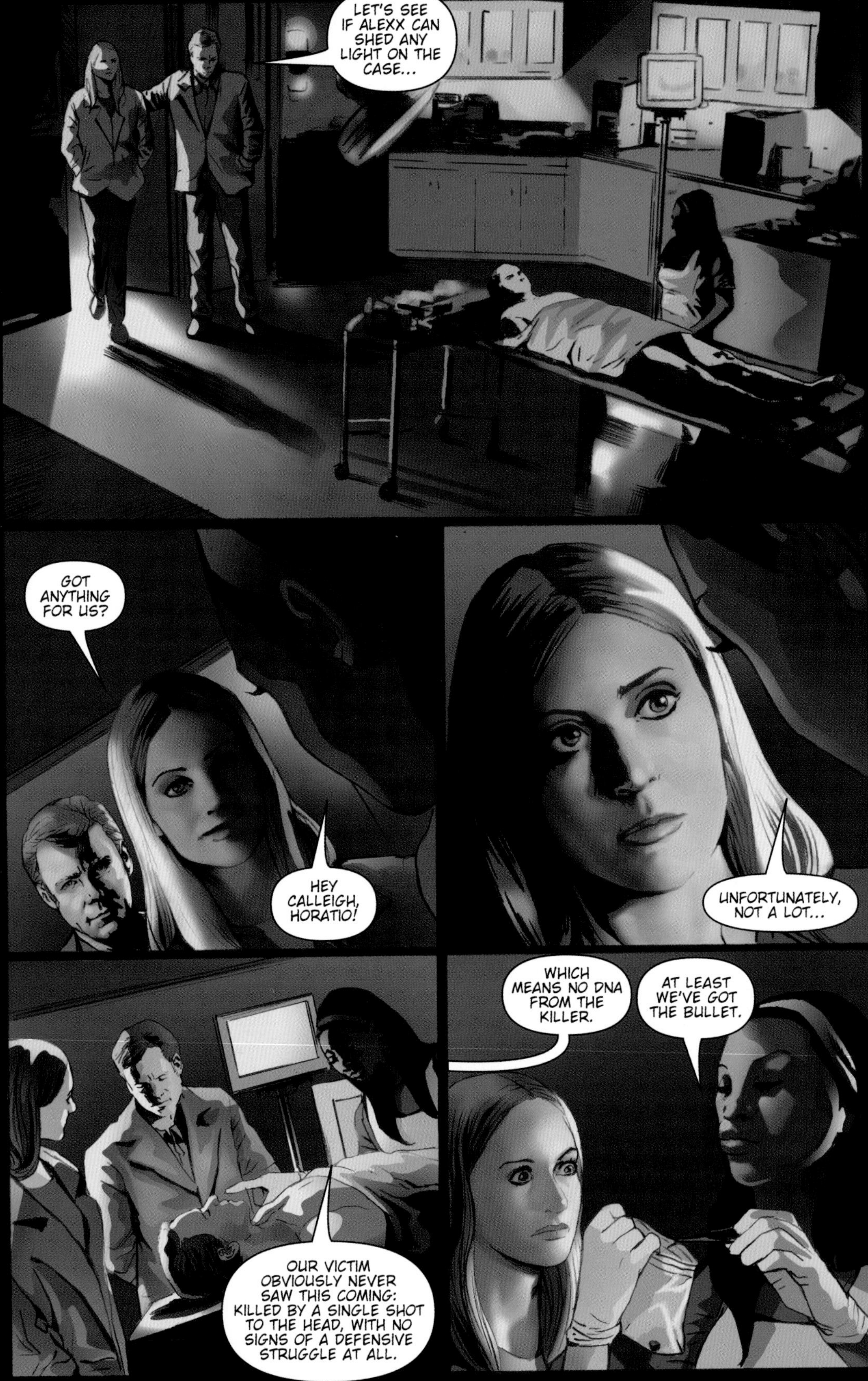
LET'S SEE IF ALEXX CAN SHED ANY LIGHT ON THE CASE...
GOT ANYTHING FOR US?
HEY CALLEIGH, HORATIO!
UNFORTUNATELY, NOT A LOT...
OUR VICTIM OBVIOUSLY NEVER SAW THIS COMING: KILLED BY A SINGLE SHOT TO THE HEAD, WITH NO SIGNS OF A DEFENSIVE STRUGGLE AT ALL.
WHICH MEANS NO DNA FROM THE KILLER.
AT LEAST WE'VE GOT THE BULLET.

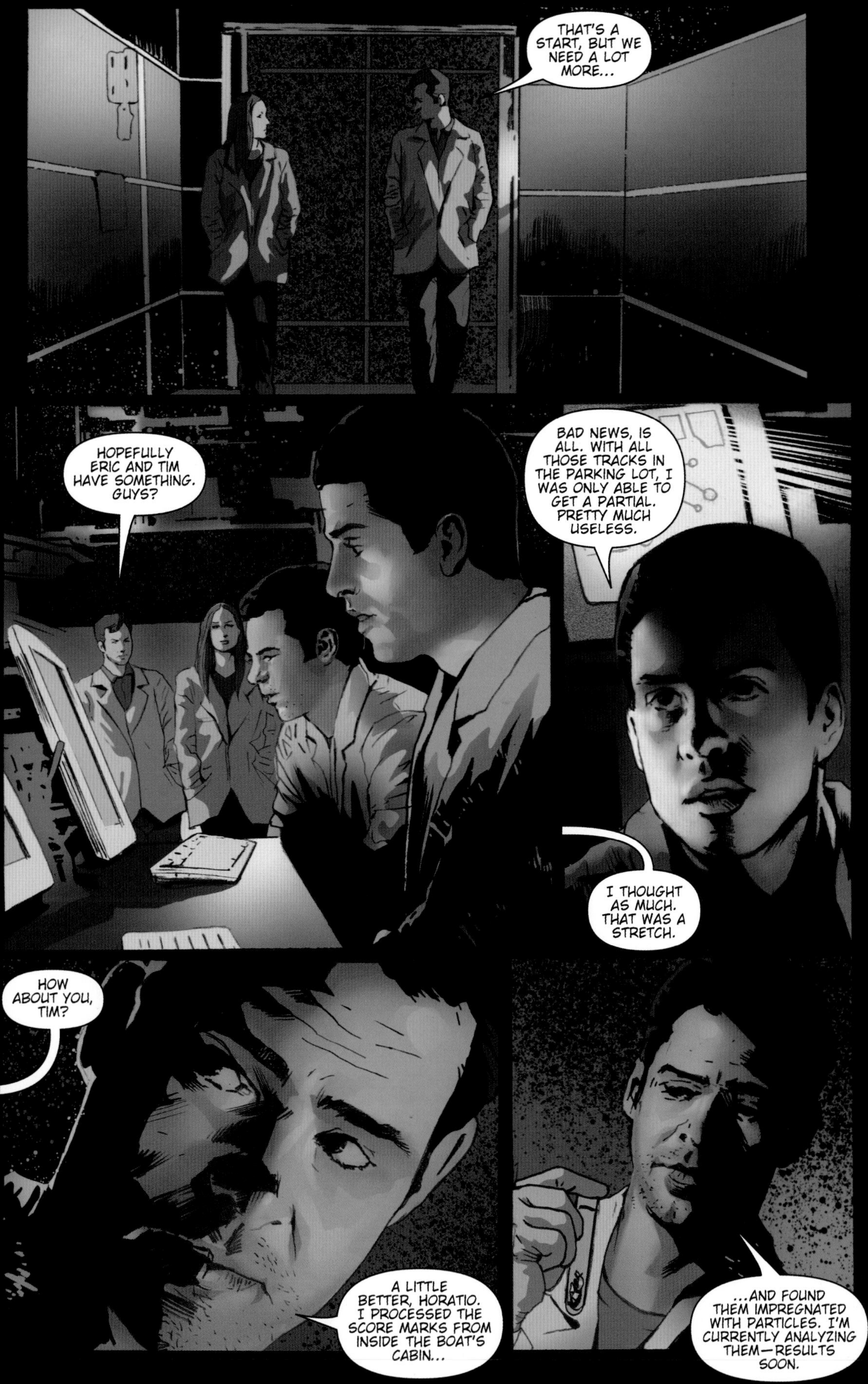
THAT'S A START, BUT WE NEED A LOT MORE...
HOPEFULLY ERIC AND TIM HAVE SOMETHING. GUYS?
BAD NEWS, IS ALL. WITH ALL THOSE TRACKS IN THE PARKING LOT, I WAS ONLY ABLE TO GET A PARTIAL. PRETTY MUCH USELESS.
I THOUGHT AS MUCH. THAT WAS A STRETCH.
HOW ABOUT YOU, TIM?
A LITTLE BETTER, HORATIO. I PROCESSED THE SCORE MARKS FROM INSIDE THE BOAT'S CABIN...
...AND FOUND THEM IMPREGNATED WITH PARTICLES. I'M CURRENTLY ANALYZING THEM—RESULTS SOON.

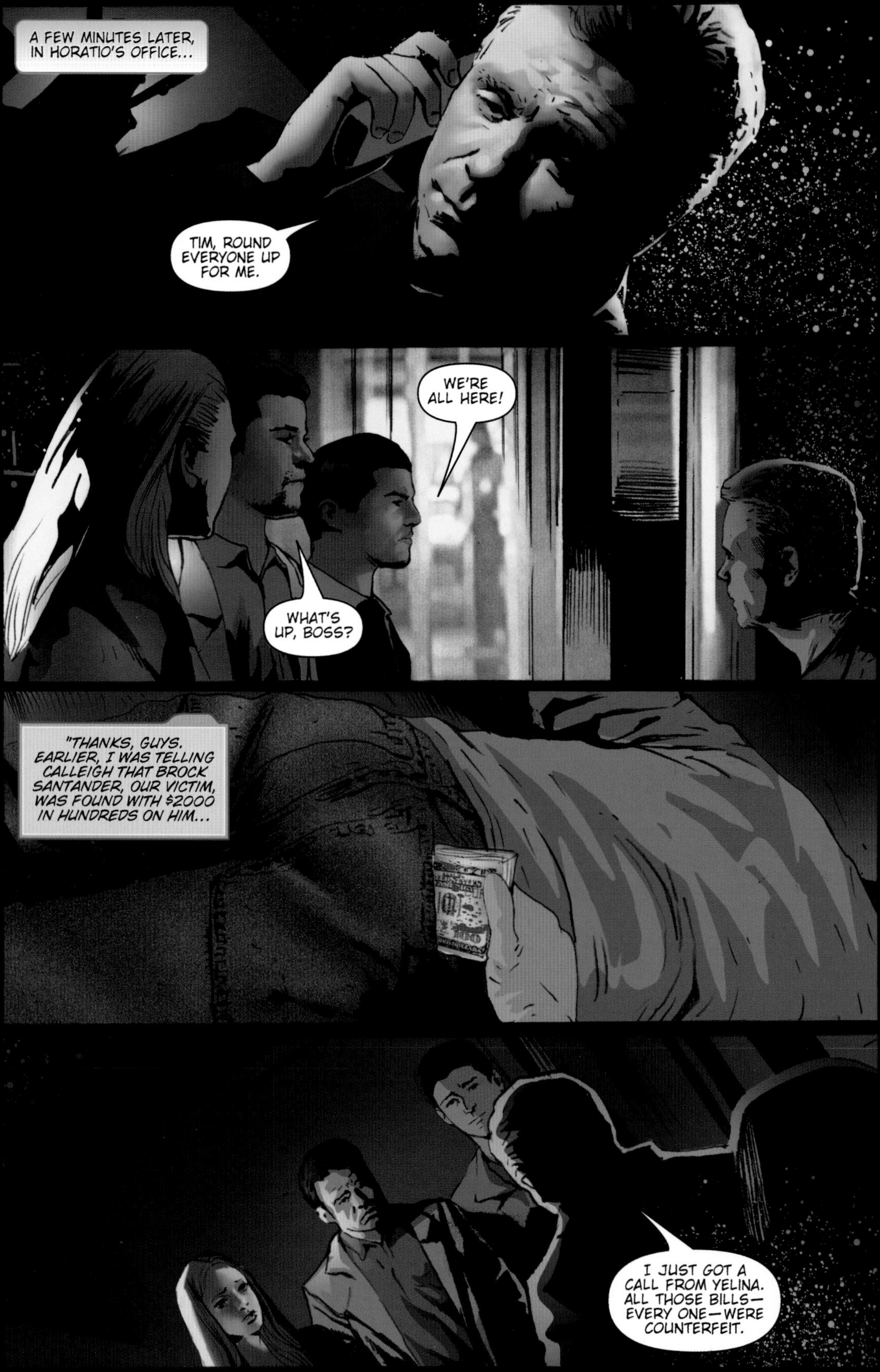
A FEW MINUTES LATER, IN HORATIO'S OFFICE...
TIM, ROUND EVERYONE UP FOR ME.
WE'RE ALL HERE!
WHAT'S UP, BOSS?
"THANKS, GUYS. EARLIER, I WAS TELLING CALLEIGH THAT BROCK SANTANDER, OUR VICTIM, WAS FOUND WITH $2000 IN HUNDREDS ON HIM...
I JUST GOT A CALL FROM YELINA. ALL THOSE BILLS— EVERY ONE—WERE COUNTERFEIT.

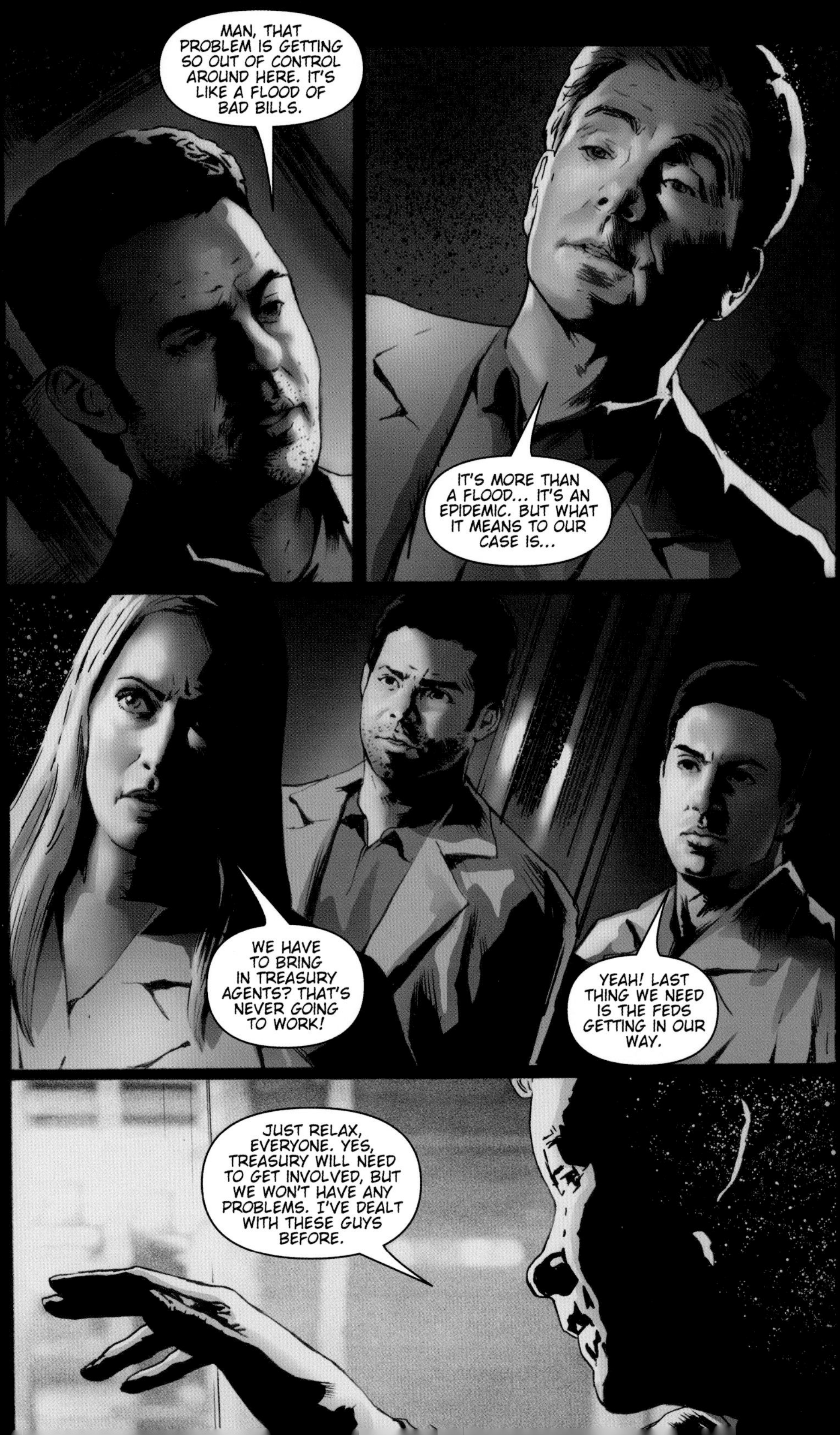
MAN, THAT PROBLEM IS GETTING SO OUT OF CONTROL AROUND HERE. IT'S LIKE A FLOOD OF BAD BILLS.
IT'S MORE THAN A FLOOD... IT'S AN EPIDEMIC. BUT WHAT IT MEANS TO OUR CASE IS...
WE HAVE TO BRING IN TREASURY AGENTS? THAT'S NEVER GOING TO WORK!
YEAH! LAST THING WE NEED IS THE FEDS GETTING IN OUR WAY.
JUST RELAX, EVERYONE. YES, TREASURY WILL NEED TO GET INVOLVED, BUT WE WON'T HAVE ANY PROBLEMS. I'VE DEALT WITH THESE GUYS BEFORE.

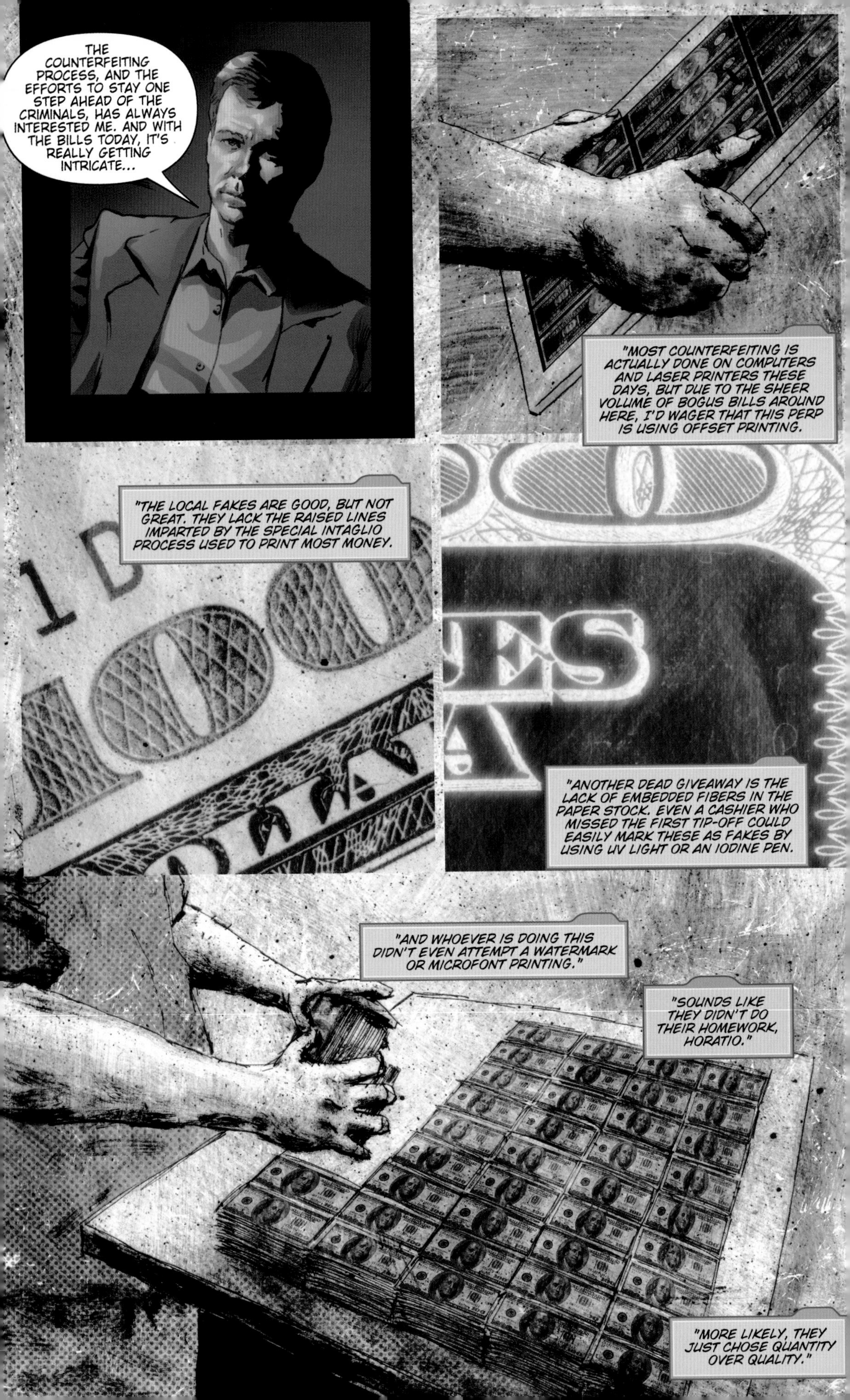
THE COUNTERFEITING PROCESS, AND THE EFFORTS TO STAY ONE STEP AHEAD OF THE CRIMINALS, HAS ALWAYS INTERESTED ME. AND WITH THE BILLS TODAY, IT'S REALLY GETTING INTRICATE...
"MOST COUNTERFEITING IS ACTUALLY DONE ON COMPUTERS AND LASER PRINTERS THESE DAYS, BUT DUE TO THE SHEER VOLUME OF BOGUS BILLS AROUND HERE, I'D WAGER THAT THIS PERP IS USING OFFSET PRINTING.
"THE LOCAL FAKES ARE GOOD, BUT NOT GREAT. THEY LACK THE RAISED LINES IMPARTED BY THE SPECIAL INTAGLIO PROCESS USED TO PRINT MOST MONEY.
"ANOTHER DEAD GIVEAWAY IS THE LACK OF EMBEDDED FIBERS IN THE PAPER STOCK. EVEN A CASHIER WHO MISSED THE FIRST TIP-OFF COULD EASILY MARK THESE AS FAKES BY USING UV LIGHT OR AN IODINE PEN.
"AND WHOEVER IS DOING THIS DIDN'T EVEN ATTEMPT A WATERMARK OR MICROFONT PRINTING."
"SOUNDS LIKE THEY DIDN'T DO THEIR HOMEWORK, HORATIO."
"MORE LIKELY, THEY JUST CHOSE QUANTITY OVER QUALITY."

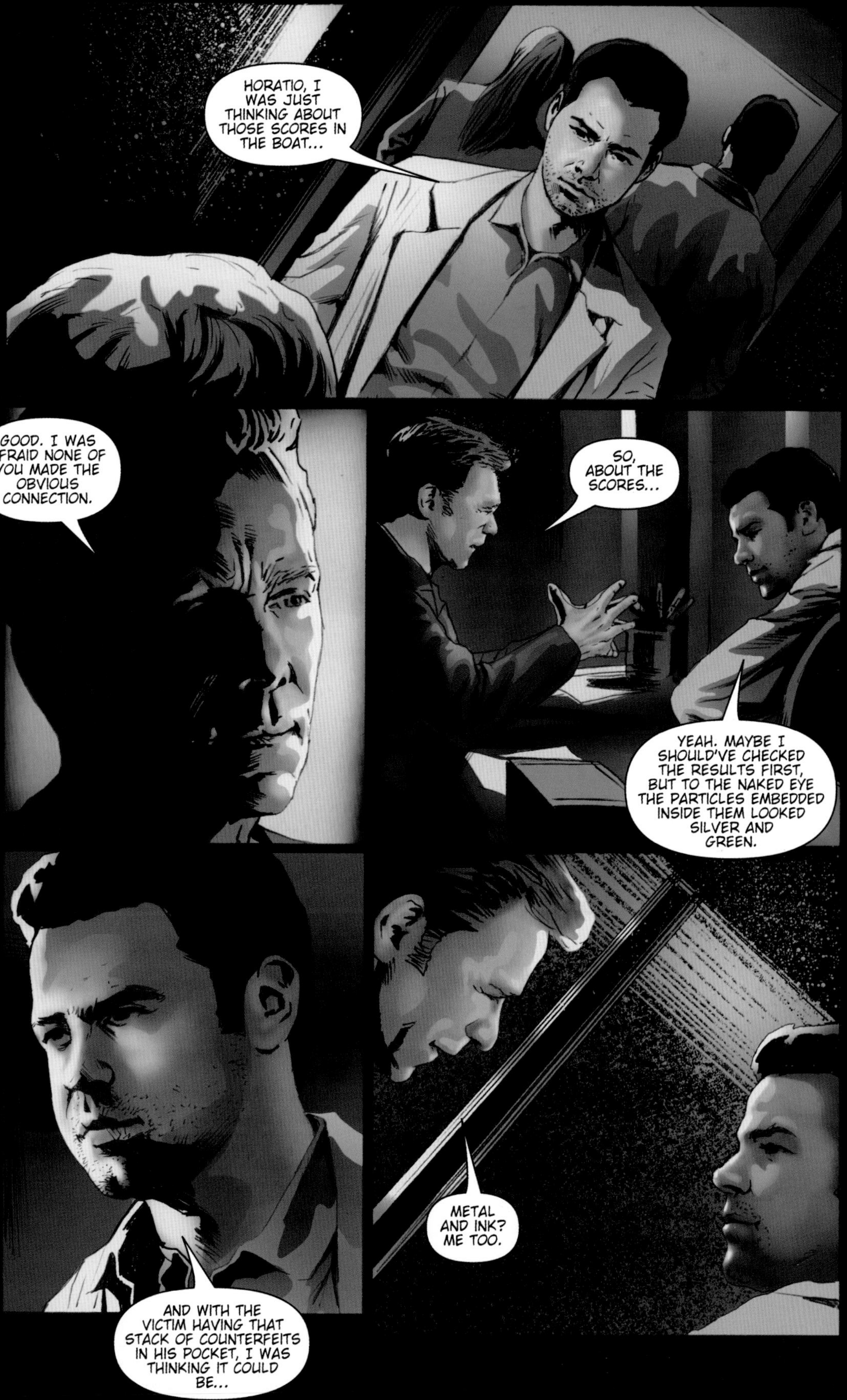
HORATIO, I WAS JUST THINKING ABOUT THOSE SCORES IN THE BOAT...
GOOD. I WAS AFRAID NONE OF YOU MADE THE OBVIOUS CONNECTION.
SO, ABOUT THE SCORES...
YEAH. MAYBE I SHOULD'VE CHECKED THE RESULTS FIRST, BUT TO THE NAKED EYE THE PARTICLES EMBEDDED INSIDE THEM LOOKED SILVER AND GREEN.
AND WITH THE VICTIM HAVING THAT STACK OF COUNTERFEITS IN HIS POCKET, I WAS THINKING IT COULD BE...
METAL AND INK? ME TOO.

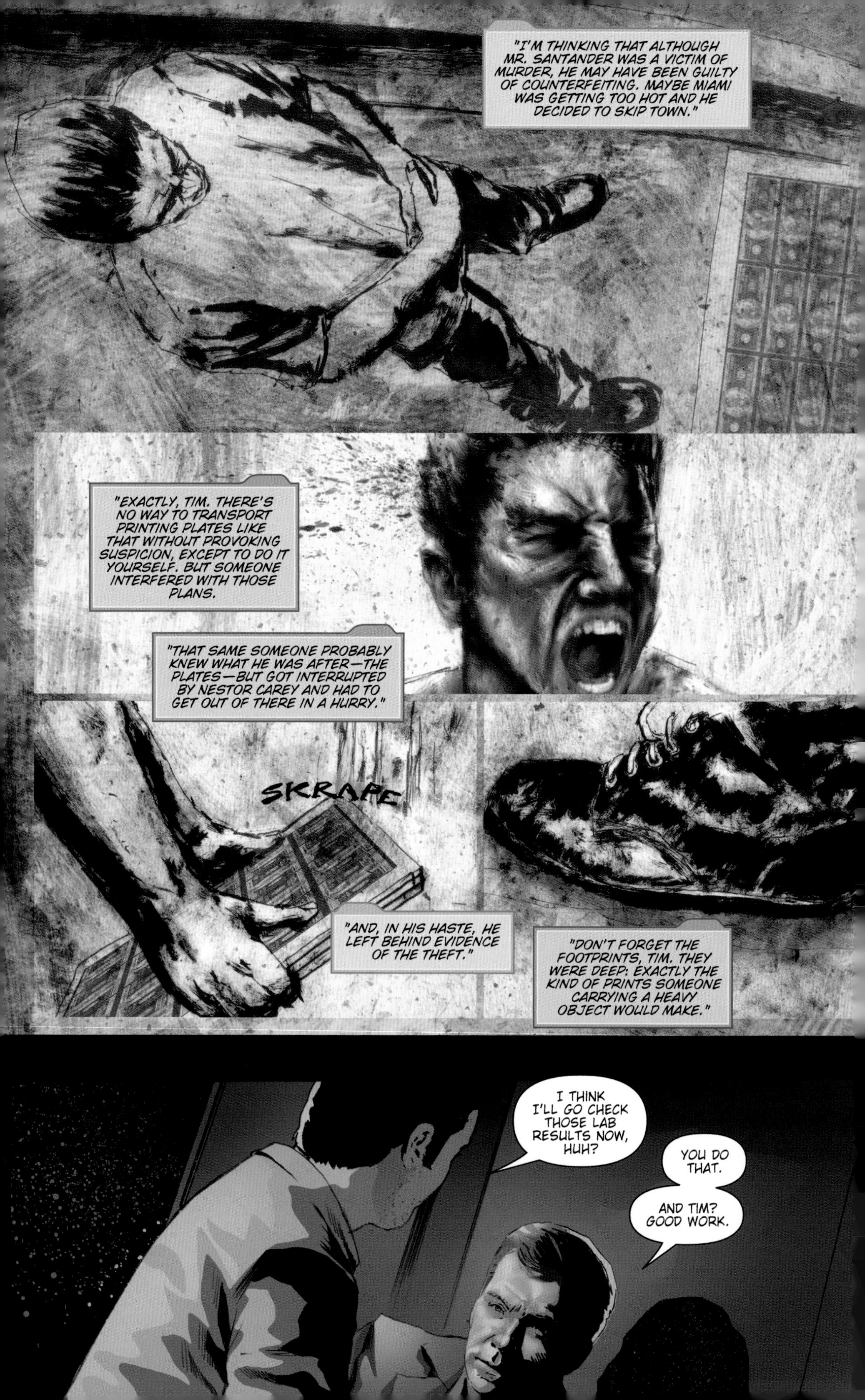
"I'M THINKING THAT ALTHOUGH MR. SANTANDER WAS A VICTIM OF MURDER, HE MAY HAVE BEEN GUILTY OF COUNTERFEITING. MAYBE MIAMI WAS GETTING TOO HOT AND HE DECIDED TO SKIP TOWN."
"EXACTLY, TIM. THERE'S NO WAY TO TRANSPORT PRINTING PLATES LIKE THAT WITHOUT PROVOKING SUSPICION, EXCEPT TO DO IT YOURSELF. BUT SOMEONE INTERFERED WITH THOSE PLANS.
"THAT SAME SOMEONE PROBABLY KNEW WHAT HE WAS AFTER—THE PLATES—BUT GOT INTERRUPTED BY NESTOR CAREY AND HAD TO GET OUT OF THERE IN A HURRY."
SKRAPE
"AND, IN HIS HASTE, HE LEFT BEHIND EVIDENCE OF THE THEFT."
"DON'T FORGET THE FOOTPRINTS, TIM. THEY WERE DEEP: EXACTLY THE KIND OF PRINTS SOMEONE CARRYING A HEAVY OBJECT WOULD MAKE."
I THINK I'LL GO CHECK THOSE LAB RESULTS NOW, HUH?
YOU DO THAT.
AND TIM? GOOD WORK.

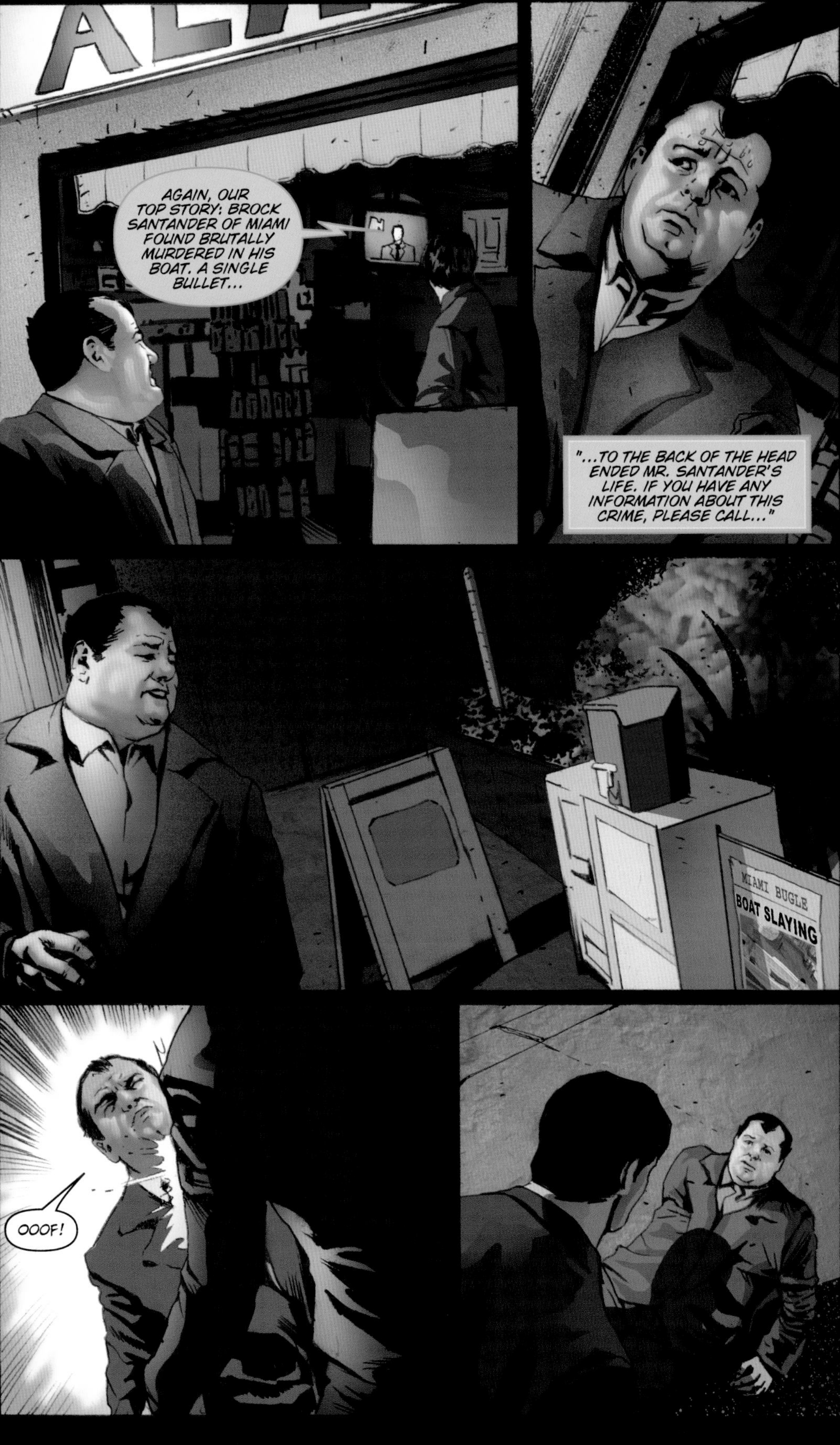
AGAIN, OUR TOP STORY: BROCK SANTANDER OF MIAMI FOUND BRUTALLY MURDERED IN HIS BOAT. A SINGLE BULLET...
"...TO THE BACK OF THE HEAD ENDED MR. SANTANDER'S LIFE. IF YOU HAVE ANY INFORMATION ABOUT THIS CRIME, PLEASE CALL..."
MIAMI BUGLE
BOAT SLAYING
OOOF!

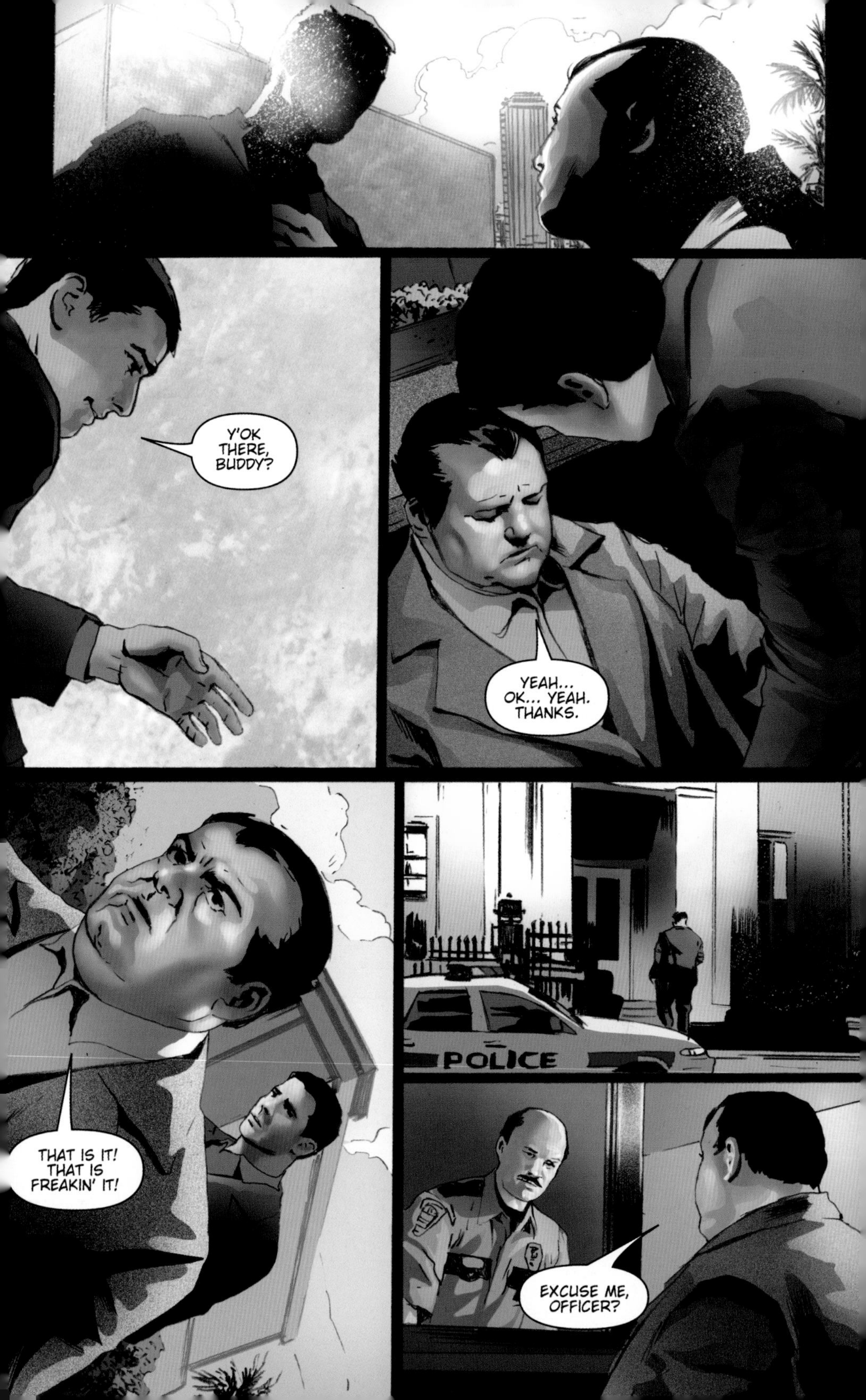
Y'OK THERE, BUDDY?
YEAH... OK... YEAH. THANKS.
THAT IS IT! THAT IS FREAKIN' IT!
POLICE
EXCUSE ME, OFFICER?

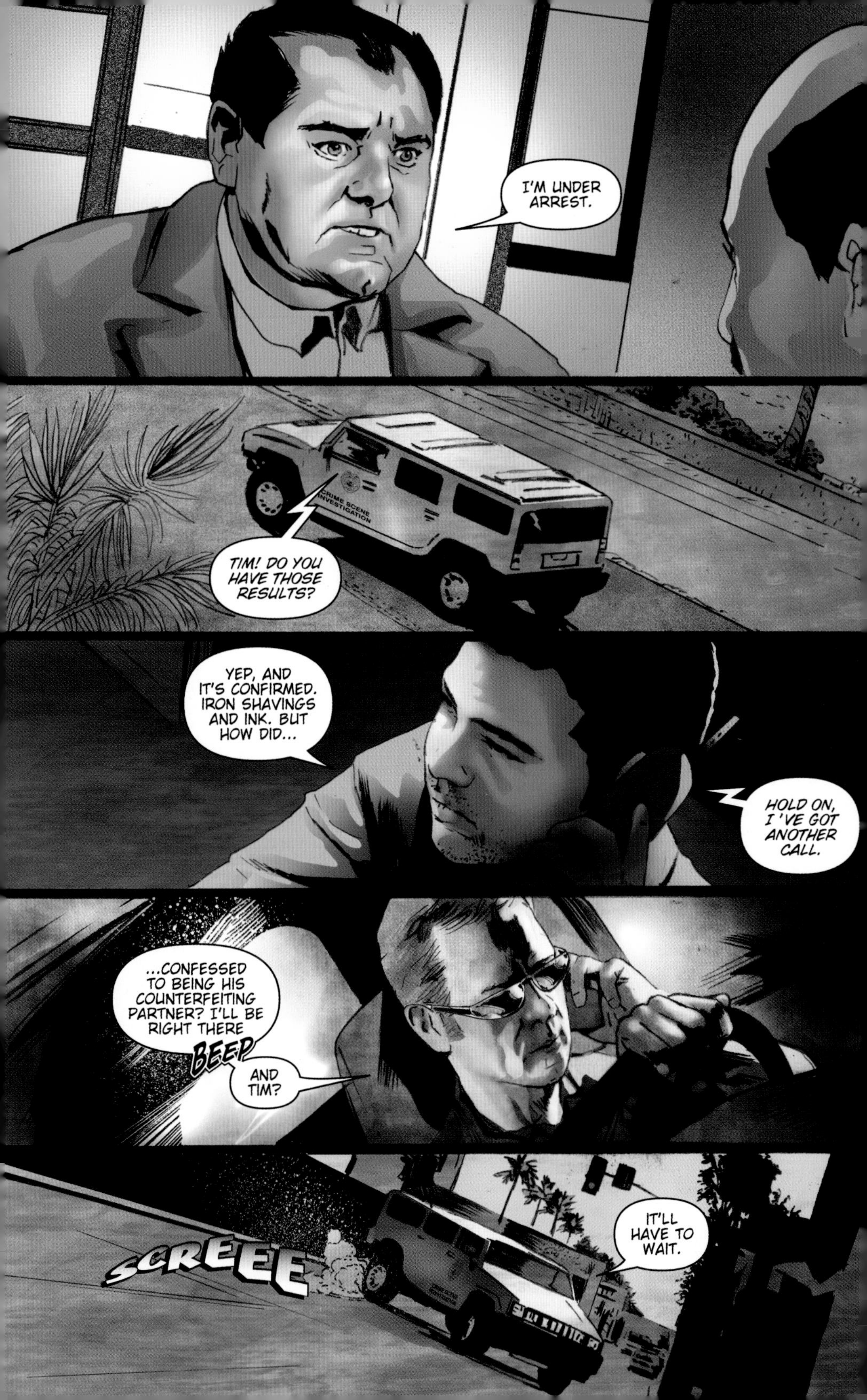

I'M UNDER ARREST.
TIM! DO YOU HAVE THOSE RESULTS?
CRIME SCENE INVESTIGATION
YEP, AND IT'S CONFIRMED. IRON SHAVINGS AND INK. BUT HOW DID...
HOLD ON, I'VE GOT ANOTHER CALL.
...CONFESSED TO BEING HIS COUNTERFEITING PARTNER? I'LL BE RIGHT THERE
BEEP
AND TIM?
SCREEEE
IT'LL HAVE TO WAIT.

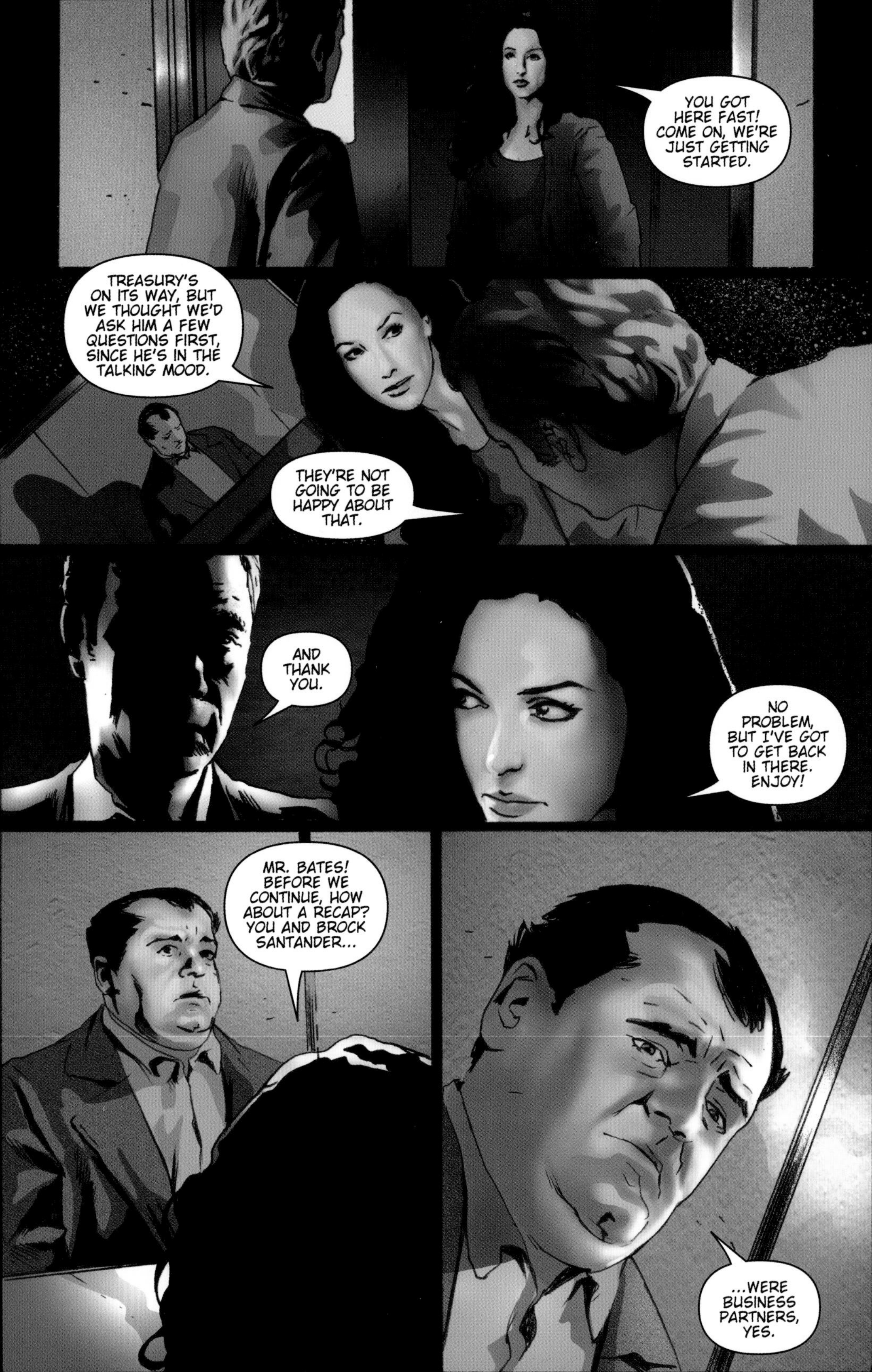
YOU GOT HERE FAST! COME ON, WE'RE JUST GETTING STARTED.
TREASURY'S ON ITS WAY, BUT WE THOUGHT WE'D ASK HIM A FEW QUESTIONS FIRST, SINCE HE'S IN THE TALKING MOOD.
THEY'RE NOT GOING TO BE HAPPY ABOUT THAT.
AND THANK YOU.
NO PROBLEM, BUT I'VE GOT TO GET BACK IN THERE. ENJOY!
MR. BATES! BEFORE WE CONTINUE, HOW ABOUT A RECAP? YOU AND BROCK SANTANDER...
...WERE BUSINESS PARTNERS, YES.

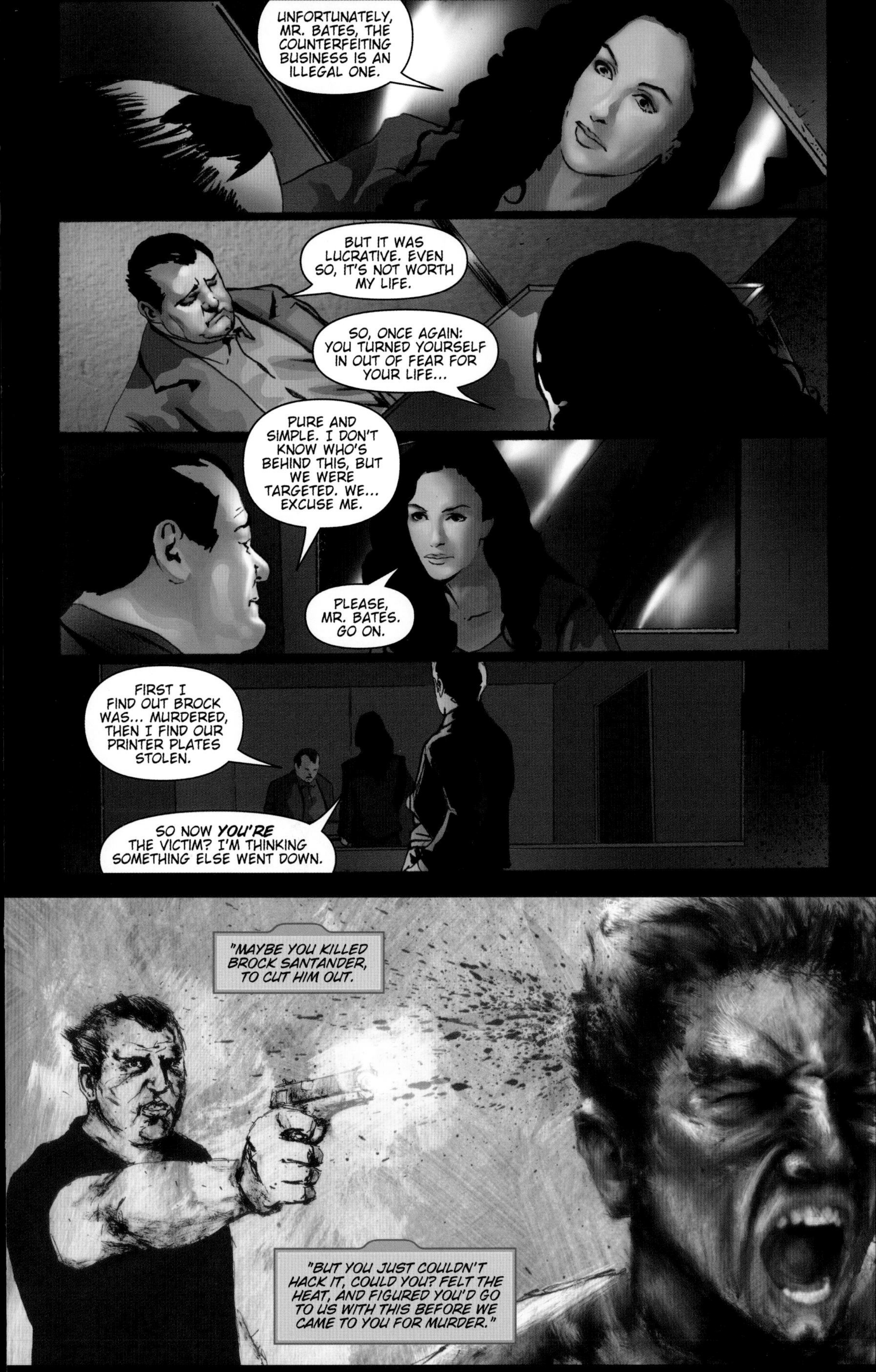
UNFORTUNATELY, MR. BATES, THE COUNTERFEITING BUSINESS IS AN ILLEGAL ONE.
BUT IT WAS LUCRATIVE. EVEN SO, IT'S NOT WORTH MY LIFE.
SO, ONCE AGAIN: YOU TURNED YOURSELF IN OUT OF FEAR FOR YOUR LIFE...
PURE AND SIMPLE. I DON'T KNOW WHO'S BEHIND THIS, BUT WE WERE TARGETED. WE... EXCUSE ME.
PLEASE, MR. BATES. GO ON.
FIRST I FIND OUT BROCK WAS... MURDERED, THEN I FIND OUR PRINTER PLATES STOLEN.
SO NOW ***YOU'RE*** THE VICTIM? I'M THINKING SOMETHING ELSE WENT DOWN.
*"MAYBE YOU KILLED BROCK SANTANDER, TO CUT HIM OUT.*
*"BUT YOU JUST COULDN'T HACK IT, COULD YOU? FELT THE HEAT, AND FIGURED YOU'D GO TO US WITH THIS BEFORE WE CAME TO YOU FOR MURDER."*

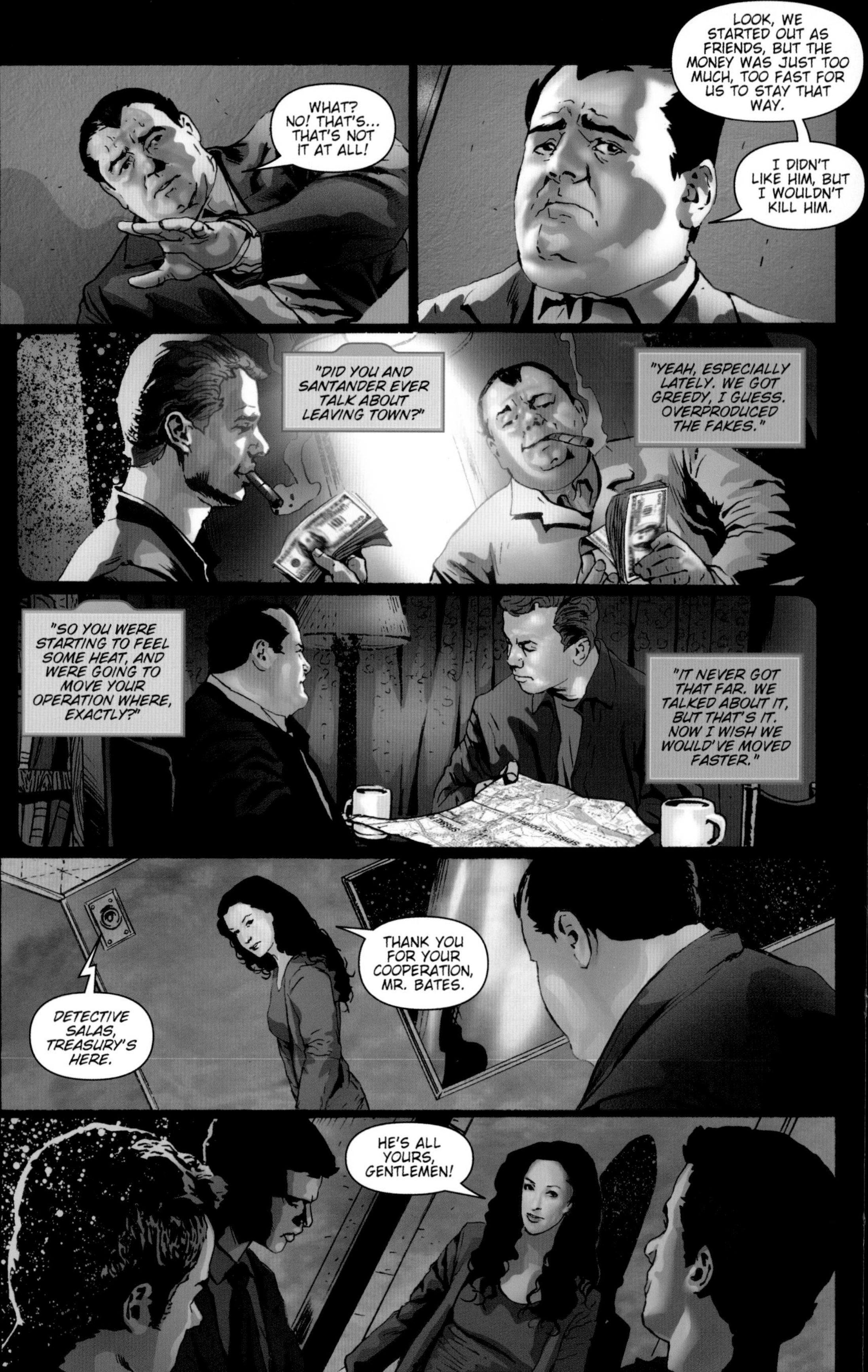
WHAT? NO! THAT'S... THAT'S NOT IT AT ALL!
LOOK, WE STARTED OUT AS FRIENDS, BUT THE MONEY WAS JUST TOO MUCH, TOO FAST FOR US TO STAY THAT WAY.
I DIDN'T LIKE HIM, BUT I WOULDN'T KILL HIM.
"DID YOU AND SANTANDER EVER TALK ABOUT LEAVING TOWN?"
"YEAH, ESPECIALLY LATELY. WE GOT GREEDY, I GUESS. OVERPRODUCED THE FAKES."
"SO YOU WERE STARTING TO FEEL SOME HEAT, AND WERE GOING TO MOVE YOUR OPERATION WHERE, EXACTLY?"
"IT NEVER GOT THAT FAR. WE TALKED ABOUT IT, BUT THAT'S IT. NOW I WISH WE WOULD'VE MOVED FASTER."
DETECTIVE SALAS, TREASURY'S HERE.
THANK YOU FOR YOUR COOPERATION, MR. BATES.
HE'S ALL YOURS, GENTLEMEN!

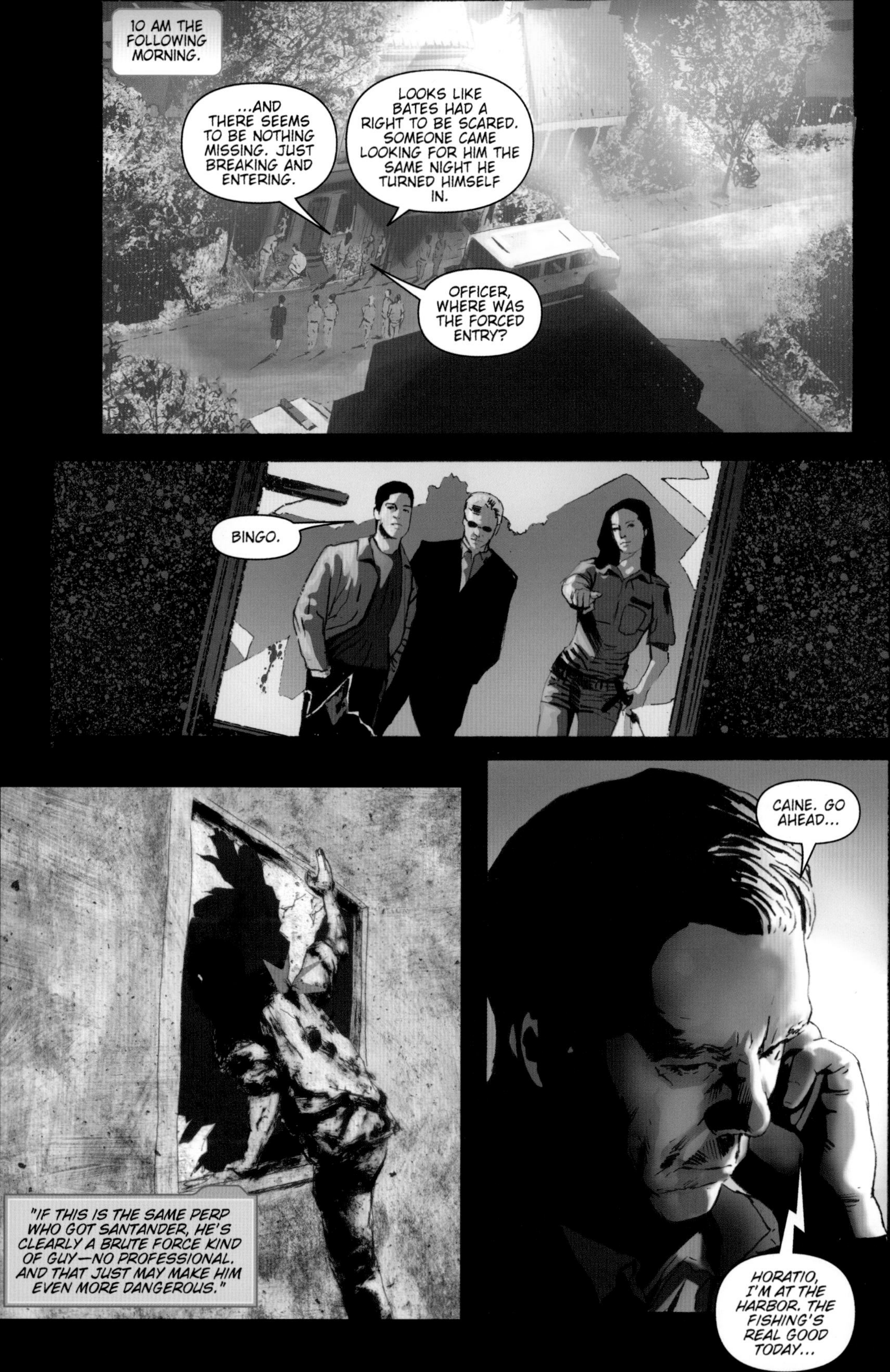
10 AM THE FOLLOWING MORNING.
...AND THERE SEEMS TO BE NOTHING MISSING. JUST BREAKING AND ENTERING.
LOOKS LIKE BATES HAD A RIGHT TO BE SCARED. SOMEONE CAME LOOKING FOR HIM THE SAME NIGHT HE TURNED HIMSELF IN.
OFFICER, WHERE WAS THE FORCED ENTRY?
BINGO.
"IF THIS IS THE SAME PERP WHO GOT SANTANDER, HE'S CLEARLY A BRUTE FORCE KIND OF GUY—NO PROFESSIONAL. AND THAT JUST MAY MAKE HIM EVEN MORE DANGEROUS."
CAINE. GO AHEAD...
HORATIO, I'M AT THE HARBOR. THE FISHING'S REAL GOOD TODAY...

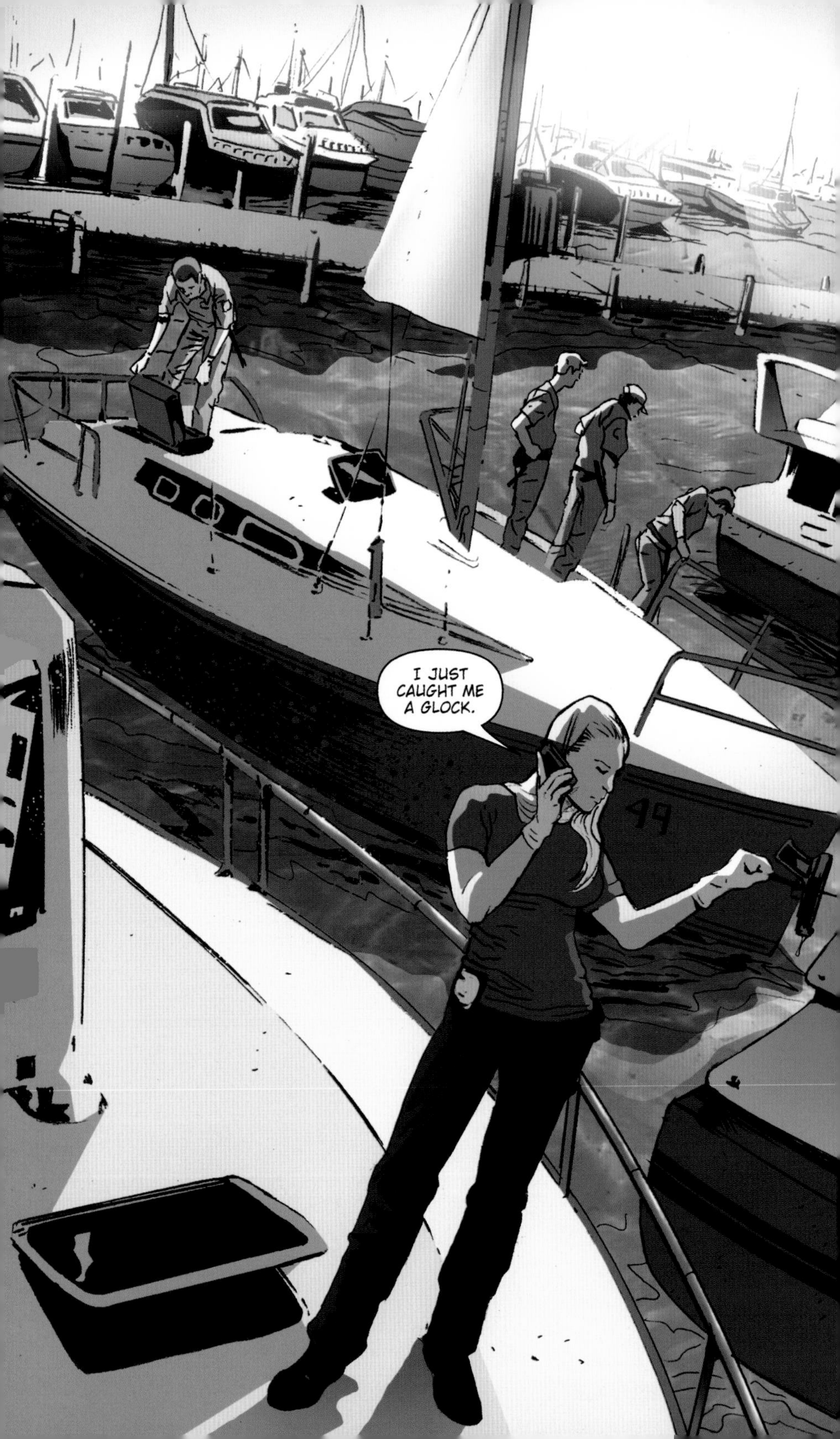
I JUST CAUGHT ME A GLOCK.

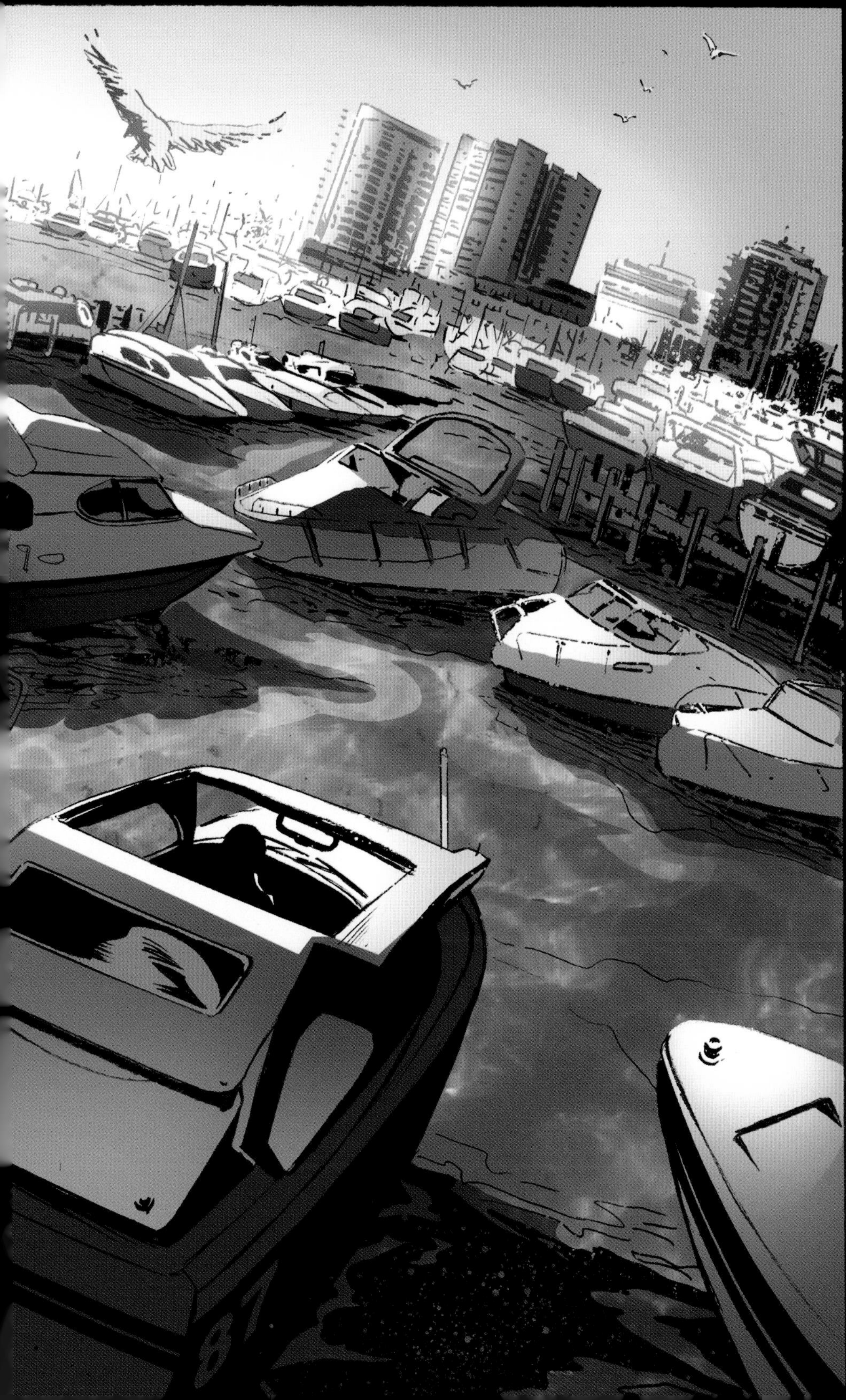

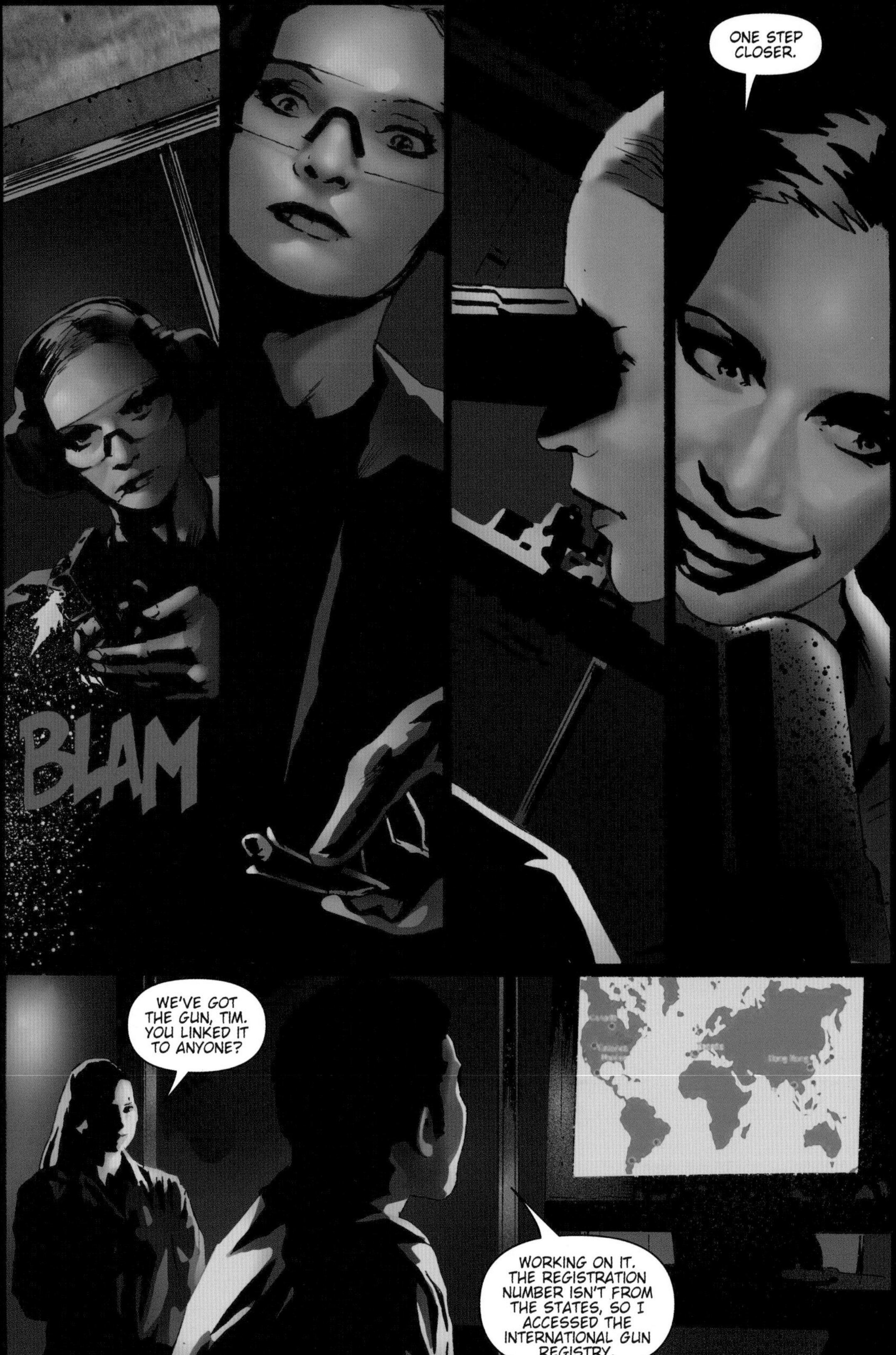
BLAM
ONE STEP CLOSER.
WE'VE GOT THE GUN, TIM. YOU LINKED IT TO ANYONE?
WORKING ON IT. THE REGISTRATION NUMBER ISN'T FROM THE STATES, SO I ACCESSED THE INTERNATIONAL GUN REGISTRY.

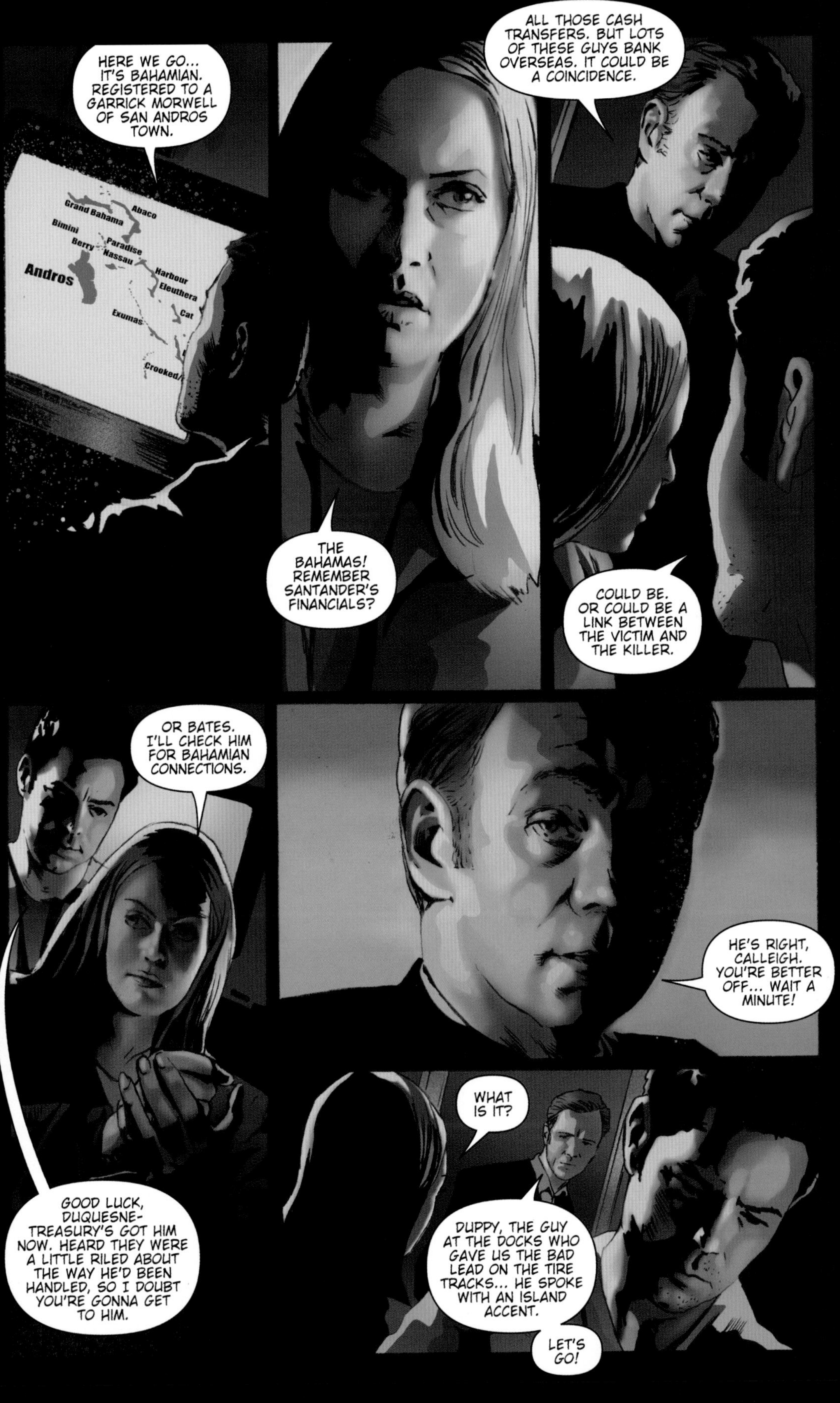
HERE WE GO... IT'S BAHAMIAN. REGISTERED TO A GARRICK MORWELL OF SAN ANDROS TOWN.
Grand Bahama
Abaco
Bimini
Berry
Paradise
Nassau
Andros
Harbour
Eleuthera
Cat
Exumas
Crooked
THE BAHAMAS! REMEMBER SANTANDER'S FINANCIALS?
ALL THOSE CASH TRANSFERS. BUT LOTS OF THESE GUYS BANK OVERSEAS. IT COULD BE A COINCIDENCE.
COULD BE. OR COULD BE A LINK BETWEEN THE VICTIM AND THE KILLER.
OR BATES. I'LL CHECK HIM FOR BAHAMIAN CONNECTIONS.
GOOD LUCK, DUQUESNE-TREASURY'S GOT HIM NOW. HEARD THEY WERE A LITTLE RILED ABOUT THE WAY HE'D BEEN HANDLED, SO I DOUBT YOU'RE GONNA GET TO HIM.
HE'S RIGHT, CALLEIGH. YOU'RE BETTER OFF... WAIT A MINUTE!
WHAT IS IT?
DUPPY, THE GUY AT THE DOCKS WHO GAVE US THE BAD LEAD ON THE TIRE TRACKS... HE SPOKE WITH AN ISLAND ACCENT.
LET'S GO!

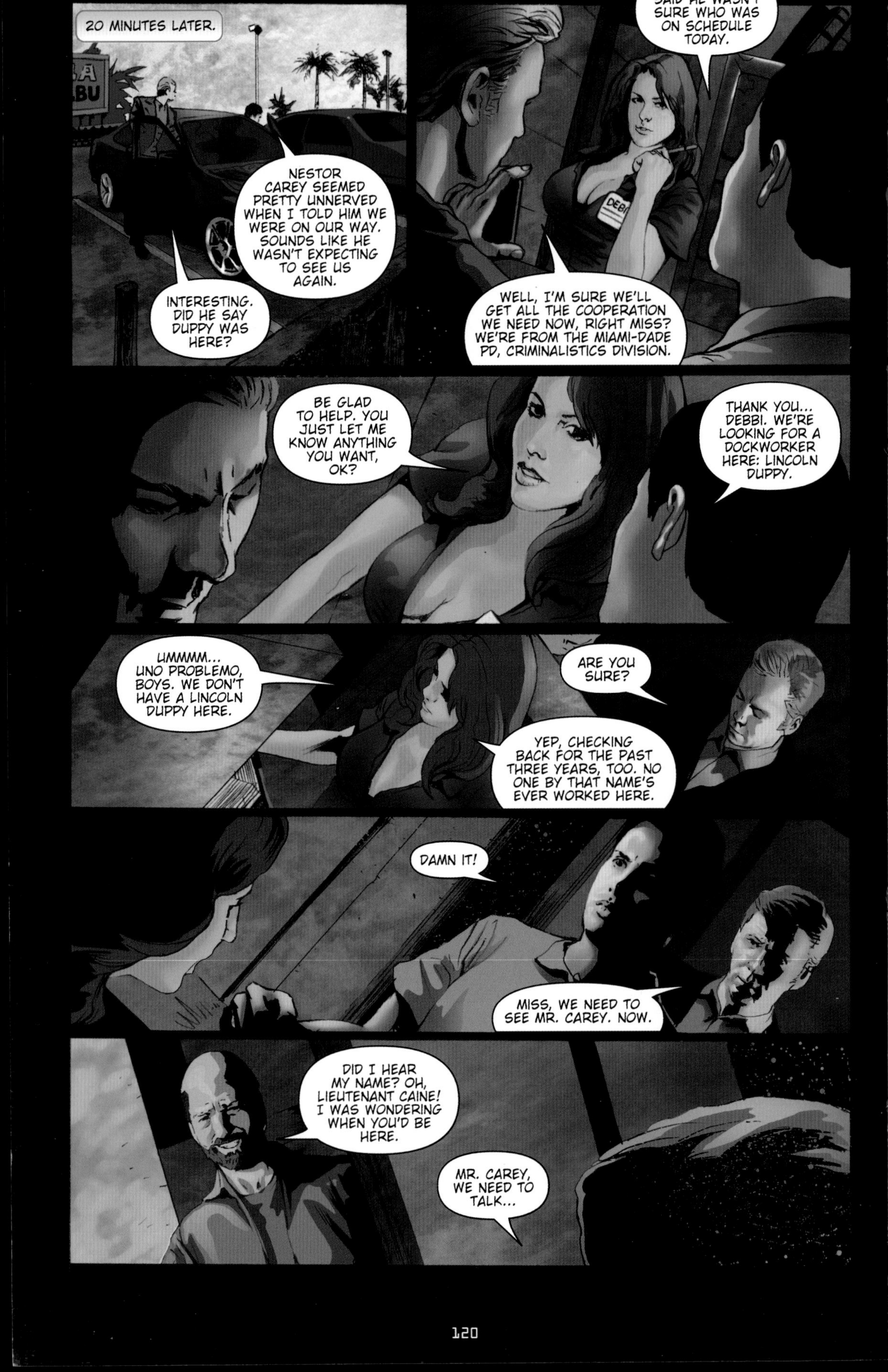
20 MINUTES LATER.
NESTOR CAREY SEEMED PRETTY UNNERVED WHEN I TOLD HIM WE WERE ON OUR WAY. SOUNDS LIKE HE WASN'T EXPECTING TO SEE US AGAIN.
INTERESTING. DID HE SAY DUPPY WAS HERE?
DIDN'T SAY. SAID HE WASN'T SURE WHO WAS ON SCHEDULE TODAY.
WELL, I'M SURE WE'LL GET ALL THE COOPERATION WE NEED NOW, RIGHT MISS? WE'RE FROM THE MIAMI-DADE PD, CRIMINALISTICS DIVISION.
BE GLAD TO HELP. YOU JUST LET ME KNOW ANYTHING YOU WANT, OK?
THANK YOU... DEBBI. WE'RE LOOKING FOR A DOCKWORKER HERE: LINCOLN DUPPY.
UMMMM... UNO PROBLEMO, BOYS. WE DON'T HAVE A LINCOLN DUPPY HERE.
ARE YOU SURE?
YEP, CHECKING BACK FOR THE PAST THREE YEARS, TOO. NO ONE BY THAT NAME'S EVER WORKED HERE.
DAMN IT!
MISS, WE NEED TO SEE MR. CAREY. NOW.
DID I HEAR MY NAME? OH, LIEUTENANT CAINE! I WAS WONDERING WHEN YOU'D BE HERE.
MR. CAREY, WE NEED TO TALK...

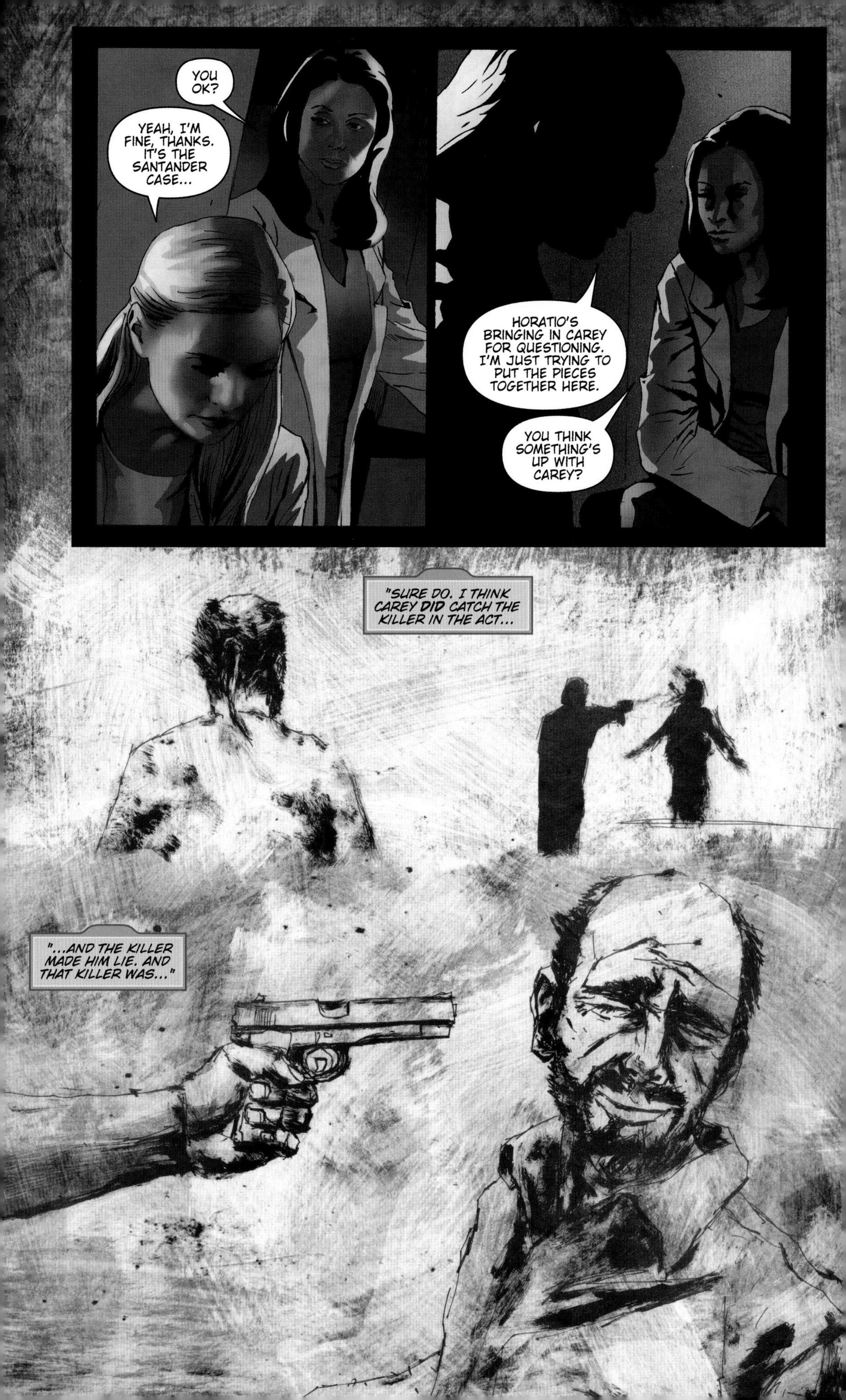
YOU OK?
YEAH, I'M FINE, THANKS. IT'S THE SANTANDER CASE...
HORATIO'S BRINGING IN CAREY FOR QUESTIONING. I'M JUST TRYING TO PUT THE PIECES TOGETHER HERE.
YOU THINK SOMETHING'S UP WITH CAREY?
"SURE DO. I THINK CAREY DID CATCH THE KILLER IN THE ACT...
"...AND THE KILLER MADE HIM LIE. AND THAT KILLER WAS..."

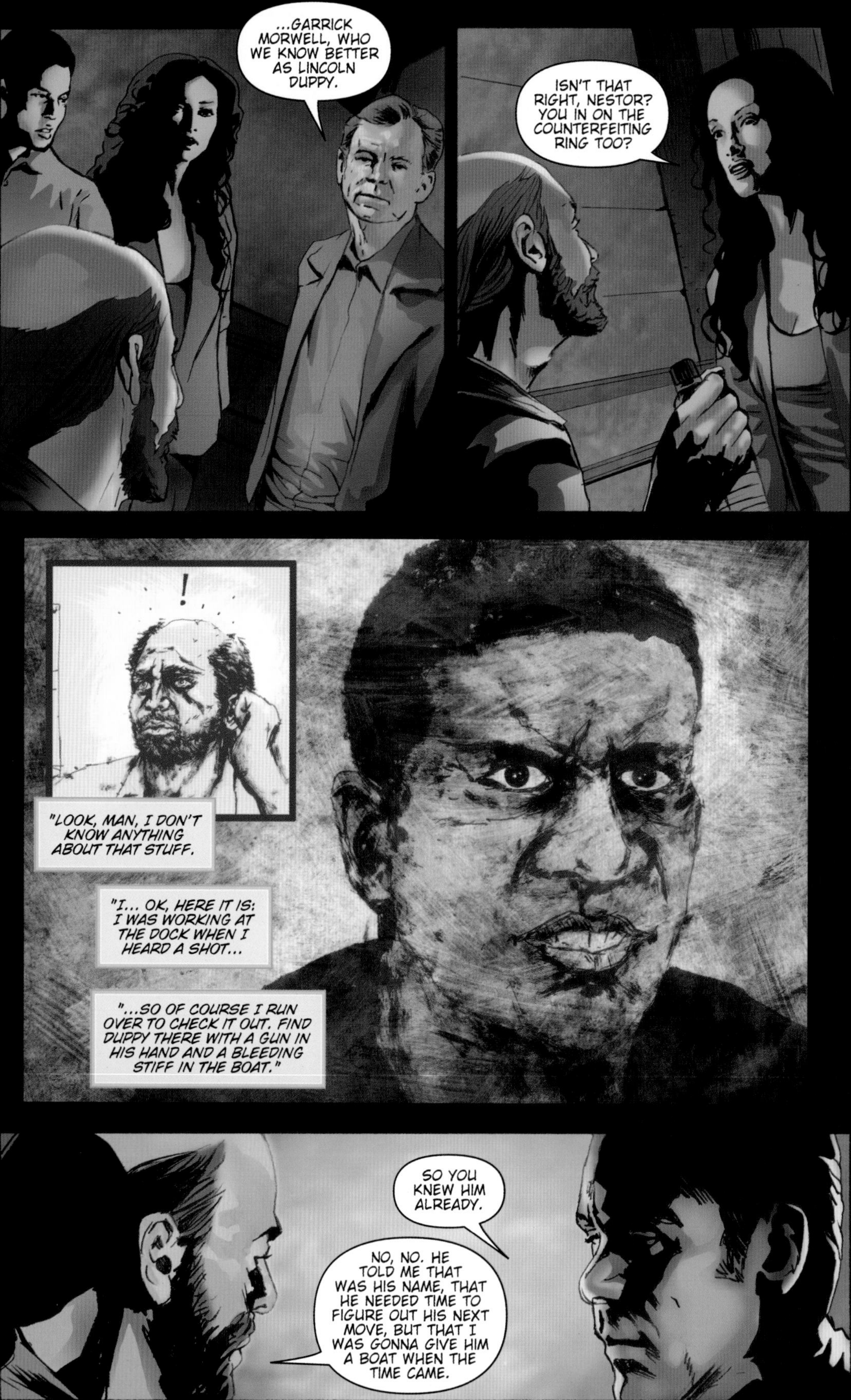
...GARRICK MORWELL, WHO WE KNOW BETTER AS LINCOLN DUPPY.
ISN'T THAT RIGHT, NESTOR? YOU IN ON THE COUNTERFEITING RING TOO?
!
"LOOK, MAN, I DON'T KNOW ANYTHING ABOUT THAT STUFF.
"I... OK, HERE IT IS: I WAS WORKING AT THE DOCK WHEN I HEARD A SHOT...
"...SO OF COURSE I RUN OVER TO CHECK IT OUT. FIND DUPPY THERE WITH A GUN IN HIS HAND AND A BLEEDING STIFF IN THE BOAT."
SO YOU KNEW HIM ALREADY.
NO, NO. HE TOLD ME THAT WAS HIS NAME, THAT HE NEEDED TIME TO FIGURE OUT HIS NEXT MOVE, BUT THAT I WAS GONNA GIVE HIM A BOAT WHEN THE TIME CAME.

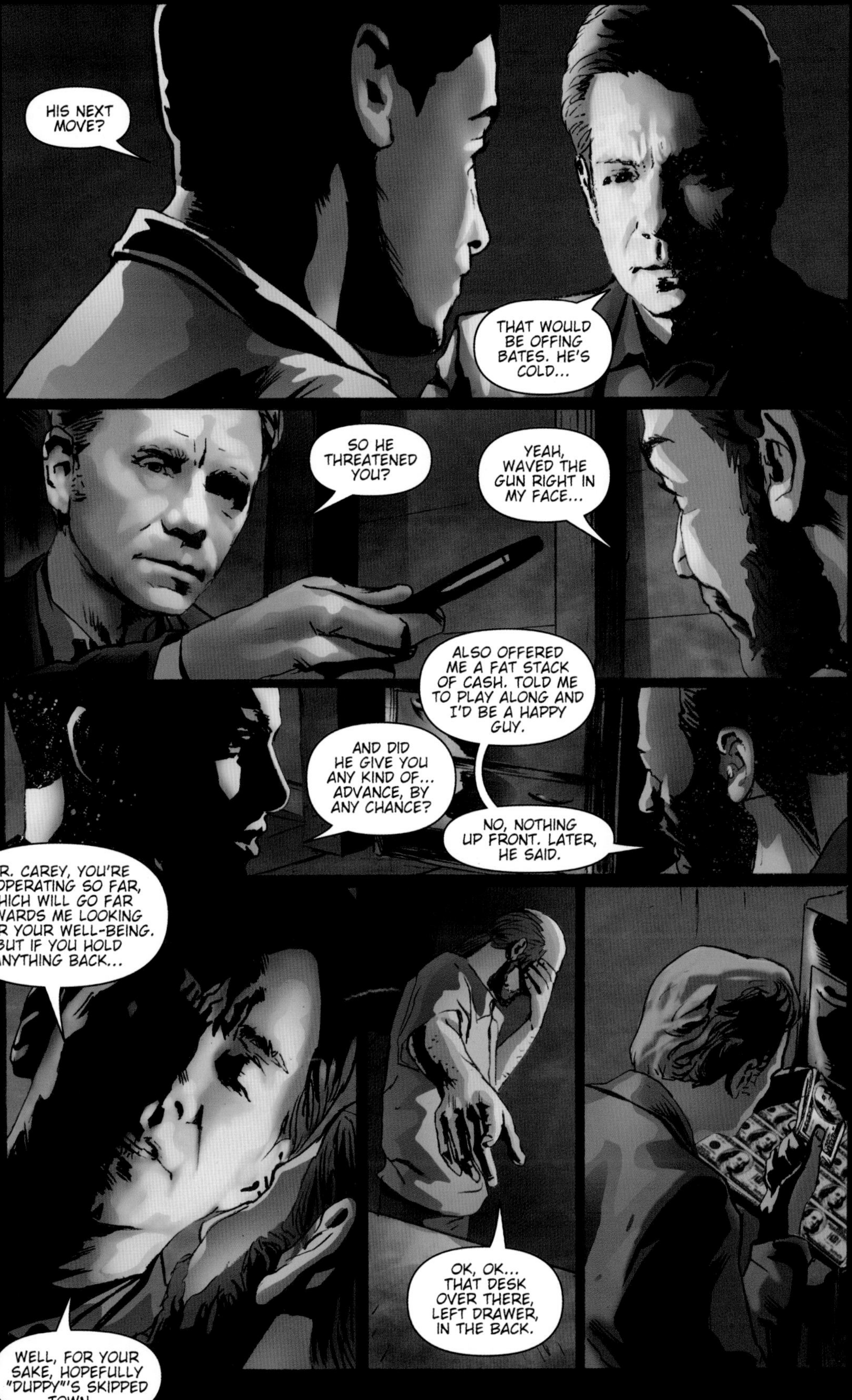
HIS NEXT MOVE?
THAT WOULD BE OFFING BATES. HE'S COLD...
SO HE THREATENED YOU?
YEAH, WAVED THE GUN RIGHT IN MY FACE...
ALSO OFFERED ME A FAT STACK OF CASH. TOLD ME TO PLAY ALONG AND I'D BE A HAPPY GUY.
AND DID HE GIVE YOU ANY KIND OF... ADVANCE, BY ANY CHANCE?
NO, NOTHING UP FRONT. LATER, HE SAID.
MR. CAREY, YOU'RE COOPERATING SO FAR, WHICH WILL GO FAR TOWARDS ME LOOKING AFTER YOUR WELL-BEING. BUT IF YOU HOLD ANYTHING BACK...
OK, OK... THAT DESK OVER THERE, LEFT DRAWER, IN THE BACK.
WELL, FOR YOUR SAKE, HOPEFULLY "DUPPY"'S SKIPPED TOWN...

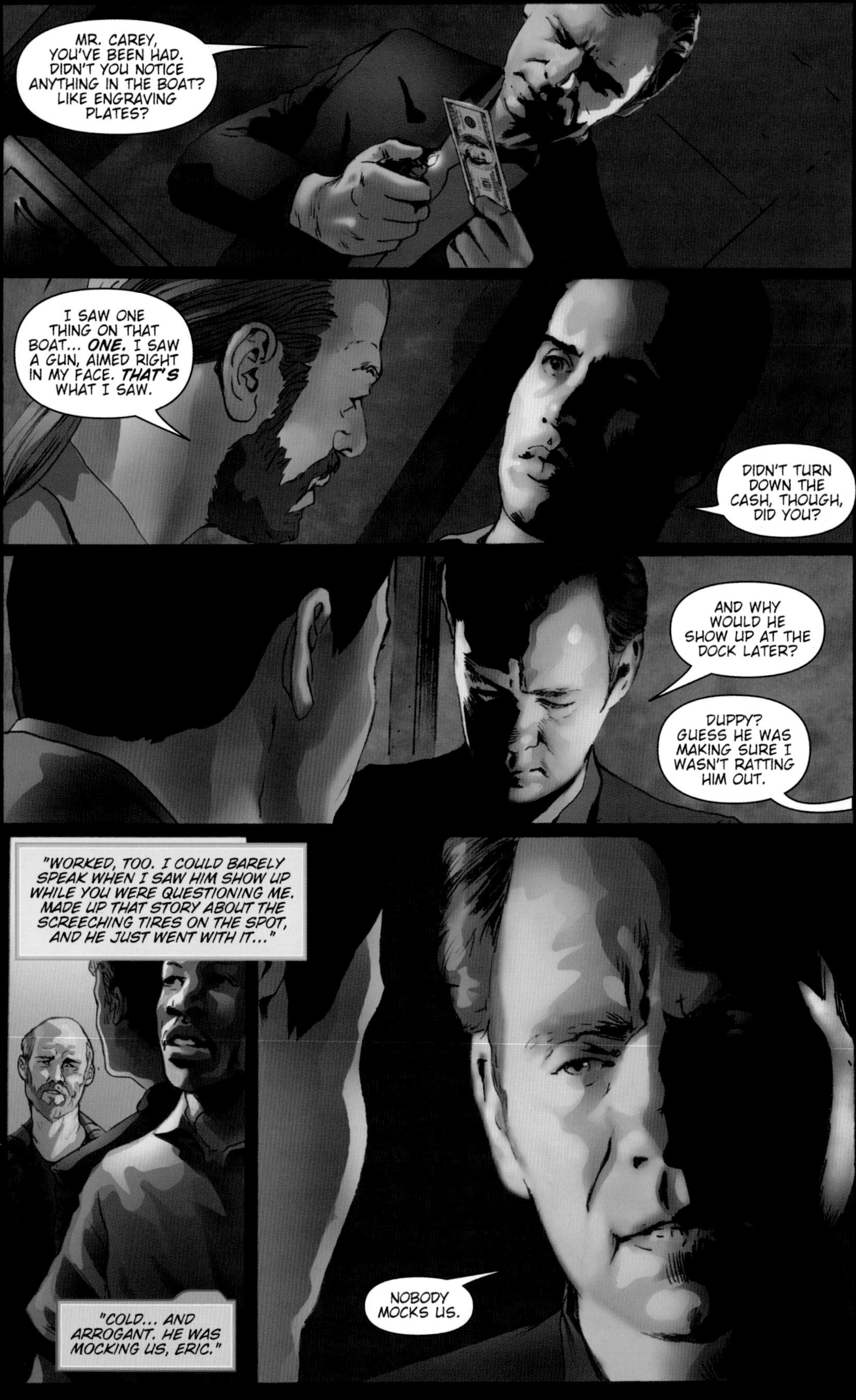
MR. CAREY, YOU'VE BEEN HAD. DIDN'T YOU NOTICE ANYTHING IN THE BOAT? LIKE ENGRAVING PLATES?
I SAW ONE THING ON THAT BOAT... ONE. I SAW A GUN, AIMED RIGHT IN MY FACE. THAT'S WHAT I SAW.
DIDN'T TURN DOWN THE CASH, THOUGH, DID YOU?
AND WHY WOULD HE SHOW UP AT THE DOCK LATER?
DUPPY? GUESS HE WAS MAKING SURE I WASN'T RATTING HIM OUT.
"WORKED, TOO. I COULD BARELY SPEAK WHEN I SAW HIM SHOW UP WHILE YOU WERE QUESTIONING ME. MADE UP THAT STORY ABOUT THE SCREECHING TIRES ON THE SPOT, AND HE JUST WENT WITH IT..."
"COLD... AND ARROGANT. HE WAS MOCKING US, ERIC."
NOBODY MOCKS US.

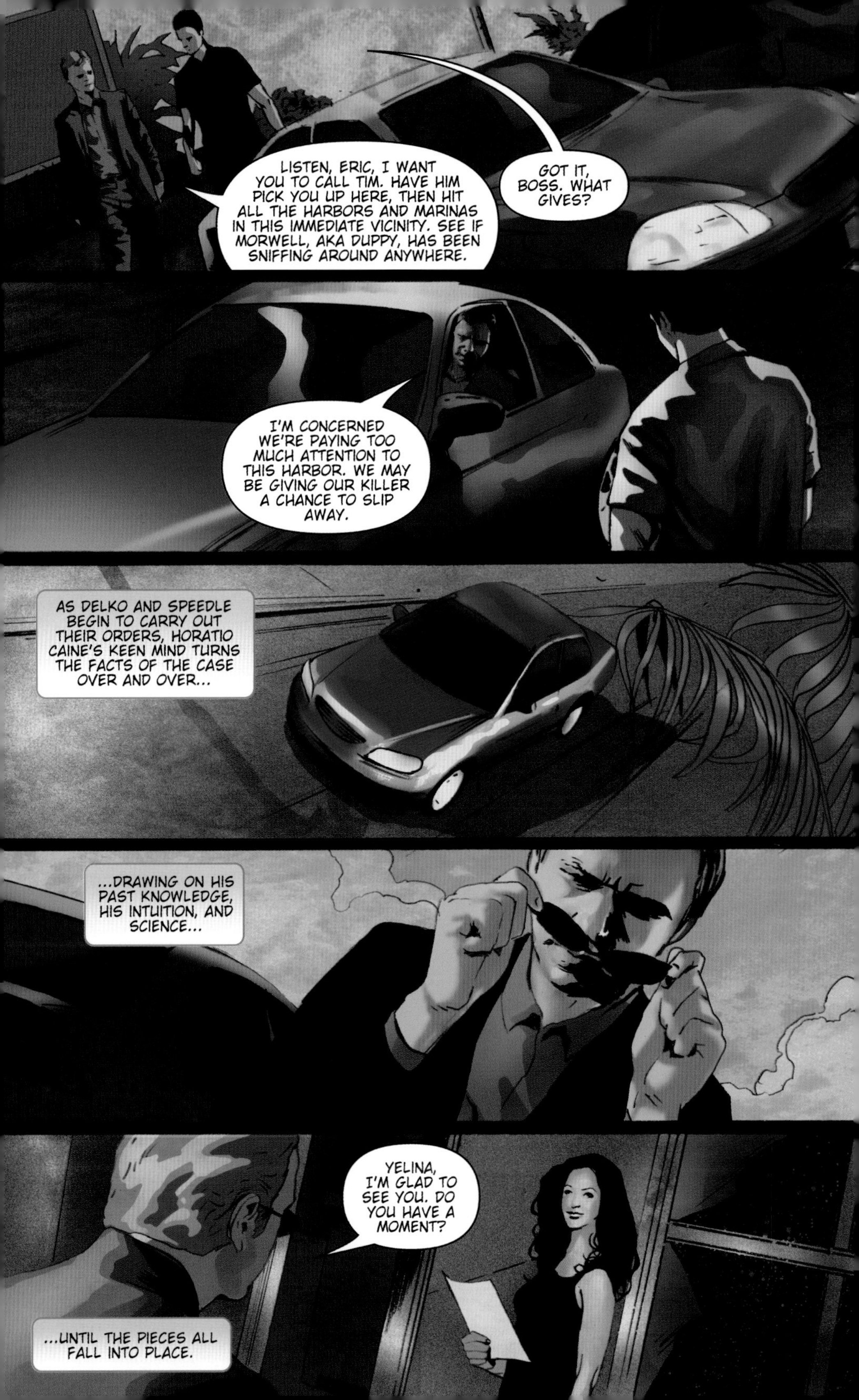
LISTEN, ERIC, I WANT YOU TO CALL TIM. HAVE HIM PICK YOU UP HERE, THEN HIT ALL THE HARBORS AND MARINAS IN THIS IMMEDIATE VICINITY. SEE IF MORWELL, AKA DUPPY, HAS BEEN SNIFFING AROUND ANYWHERE.
GOT IT, BOSS. WHAT GIVES?
I'M CONCERNED WE'RE PAYING TOO MUCH ATTENTION TO THIS HARBOR. WE MAY BE GIVING OUR KILLER A CHANCE TO SLIP AWAY.
AS DELKO AND SPEEDLE BEGIN TO CARRY OUT THEIR ORDERS, HORATIO CAINE'S KEEN MIND TURNS THE FACTS OF THE CASE OVER AND OVER...
...DRAWING ON HIS PAST KNOWLEDGE, HIS INTUITION, AND SCIENCE...
YELINA, I'M GLAD TO SEE YOU. DO YOU HAVE A MOMENT?
...UNTIL THE PIECES ALL FALL INTO PLACE.

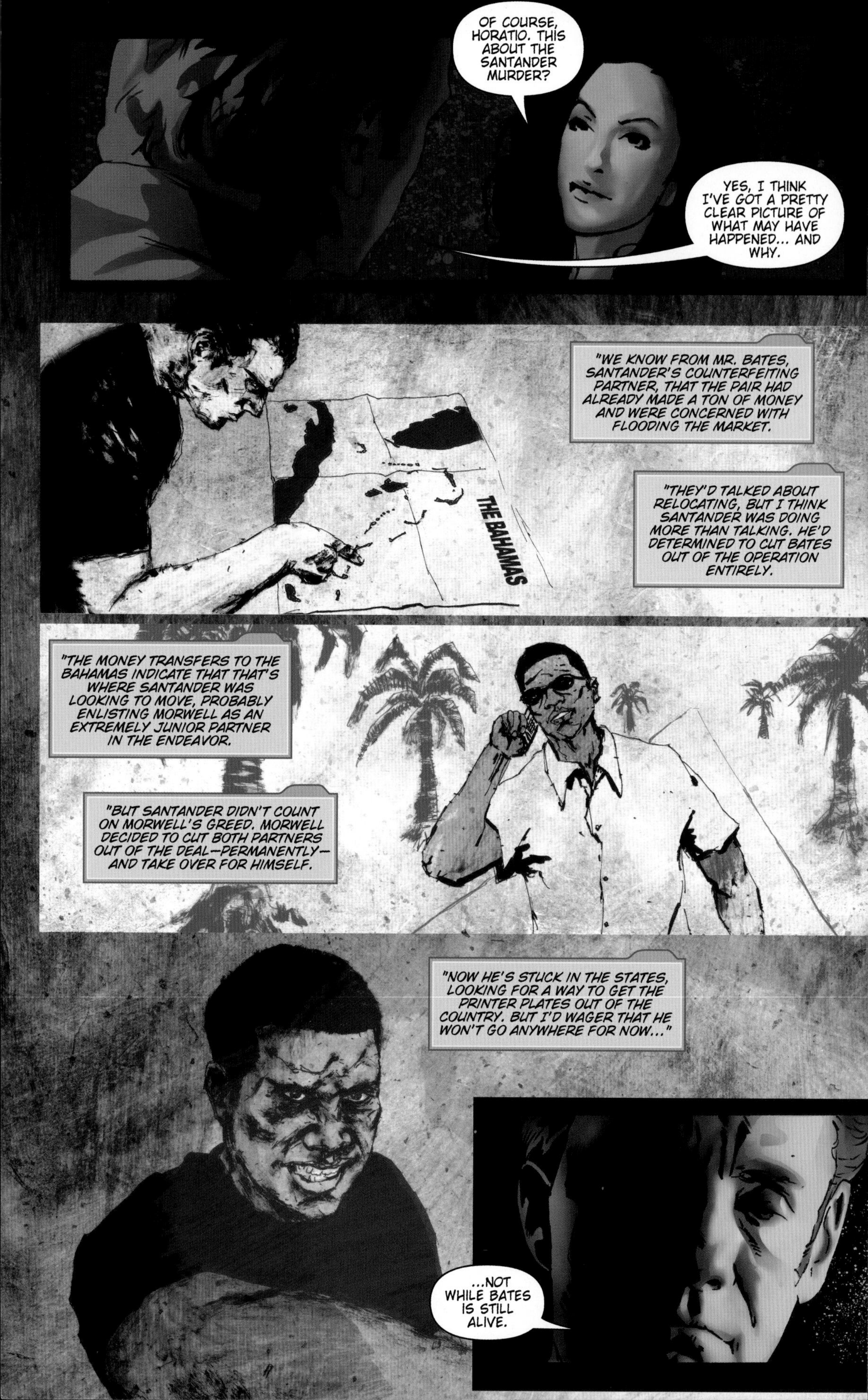
OF COURSE, HORATIO. THIS ABOUT THE SANTANDER MURDER?
YES, I THINK I'VE GOT A PRETTY CLEAR PICTURE OF WHAT MAY HAVE HAPPENED... AND WHY.
"WE KNOW FROM MR. BATES, SANTANDER'S COUNTERFEITING PARTNER, THAT THE PAIR HAD ALREADY MADE A TON OF MONEY AND WERE CONCERNED WITH FLOODING THE MARKET.
THE BAHAMAS
"THEY'D TALKED ABOUT RELOCATING, BUT I THINK SANTANDER WAS DOING MORE THAN TALKING. HE'D DETERMINED TO CUT BATES OUT OF THE OPERATION ENTIRELY.
"THE MONEY TRANSFERS TO THE BAHAMAS INDICATE THAT THAT'S WHERE SANTANDER WAS LOOKING TO MOVE, PROBABLY ENLISTING MORWELL AS AN EXTREMELY JUNIOR PARTNER IN THE ENDEAVOR.
"BUT SANTANDER DIDN'T COUNT ON MORWELL'S GREED. MORWELL DECIDED TO CUT BOTH PARTNERS OUT OF THE DEAL—PERMANENTLY—AND TAKE OVER FOR HIMSELF.
"NOW HE'S STUCK IN THE STATES, LOOKING FOR A WAY TO GET THE PRINTER PLATES OUT OF THE COUNTRY. BUT I'D WAGER THAT HE WON'T GO ANYWHERE FOR NOW..."
...NOT WHILE BATES IS STILL ALIVE.

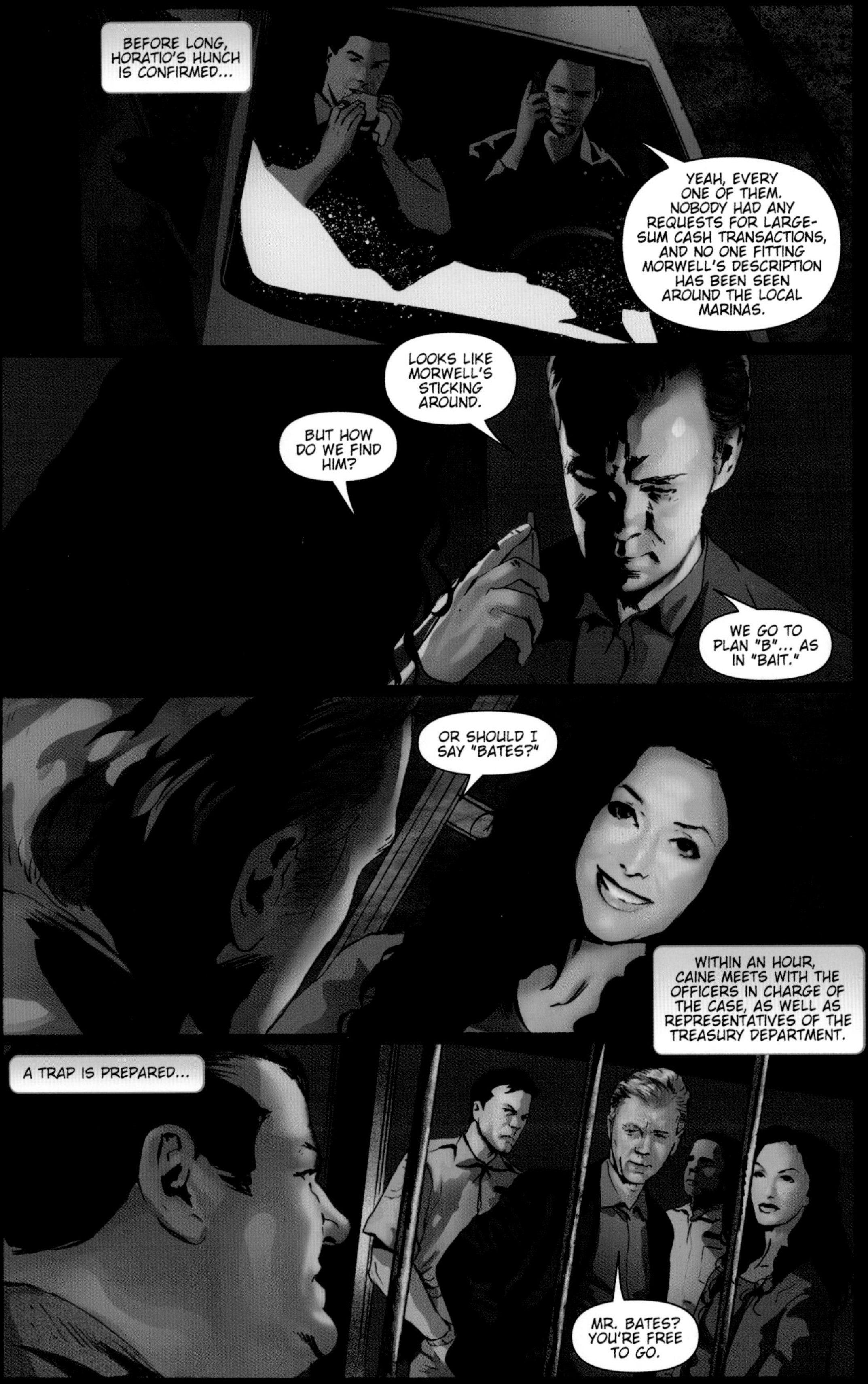
BEFORE LONG, HORATIO'S HUNCH IS CONFIRMED...
YEAH, EVERY ONE OF THEM. NOBODY HAD ANY REQUESTS FOR LARGE-SUM CASH TRANSACTIONS, AND NO ONE FITTING MORWELL'S DESCRIPTION HAS BEEN SEEN AROUND THE LOCAL MARINAS.
LOOKS LIKE MORWELL'S STICKING AROUND.
BUT HOW DO WE FIND HIM?
WE GO TO PLAN "B"... AS IN "BAIT."
OR SHOULD I SAY "BATES?"
WITHIN AN HOUR, CAINE MEETS WITH THE OFFICERS IN CHARGE OF THE CASE, AS WELL AS REPRESENTATIVES OF THE TREASURY DEPARTMENT.
A TRAP IS PREPARED...
MR. BATES? YOU'RE FREE TO GO.

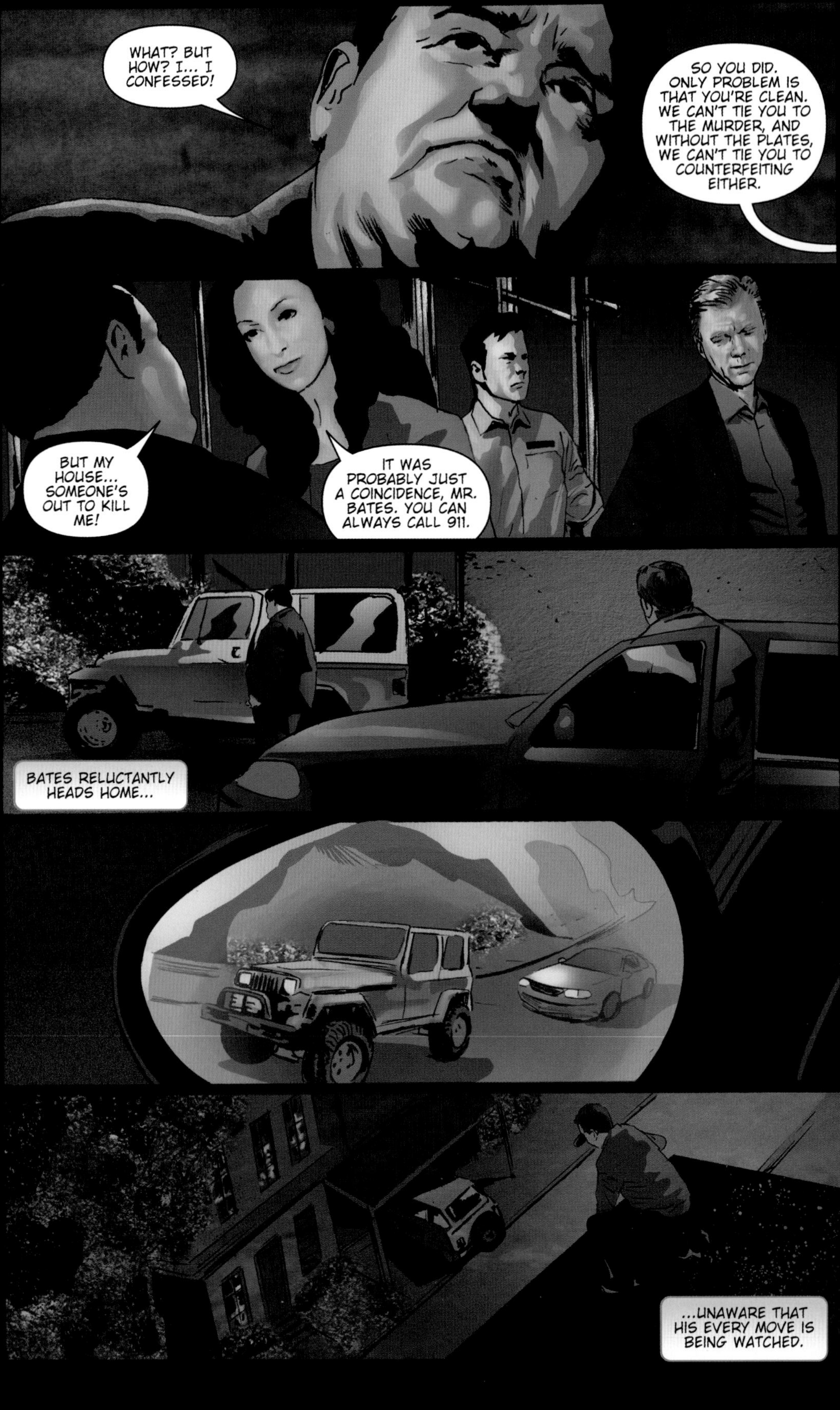

WHAT? BUT HOW? I... I CONFESSED!
SO YOU DID. ONLY PROBLEM IS THAT YOU'RE CLEAN. WE CAN'T TIE YOU TO THE MURDER, AND WITHOUT THE PLATES, WE CAN'T TIE YOU TO COUNTERFEITING EITHER.
BUT MY HOUSE... SOMEONE'S OUT TO KILL ME!
IT WAS PROBABLY JUST A COINCIDENCE, MR. BATES. YOU CAN ALWAYS CALL 911.
BATES RELUCTANTLY HEADS HOME...
...UNAWARE THAT HIS EVERY MOVE IS BEING WATCHED.

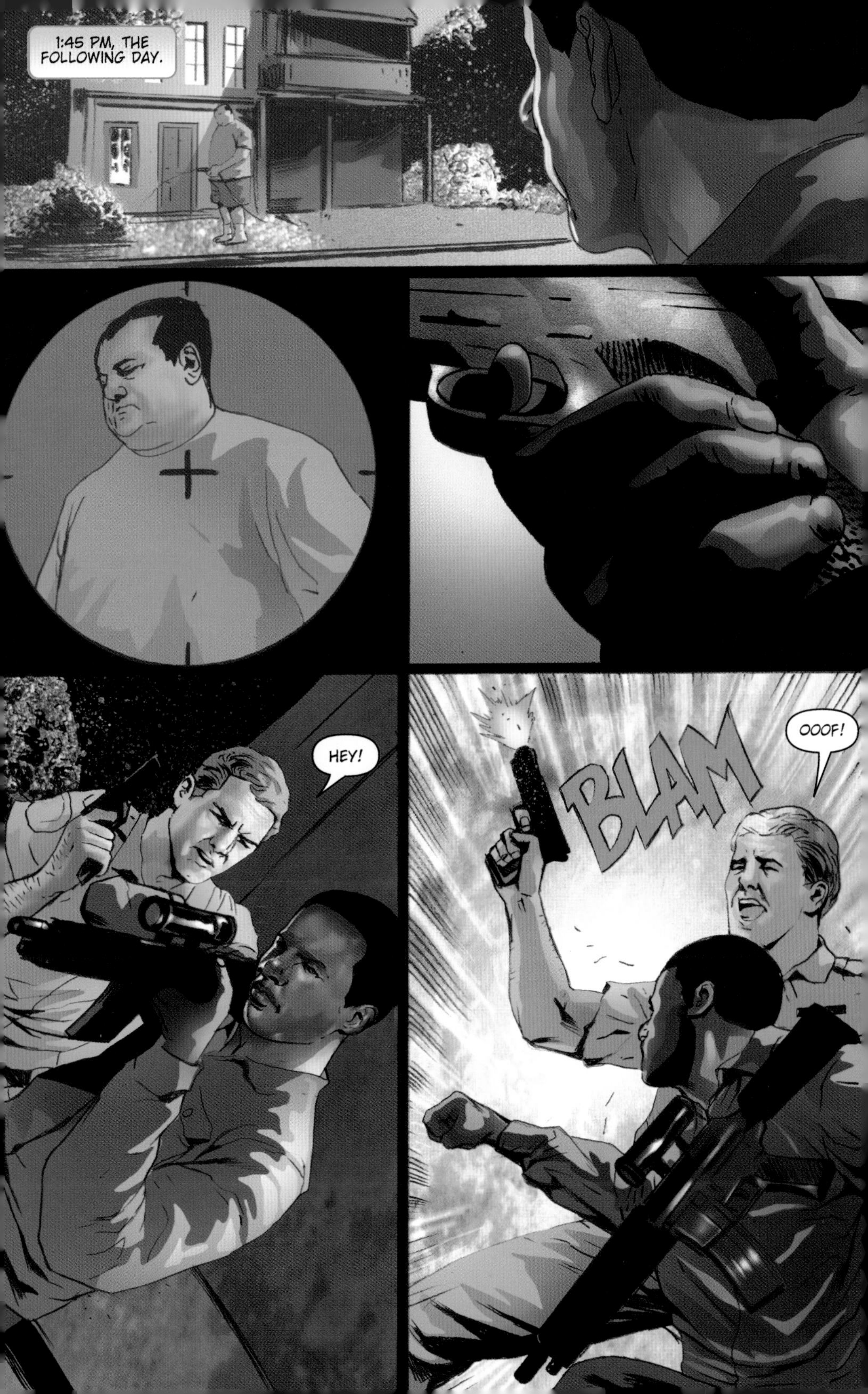
1:45 PM, THE FOLLOWING DAY.
HEY!
BLAM
OOOF!

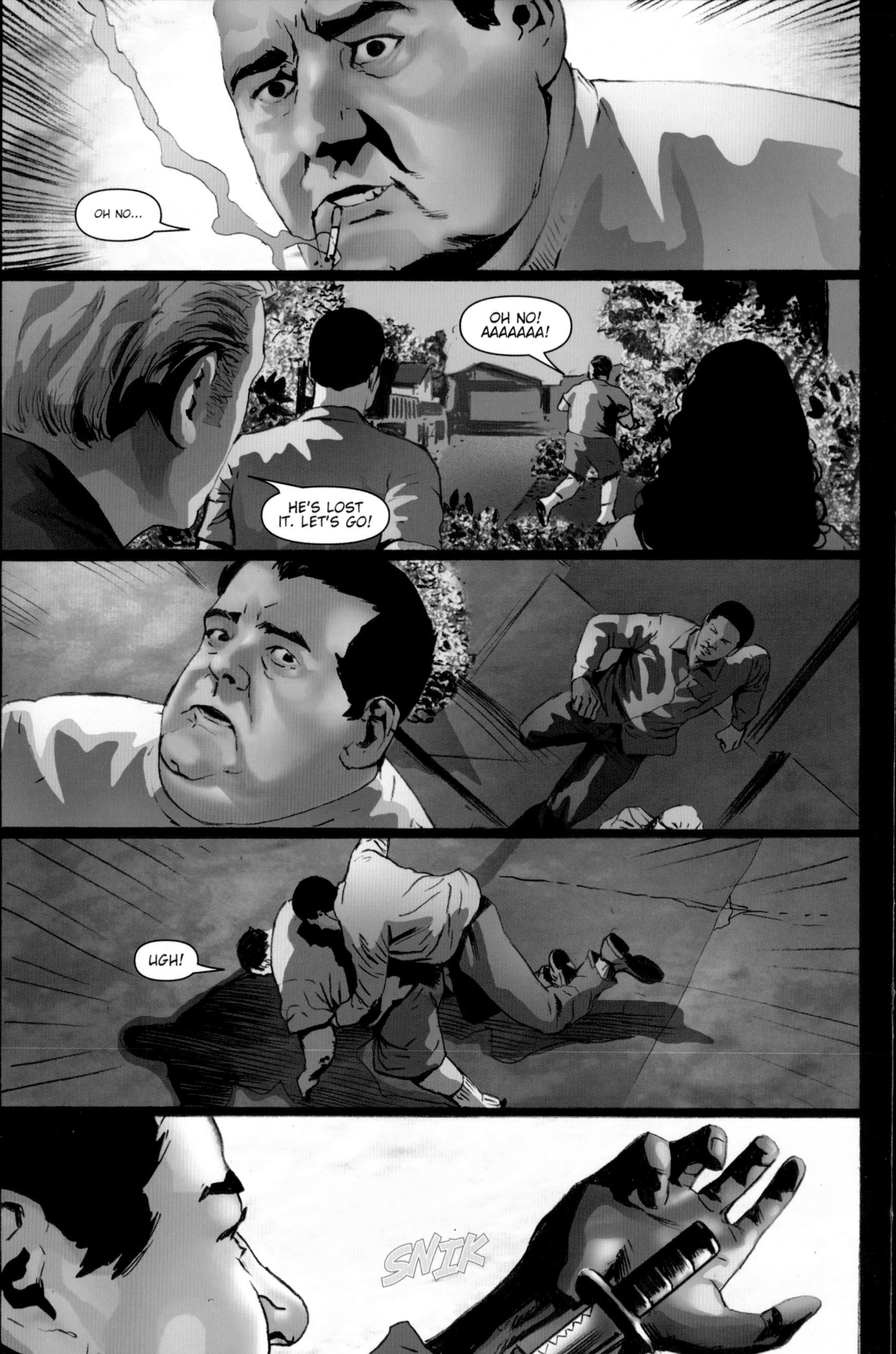
OH NO...
OH NO! AAAAAAA!
HE'S LOST IT. LET'S GO!
UGH!
SNIK

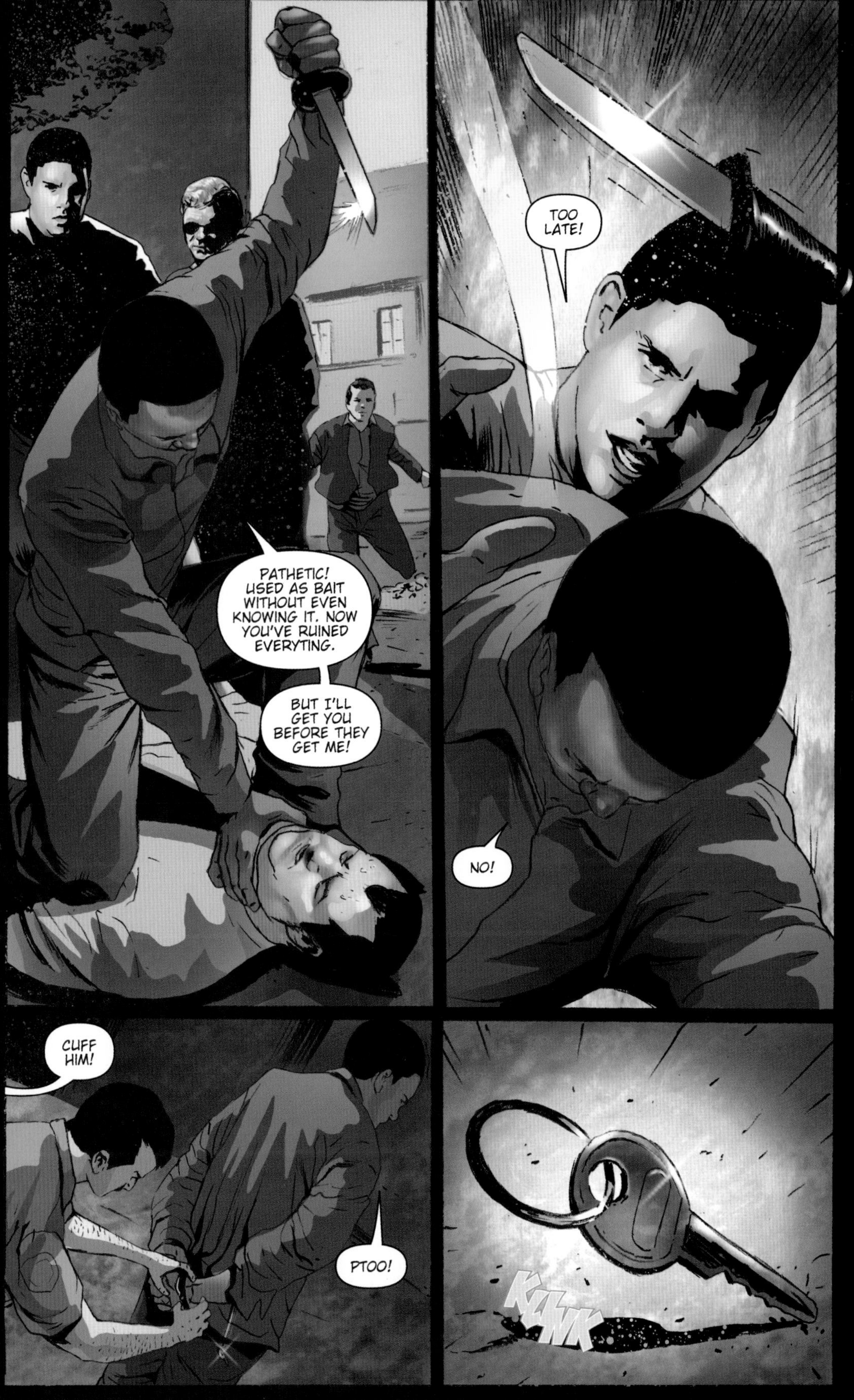
PATHETIC! USED AS BAIT WITHOUT EVEN KNOWING IT. NOW YOU'VE RUINED EVERYTING.
BUT I'LL GET YOU BEFORE THEY GET ME!
TOO LATE!
NO!
CUFF HIM!
PTOO!
KLINK

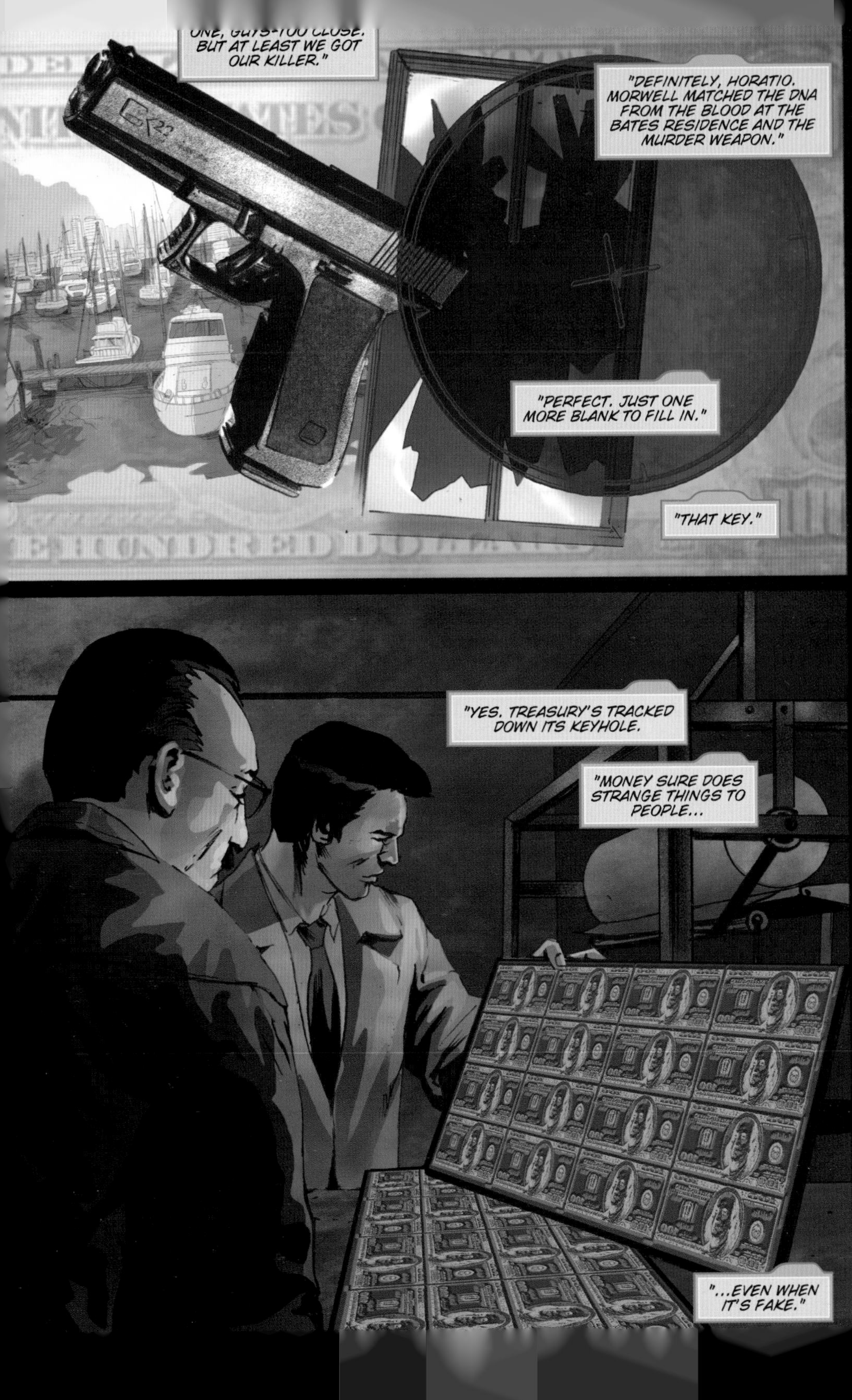
BUT AT LEAST WE GOT OUR KILLER."
"DEFINITELY, HORATIO. MORWELL MATCHED THE DNA FROM THE BLOOD AT THE BATES RESIDENCE AND THE MURDER WEAPON."
"PERFECT. JUST ONE MORE BLANK TO FILL IN."
"THAT KEY."
"YES. TREASURY'S TRACKED DOWN ITS KEYHOLE.
"MONEY SURE DOES STRANGE THINGS TO PEOPLE...
"...EVEN WHEN IT'S FAKE."